PRAISE FOR
AS WE BLOOM

"*As We Bloom* is a luminous, heartfelt journey into resilience, identity, and collective healing. Through raw honesty and tender storytelling, Mia Bolton weaves together her own transformative road trip with the lived wisdom of extraordinary people. Against a backdrop of personal heartbreak and societal injustice, *As We Bloom* is a reminder that even in the harshest landscapes, beauty, bravery, and connection still bloom. Bolton's voice is intimate and courageous — a beacon for anyone seeking belonging, meaning, and hope."

– **Jeremy Bradley-Silverio Donato**, Writer and Wishing Shelf Book Award Winner

"Mia has written a brave adventure story, sharing her heart and experience along her travels in life and love. It will transport you to new places and just might give you a new understanding of yourself or someone you love."

– **Shelby Stanger,** author of *Will to Wild: Adventures Great and Small to Change Your Life* and host of REI's *Wild Ideas Worth Living* podcast and Vitamin Joy podcast

"Mia Bolton is a writer and storyteller of enormous grace, wit, compassion and curiosity, with just the right elements of self-reflection and vulnerability. It is her endless capacity and desire to seek out the best in herself, her friends, her lovers, her family members, and the strangers she meets along the way that make *As We Bloom* a thoroughly enjoyable roadtrip of a book. But woven throughout the book is another layer — a complex, deeply personal tale of love, hope and loss to which almost any reader will most likely relate. Finding and losing love, and then finding it again in the most unlikely location, is one of this book's most heart-tugging, rewarding byways. Take *As We Bloom* to the beach, take it to a bustling coffee shop, read it aloud to your traveling companion on a long stretch of open highway, or curl up with it by lamplight in bed. The hours you spend in Mia's company will repay you over and over."

– **Mason Funk,** Founder of The OUTWORDS Archive

"Heartbreak often leads us to retreat, Mia does something far more courageous—she sets out on a journey, not only to heal but to connect. *As We Bloom* is a beautifully woven memoir that blends her personal narrative with voices from people she meets along the way, a profound exploration of connection. Mia takes to the road—not in search of distraction, but in pursuit of meaning. During her journey, she interviews strangers and friends. The narrative oscillates between the author's inner world and the external stories she uncovers, creating a rhythm that feels both intimate and expansive. What makes this book particularly resonant is its authenticity. It is a gentle reminder of the power of human connection."

– **Carolina Amell,** book packager and editorial designer behind *Surf Like a Girl, Every Body Surf,* and more

"*As We Bloom* is thought provoking, delicate yet courageous. This kind of storytelling is needed right now more than ever and it is delivered in a way that both moves and calls on us to act."

– **Lucy Small,** Surfer and Feminist Activist

AS WE BLOOM

Wisdom From Extraordinary Everyday
Women & Gender Nonconforming People

AS WE BLOOM

MIA BOLTON

As We Bloom: Wisdom from Extraordinary Everyday Women and Gender Nonconforming People

© 2025 by Mia Bolton

All rights reserved. No portion of this publication may be reproduced, stored in a retrieval system, or transmitted by any means—electronic, mechanical, photocopying, recording, or any other—except for brief quotations in printed reviews, without the prior written permission of the publisher.

Library of Congress Control Number: 2025902813

ISBN: 978-1-964686-34-9 (paperback) 978-1-964686-35-6 (ebook)

This book is based on true events reflecting the author's memory of them. Some names and characteristics may have been changed, some events compressed, and some dialogue recreated.

Editors: Deborah Froese, Dianna Graveman, Mary Ward Menke
Cover Design: Emma Elzinga, Karina White
Interior Design: Emma Elzinga
Illustrations: Karina White

Printed in the United States of America

First Edition

3 West Garden Street, Ste. 718
Pensacola, FL 32502
www.indigoriverpublishing.com

Ordering Information:

Quantity sales: Special discounts are available on quantity purchases by corporations, associations, and others. For details, contact the publisher at the address above.

Orders by US trade bookstores and wholesalers: Please contact the publisher at the address above.

With Indigo River Publishing, you can always expect great books, strong voices, and meaningful messages. Most importantly, you'll always find . . . *words worth reading*.

To everyone who shared pieces of themselves with me along the way.

INTRODUCTION

Since I began this journey in July 2018, humanity has witnessed both progressive and painfully regressive moments in the movement for gender equality and representation. Fans throughout the Stade de Lyon in France chanted, "Equal pay!" as the US Women's National Soccer Team became world champions for the fourth time in 2019. Two LGBTQIA+ women—Sue Bird and Diana Taurasi—became the most decorated basketball players of any gender in US Olympic history. Maia Chaka became the first Black woman to officiate in the National Football League for the 2021 season.

Meanwhile, pro surfer Bethany Hamilton and former competitive swimmer Riley Gaines disgracefully led a transphobic cross-country book tour and lobbied to ban transgender athletes in women's sports. During this time, lawmakers wrote a multitude of bills attempting to keep transgender athletes from participating in sports consistent with their non-biological gender identity.[1]

Off the fields, courts, and mats, America elected its first-ever female vice president, Kamala Harris. A 2019 documentary about menstruation

---

1 "Transgender Exclusion in Sports: Suggested Discussion Points With Resources to Oppose Transgender Exclusion Bills," American Psychological Association, accessed July 23, 2024, https://www.apa.org/topics/lgbtq/transgender-exclusion-sports.

from Rayka Zehtabchi won an Oscar. Victoria's Secret featured its first openly transgender model in August 2019, and *Sports Illustrated* put a transgender woman, Grammy-winning Kim Petras, on the cover of its 2023 Swimsuit Issue.

We endured moments of upheaval and heartache as the COVID-19 pandemic exposed how American institutions and systems—law enforcement, healthcare, education, housing, and more—by design, keep communities on the margins in perpetual struggle. Hate crimes surged against people of color as the murders of George Floyd, Breonna Taylor, Michelle "Tameka" Washington, and too many more sent the world into the streets, demanding justice. Asylum seekers and women in border detention centers faced horrific conditions, including Roxsana Hernández, a transgender woman from Honduras who died at the hands of Immigration and Customs Enforcement (ICE) in May 2018. American legislators continued to criminalize abortion, resulting in the overturn of Roe v. Wade—the constitutional right to an abortion—in June 2022, followed by fourteen states completely banning abortion and twenty-seven states banning abortion after a certain point in pregnancy.[2]

And since October 2023 (although it has been going on much longer), the world has watched a genocide unfold before our eyes as Israeli Defense Forces kill women, children and families in Palestine using American weapons and funds.

We said goodbye to Toni Morrison in 2019, a powerful literary icon and the first Black woman to win a Nobel Prize in Literature; Ruth Bader Ginsburg in 2020, the Supreme Court justice with a long history of defending women's rights; and Cecilia Gentili in 2024, an extraordinary advocate for sex workers and the transgender community. And in early 2025, a new federal administration declared war on DEI and blatantly attempted to erode our rights and erase our histories.

---

2 "State Bans on Abortion Throughout Pregnancy," Guttmacher, State Laws and Policies, July 20, 2024, https://www.guttmacher.org/state-policy/explore/state-policies-abortion-bans.

While this may feel unprecedented in our lifetimes, history teaches us that every struggle for justice is dotted with fantastic progress and equally fantastic turmoil. We turn to each other through our joy and grief to try to make sense of it all, but the truth is, it rarely makes any sense.

For me, transcribing the conversations I had with twenty extraordinary everyday women and gender nonconforming people into this book was my way forward – my own act of healing and resistance. The people you're about to meet are our mechanics, our coaches, the owners of our favorite small businesses, our neighbors, and our friends. They're the person across the table or sharing our park bench. They are all around us. They are us. I've compiled their recorded interviews in the hopes that hearing from them can feel like a way forward for you, too.

This story begins with the discovery of the brave people surrounding me, which sent me stumbling into discovering the bravery within myself. May we all find pieces of ourselves in the following pages and realize that we are more magnificent than we think, more alike than we know, and never, ever alone.

"I hope you will go out and let stories, that is life, happen to you, and that you will work with these stories from your life—your life—not someone else's life—water them with your blood and tears and your laughter till they bloom, till you yourself burst into bloom.
That is the work.
The only work."

~ Dr. Clarissa Pinkola Estés, *Women Who Run With the Wolves: Myths and Stories of the Wild Woman Archetype*

1

"No one will ever create what you will create, because no one else is you."

JULY 30–SAN DIEGO, CALIFORNIA
0 DAYS ON THE ROAD, 0 MILES

I've loved to tell stories for as long as I can remember. My parents once showed me the first book I ever made—a collection of small, pink papers ripped from a notepad on my hardworking mother's desk and bound together by three neatly placed staples. The front read: LEITTEL SEEDS WET FLOOTING BY, BY MIA B. The pages told a pleasant story about a little seed that gets put in the ground, and when the rain comes, it grows into a flower—or, as I wrote it, "the begist flawr you ever Saw!" On the back of the last page, it said "$1" in my best six-year-old handwriting. My dad maintains it's still his favorite book, even though "it's expensive."

As years passed, the back of Mom's pink notepads became countless journals packed with doodles. Doodling became a degree in communications, and after college, that degree transformed into a young career as a freelance writer. By the time I was twenty-nine years old, I'd written and taken photos for national and international swimming, surfing, and outdoor adventure magazines.

Growing up in a suburb equidistant to Baltimore, Maryland, and Washington, DC, I had access to big, bright, beautiful cities while also enjoying the comforts of a quiet neighborhood I called home. Mom and Dad were each other's second marriage, and my dad had three daughters from his first—Angela, Grace, and Mercy—who were about ten years older than me. Although my half sisters lived in California, my younger brother Nathan and I loved them like we'd grown up in the same house together our entire lives. Every summer for years, they flew across the country from the San Francisco Bay Area to spend a few sunny, humid months rotating between the football field, the playground, and the pool within walking distance of our small Maryland townhouse. When I think of my childhood with four siblings, I feel sticky hands from melted popsicles that we got from the ice cream truck and sunburnt bodies that became swimsuit tan lines. I also feel the tall grass scratching my mosquito-bite-ridden legs and the sadness of tearfully saying goodbye to my sisters when the summer was over. Nathan and I lived far from them and missed them when we weren't together, but we all loved each other deeply, nonetheless.

My siblings in the Maryland house I grew up in. From the left: Angela, Nathan, our neighbor, Mercy, me and Grace.

From what I could tell, my parents had a happy relationship. They fought so rarely that I distinctly remember each time they did, notably the one time my dad kicked over the trash can, and the whole house smelled like garbage for a few days. Mostly I remember them hugging in the kitchen and kissing me on the head as they told me how much they love me. They never let me wonder.

They were hardworking and kind parents who made sure their children always felt supported—within reason, of course. When I was tired of getting participation ribbons at local swim meets, they signed me up to swim with the year-round swim club. It didn't matter that they called swim lanes "aisles" and never remembered the order of strokes in the individual medley. They cheered no matter how I did, and I could always count on them to wrap me in towels afterward and drive me home while I slept in the car.

As a young teenager, my life revolved around school and swimming, with your usual young girl drama and a smattering of good friends from the various parts of my life: school, my neighborhood, my babysitter's neighborhood, my summer swim team, and my year-round swim team. Getting my friends together for birthday parties was awkward for everyone but me; none of them knew each other, but I knew them all. I was the only common denominator in my friend groups for a long time. Not until much later would I recognize the gift of finding friends anywhere, with all kinds of people.

When I was fourteen, I became a competitive swimmer, and as many young girls do, I thought the world of my coach. He seemed like the key to unlocking my potential as an athlete, and as I leaned on him for emotional support, I also became dependent on his approval—both in and out of the water. I craved his wisdom and felt validated when I was the object of his attention, at least for a while.

At the time, I didn't realize that our close relationship was abnormal for a man in his late twenties and a girl in her early teens. I didn't realize it was abnormal that we kissed one time, and I had to get up and check my underwear because they were wet, and I didn't understand why.

After that, I noticed that my coach paid me special attention in a way that felt confusing and unpredictable. Sometimes, he was extra kind and thoughtful, and other times it felt like he was taking out a personal vendetta on me in front of my teammates. Over time, I found myself uncomfortable with how involved he was in my life. The tiresome saga came to an end when I graduated high school and moved to Baltimore for college, though it took much longer than that to process his impact on me.

As years passed, I had boyfriends—well, boys who were friends, and boys who were more than friends. In retrospect, I'm not sure how much mind I truly paid those relationships. It was as if every interaction fell under a hazy veil of "I like him. Let's see where this goes." More often than not, it didn't go at all. There were heartbreaks and assholes, and of course unrequited, out-of-the-blue crushes on long-term friends. (The agony!)

There was also the unwanted attention from boys—like the guy who came back to my room my freshman year of college and, despite me telling him that I didn't want to have sex, decided that he did, and that that was more important. I remember pushing him off me and forcing him out of my apartment. The next morning, I went for a four-hour swim to clear my mind, and memories of my swim coach began to resurface and insert themselves into the mix. Two experiences with abusive men left me feeling like I was crawling out of my own skin. I hadn't yet used words like, "boundaries," "abuse," "sexual assault," or "rape" to describe what had happened. I was terrified that admitting these words to myself would be life altering. I might never be able to go back to the way I was before. It took me a long time to understand how to talk about these moments and the power in owning my own story. I'm still working on it.

Despite how much we loved each other, my mother and I butted heads as I got older. It's hard to remember exactly why, just that everything she did felt wrong. She cared too much. She didn't say the right thing.

She embarrassed me. We walked on eggshells around each other for a while, often ending our interactions with yelling or slamming doors. Still, when I was eighteen years old, she paid for me to have breast reduction surgery, and I was grateful. As a young girl with a large chest, I had been constantly aware of my big boobs—how to manage them, the way they looked, or the way other people looked at me because of them. This one part of my body didn't fit me. I admired girls with small chests, who didn't have to wear bras or worry about their cleavage and the icky attention it drew. It wasn't something I thought of on my own—my mom had had the surgery, and she posed breast reduction as an option. Overnight, I was down two cup sizes. The recovery was intense, but the relief was immediate.

I've never regretted having breast reduction surgery, but looking back, I do wonder what might have happened if I talked more about why I wanted the surgery and how to love myself and the body I had first, the same way I wonder what would have changed if I had talked about my coach or the guy in college. I feel shaken when I realize just how the effects of a silencing, patriarchal culture have manifested in my own life. But young Mia didn't know what she didn't know, and I won't let her feel shame for that.

When I was twenty-three, I moved from Maryland to San Diego. My entire thought process went like this: *My friends are doing it, and I don't have anything keeping me here, so why not?*

For my parents, particularly my mom, the transition was hard. It broke her heart that I wanted to be so far away from her. She called me crying almost weekly, while my dad simply reminded me to "Have fun, baby," even when his voice sounded sad. I knew they missed me, but underneath the temporary sorrow, they still supported me the way they always had. Cheering me on. Calling the lanes "aisles." Wrapping me in a towel. A few years after I moved to San Diego, they packed up the small house I grew up in and began a new chapter in Destin, Florida.

Across the country, the sunny-and-70 adventure turned into almost ten years in San Diego. The city changed me in ways that I'm still discovering, but two big revelations feel clear.

The first: I found a career I loved. With a communications degree, I wasn't sure how to narrow down a broad set of skills, like knowing how to talk to people and write well. I knew I could tell stories, but what did that translate into? I spent close to a year juggling part-time jobs at a surf shop and as an executive assistant before I met Jamie. That changed everything.

Jamie had started a communications agency in 2012, now called Mixte Communications, that supports environmental and social justice organizations in San Diego. I still remember the outfit I wore to my first interview: a black cotton dress with tiny flowers and buttons down the middle, and a pair of black Vans with holes in the toes. We had an incredible conversation for more than two hours, and the following week, I became the company's first full-time employee.

Each day after that, I rode my bike to Jamie's condo a few miles from my house and spent the day in her second bedroom-turned-office. We sat at our desks facing opposite directions, wheeling around in our chairs to verbally workshop whatever was on our minds. One day, Jamie turned to me with tears in her eyes.

"I'm getting a divorce," she confessed shakily, admitting she didn't know what that would mean for anything—including me.

"I'm not going anywhere," I reassured her. "We'll figure it out."

After that, we became not only colleagues but very close friends. When she moved out of her condo, I followed her to all the places she relocated, dutifully showing up each day to new friends' houses and coffee shops for work. On the weekends and after work, we'd hang out and watch movies, go on bike rides, and explore San Diego together. When we weren't on bikes, we took trips in her 1981 Vanagon up the coast for an adventurous combination of work and play. In my eyes, Jamie had it all figured out. Even in her hard moments, my confidence in her never wavered.

The second way San Diego changed me? I realized I wasn't straight.

I vaguely remember the first time I met KC. I was twenty-five and had just started working at Mixte. One day, Jamie took me to her favorite bike shop in San Diego, which happened to be where KC worked. I watched them wrap my handlebars in red tape with careful focus and precision. Then I said thank you, and we left. There was nothing exceptional or memorable about that particular interaction, except for when I look back and realize that it was the beginning.

Two years passed before I crossed paths with KC again. This time, they owned their own bike shop and were active and outspoken about making biking accessible for all people. As our lives mutually centered on bikes, we began to see a lot more of each other—on group rides, at community events, art shows, and the like. Through these interactions, I began to see them. Their gritty sense of humor. Their stained hands, neck tattoos, and strawberry-blonde curls peeking out from under their hat. Their consistently mismatched socks. How they never tried to impress anyone. How their laugh made everyone around them smile—including me.

We eventually began hanging out as friends, spending our days going to the Anza Borrego desert or to a Dolly Parton show, and evenings on my back patio, talking and looking up at the sky as they smoked cigarettes and I drank beer. We made each other art. We texted constantly. When I left on trips, they were the last person I'd see. When I got back from trips, they were the first person I'd call—I never could wait to show them all the photos. When we spent time in groups, we were never far from each other's side. They came to events I hosted to support me, driving me home afterward and telling me they were proud of me. I showed up to their bike shop to support them, whispering that I was proud of them too. We flirted and laughed and snuck in compliments about each other subtly, the way people do when they're trying to figure out if someone likes them back.

One year, I won a contest hosted by New Belgium Brewing that gave me the opportunity to trade in my very old car and use only a bicycle for a year. When I won, I gave the prize money to KC and asked them to build me a custom bike.

"The only thing I know is that I want enormous panniers," I told them, sitting in their bike shop on a Sunday morning, hungover.

"Mia, I've seen you bike commuting for years. I already know how I'm going to build your bike," they said. "You just have to trust me. Do you?"

"I trust you," I told them, smiling.

I became infatuated with the person I saw—this person full of creativity, talent, and wit, with a big heart for the people they cared for.

The first time we kissed, they had invited me camping with them and a few friends. In the tent that night, I planted my lips on theirs from the safety of my sleeping bag. The next day, I called my parents to tell them the simple truth: I was pansexual.

I was met with initial silence, followed by a simple question: "Are you happy?"

"Yes, I am."

"Then that's all that matters to us," they said simply, followed cautiously by, "Also, what is pansexual?"

I smiled to myself as I told them it means being attracted to people regardless of their gender.

When I remember the acceptance from my parents in this moment, I always tear up, especially knowing how unusual this experience is for too many LGBTQIA+ people.

So yeah, life was good for a while. I had a job I loved while doing work that mattered. I was understanding my own sexuality, and I had a partner who made me feel a way I'd never felt before.

A few months passed like this before KC called to tell me it would be best if we stopped seeing each other. I was stunned. Out of stubbornness and a sheer inability to understand what they were saying, I called a Lyft to drive me to their shop. I cried the whole way there, and when the poor driver asked where I was headed, I said, "To convince my partner to not break up with me," and continued sobbing in his backseat.

Ultimately, it wasn't worth the cringeworthy drive; nothing came of talking to them. They'd made up their mind and barely made eye contact with me as they told me we were done. I texted them after I left, desperately seeking clarity while trying not to appear as distraught as I felt. They ignored my messages.

Barely a week later, I got an email reminder for the upcoming trip to Alaska that KC and I had planned together. I decided to go alone. Fuck it—I wouldn't let our breakup keep me from doing something I wanted to do.

So I went. Alone. I camped, explored, hiked, drank beer, and asked strangers to take pictures of me as I tried to not look sad in front of pretty stuff. But no amount of guided glacier tours and fresh air made me any less distraught about my situation. One minute I could've sworn we were happy. The next minute, they'd brushed me off. Like I was disposable. Like we hadn't known each other for years. Like I hadn't loved them.

On my last day in Alaska, social media served me a picture of KC camping with their ex-girlfriend. It had been less than a month since we'd split, and they had already moved on with a girl they used to date—or maybe had been dating this whole time? Did everyone know I'd been so quickly replaced? Did I ever even matter at all? It was like I'd walked into a cement wall, and all the healing I'd been stitching together unraveled. I left Alaska the next day.

When I got home, a combination of internet stalking and talking with friends made my new reality clear: They were together, and I had been blocked—both literally and emotionally. I had already been devastated about the abrupt loss of a special person in my life. It didn't take long for that devastation to become bitterness—the kind of bitter where you cringe when you see happy couples holding hands. I avoided hanging out with friends in happy relationships because pretending to be happy was exhausting. After almost a year, the confusion, anger, and longing for closure faded into the dull acceptance that we simply weren't in each other's lives anymore.

To cope with heartbreak, I buried myself in work, which after a year, meant burnout. I'd been working exceptionally long days and making more mistakes than I ever used to, missing deadlines and sending emails to important clients with glaring typos or entire sentences missing. More importantly, I didn't feel like myself. I cried. A lot. I lost my purpose and passion for the work. I couldn't shut my brain or my heart off, even though it was what I wanted most desperately to do.

When I started to lose my footing, I craved being able to talk to someone who knew Mixte but wasn't in the day-to-day of it with me. I hadn't talked to KC in a year, but I texted them impulsively anyway.

> Hey, can you talk?

Thirty seconds later, they called me.

"I think I need to leave Mixte," I choked. I couldn't believe I had said the words out loud or who I had said them to. The whole situation was a mindfuck. Finally admitting to myself that I had to leave the company I'd helped build brought on a wave of emotions I was barely ready to face. I had tethered my identity to Mixte so tightly—what would I be without it? It was like I would lose myself in the abyss of the world, like the astronaut in that movie who goes outside to fix the ship and accidentally floats off into space.

"You can do anything," KC said. "You're the most amazing person I know."

Their support only made me cry. Suddenly I stopped thinking about Mixte, and the ache I had worked to bury for the past year came rushing back to the surface, demanding to be felt. The wound of losing the person I had loved was instantly fresh all over again. I had no idea what to do—with any of it.

A few months later, in the spring of 2018, I found myself saying goodbye to a job that had defined me for years. I untangled myself from long relationships with clients, colleagues, and even Jamie—at least as my boss. And while a piece of me felt lost without her by my side day in and day out, there was another piece of me that acknowledged the quiet liberation of being able to enjoy our friendship without the undercurrent of her as my supervisor.

"I have no idea what I'm doing, Jamie, but I think I have to go," I told her as tears welled in my eyes. "I will always love you and Mixte, and I'm so grateful for every opportunity you've given me."

"I know," Jamie said, putting her hand on mine. "And as your friend, I'm not going anywhere."

I nodded, at a loss for words. A blink sent the tears spilling down my cheeks.

Meanwhile, that phone call with KC had brought us barreling back into each other's lives. After our short conversation about Mixte, we didn't really stop talking, despite the fact that they were in a relationship with someone else. At first it was a few texts. Another phone call. A few more texts and a few more phone calls. After a few weeks, we developed the habit of talking on the phone almost every night. We always started out light and humorous before drifting back to the achingly familiar long stretches of silence. It wasn't long until we started to acknowledge what the silence implied, telling each other the truth of what brought both of us to the phone every night: we missed each other. We missed each other's voices, laughs, and company.

One night, I got brave enough to ask if they ever regretted ending things.

"I play the what-if game," they said hesitantly, "but it's not a good game. It never gets me anywhere."

"Well . . . everything happens for a reason, right?" I responded with my untimely optimism. "You just have to do what's best for you."

"Yea-a-ah," they said slowly, as if their mind had wandered off. As if they didn't believe me. I also didn't believe me. I wanted to be with KC.

Despite being so confused, I didn't push any harder for clarity from them. Instead, I relished this time with just the two of us in our own space, the way it used to be. My nightly routine of climbing into bed and pulling the covers up over my head as we talked for hours made me feel like we were in our own world—a world that no one knew about except us. It felt precious and tender. Untainted by anything or anyone else. But I also didn't trust it or know if it was real, which made it hurt. More times than not, our calls left me with conflicting emotions—energized yet empty, alive yet alone—which usually resulted in crying myself to sleep. To me, we were clearly in love with each other, but we were still so far from being together

The first time I saw them in person again, they were exactly as I remembered, which made me feel weak and comforted all at once. We drank too much for too long. Outside one of our favorite bars, they played delicately with a ring on my finger in between drunken laughs.

"Were you in love with me?" they asked suddenly.

The question surprised me. I almost thought they were joking, but when I looked at them, I could tell they were serious, their gray-blue eyes fixed on me earnestly.

"Yes."

Then, they kissed me, and we spent a stolen, foggy night together.

In the morning, I couldn't face myself. Not only did I feel hungover, I felt like a terrible person to my core. They were in a relationship with someone else. I didn't want to be a homewrecker; I was just in love. And if I was being honest with myself, which I finally was, my feelings for KC had never gone away.

Tormented, my self-doubt and anxiety hit an all-time high as I questioned my own character and moral compass. What had I done?

Finally, I told KC I needed to know what we were doing. While they didn't know what the future held for us, they promised to break up with their girlfriend so we could figure it out. I felt a familiar tightness clenched in my chest. I didn't know right from wrong or up from down, and the Mia-KC saga resembled a twisted game with tons of collateral damage and no real resolution. We resumed our emotional and physical intimacy as if no time had passed. But time had passed. And that time had been defined by unreconciled hurt and sadness.

Over the next few months, we attempted to find moments of lightness in our relationship 2.0, but the foundation was undeniably shaky and unsettled. One night, I met them at a bar, and they had their ex-girlfriend's dog with them. They assured me they were just doing their ex a favor. Another day, I drove past them on the street while they were running an errand, also for their ex. A favor. My friends urged me not to trust them while the rose-colored mantra in my head went something like this: If we just spend more time together, if we just talk more, if we just make more new, happy memories, I will eventually trust them again, and the ground will stabilize beneath us. It will get better.

One evening, we were in the kitchen making dinner after spending a night out with their friends. We had a nice time, but I couldn't shake the feeling that they all knew something I didn't. I caught them darting looks at KC that I didn't understand, as if they were speaking a language I didn't speak.

When KC and I got home, I propped myself up on the counter as they searched the kitchen to find the utensils. Suddenly, as they were shuffling through drawers, I started to cry, and I couldn't stop. I had my head in my hands, sobbing while they looked for the forks.

They stood in front of me with their hands on my knees, asking why I was crying.

Without thinking, I said, "I don't trust you anymore."

Hands still on my knees, they hung their head. They didn't argue with me or try to convince me otherwise. Instead, they said, "You shouldn't."

That's when I learned that new, happy memories can't fix what's still broken.

On a rollercoaster of temporary bliss, turmoil, and every red flag imaginable, I carried on loving them. I knew the other shoe was going to drop, and it was going to be awful, but I couldn't walk away. KC would tell me they loved me, they always had and always would. My friends and family warned me. I'd tell KC I loved them back. They would spend the night. I'd cry the next day, then invite them back. They'd text me, and I'd be happy. They wouldn't text me back, and I'd feel anxious. Warnings. Crying. Texting. Anxiety. Round and round we went.

A few weeks later, I was at breakfast with my family when I got a text from KC that said:

> She knows about you, and she's really mad. I don't know what she's going to do. I'm sorry.

As I stared at my phone, my heart sank into my stomach. I suddenly felt nauseous. My vision tunneled and blurred on the sides, the way it does just before you pass out. The shoe had dropped. When I called KC, the defeated voice on the other end told me their ex had demanded to see their phone and had read our texts. She knew everything.

I was confused. Why would you let your ex-girlfriend go through your phone? Why didn't you just say no? This doesn't make sense.

In a moment that was both excruciatingly slow and instantaneous, it clicked: *KC had never broken up with her at all. I had been the other woman all this time.*

KC didn't have to say it; in fact, they never did. I hung up the phone, swirling in a collection of feelings I knew all too well. I couldn't believe I'd thought it would be different this time. I couldn't believe how naive I'd been, that after everything, I was here, heartbroken by the same fucking person.

San Diego changed for me after that. With Mixte and KC both gone, a light inside me went out. I felt broken. Places I used to cherish lost their magic, and I started avoiding them for fear of running into KC or someone who would recognize me in relation to them. When I had to go to those places, I'd be so overcome with memories that I just wanted to—and often did—cry and leave. A city that had once been full of excitement and possibility became a collection of places that didn't feel safe—emotional minefields of things I once loved. Paramore's "Fake Happy" played on repeat as my carefully chosen bike routes took me the long way home, avoiding anywhere that might unleash the flow of painful memories I didn't know how to manage. San Diego was caving in on me, and I was caving in on myself.

I don't remember when I got the idea to leave, but once I did, it became impossible to think of anything else. Instead of a week in Alaska, this time I wanted to spend a few months driving around the country.

My trip was initially just to get out of San Diego, but with further thought and more conversation, it transformed into an opportunity to meet women and gender nonconforming people who embodied everything I felt like I had lost: courage, bravery, determination, purpose, and wisdom.

I longed for exposure to ways of life that jolted me awake. I wanted to find myself overcome with inspiration and possibility so immense and so grand that I couldn't help but feel alive—everything I felt achingly far away from in San Diego.

The proud new owner of my Toyota Previa van.

I went all in. I gave up two-wheeled transport and bought a 1999 Toyota Previa, a car KC had once told me they liked because it "looked like a spaceship." *Funny how you can want so badly to get away from someone and want to keep them close at the same time*, I thought. I took too many freelance jobs at once and, instead of putting a third of that income aside for taxes, I poured it all into getting my van ready for the trip, leaving her at the mechanic for weeks and paying thousands of dollars for them to replace anything that seemed problematic for such a long journey. I also bought a lot of equipment I thought I would need for months on the road, like a Goal Zero battery to charge electronics, camping equipment, and various other things (snacks) to make life on the road easier. I took out the seats, and my friends built a wooden bed out of two-by-fours for the back of my van. I ordered a three-inch memory foam pad to fit. I bought a series of long, thin Tupperware containers to store clothes, toiletries, cameras, and other miscellaneous provisions, and I tucked my mid-length surfboard underneath the wooden bed frame next to the extra engine oil and tire pressure gauge. Finally, I topped the bed with a quilt from my grandmother and two pillows.

One day, I was telling a friend about my trip, and he suggested I meet his friend, Erin. She was just getting certified as a life coach and needed practice hours, and I was apparently an excellent candidate for some coaching on life.

Erin and I started talking once a week over the phone leading up to my trip. She listened as I shared everything going through my mind and reflected things back to me objectively, helping expand my perspective and making her one of my closest confidants. She gently challenged my negative self-talk and any limiting beliefs I had about myself while sweetly supporting the journey I was preparing for. To that end, I began calling her "sweet Erin."

The final, hardest piece to figure out was where I would go and who I would talk to. I had no idea what I was doing and felt a tremendous amount of impostor syndrome, which I coped with by becoming hyper-organized. I started a detailed spreadsheet outlining exactly what city I'd be in for exactly how many days, with exactly who I'd talk to and exactly where I would stay. The only concrete date I had was in October for my friend Steph's wedding on the East Coast. I planned everything else around that with so much precision that there was zero margin for error.

My roommate and one of my best friends, Kaley, pointed out that I wasn't accounting for possibilities of life on the road, such as a postponed interview, a mechanical issue with my car, or a spontaneous detour. She made the case that there was only so much planning I could do, and the rest would fall into place. If I tried to do it all now, it would only be more painful later when I inevitably had to change plans. Even though I knew she was right, this perceived lack of organization made me deeply uncomfortable at a time when I craved control over something.

As I got ready to leave, sans spreadsheet, my self-doubt gained momentum. *What qualifies me for this adventure? Why would anyone talk to me? What if I do it wrong? What if I run out of money? What will I do when I come back? When will I come back, and who will I be when I do?*

Still swimming in my sea of self-doubt a few days before my trip, I went surfing with my friend Cori—three-time longboard world champion, queer environmental activist, city council member, and one of my personal heroes. Cori's unwavering commitment to justice, demonstrated at one point when she quit professional surfing because the industry didn't accept or support her as a gay woman, drew me to interview her for a piece I was writing a for a magazine. We'd become friends after that, going for the occasional surf whenever I got lucky enough to align my schedule with hers.

As we paddled next to each other, I mentioned my trip to Cori, still grappling with how to explain it in a way that felt right.

"I've been planning this trip around the country to talk to women and gender nonconforming people who are living in unconventional ways," I told her before the self-sabotage began. "But I don't know what I'm going to do with any of it, and there are so many other people doing similar work out there that I might not. It might be too redundant—I don't know that anyone will care."

I'll never forget the way Cori stopped dead in her tracks and reached her hand out to grab the rail of my surfboard. She looked me so squarely in the eyes that it startled me.

"Don't ever say that," she said, her eyes a crisp, bright blue. "Your project will be different because it's coming from you. No one will ever create what you create, because no one else is you."

After that moment with Cori, I settled on one straightforward statement that was enough to get me to day one: just try. I didn't know if I was the "right" one to do this, whatever that meant, but I was going to do it anyway. I didn't have much money, but I had enough to go. I didn't have a vision for where I saw myself in the next five or ten years or a way to explain the future gap in my resume. I didn't have a backup plan. I didn't have a perfectly planned spreadsheet. I didn't even have a car from the twenty-first century.

None of it mattered.

What mattered was that I needed to do something about the layer of perpetual gray that covered everything. I wanted to see in color again. I longed to rediscover my self-worth and self-love, my general enthusiasm for life, my sense of potential and possibility that had slowly slipped away from me. My entire being felt fueled by the fear of waking up twenty years down the road, listless and depleted. No spark. No drive. No joy. Unable to see the beauty around me or feel the life within me.

I wanted to be as simple and unfettered as a little seed dancing with the wind across unfamiliar places, but that felt unfathomably far away. I had no clue where to begin, but I couldn't stay. Without knowing much, I knew the best way to start was to go.

2

*"I'll go anywhere I can admire nature.
She is the grand architect—the best artist I know of."*

AUGUST 1–MALIBU, CALIFORNIA
1 DAY ON THE ROAD, 151 MILES

Anna Gudauskas (formerly Anna Ehrgott) and I had friends in common but had never gotten to know each other. I admired her surf adventures in remote places around the world, and I enjoyed watching her from an environmentally conscious, entrepreneurial perspective; she made handmade board bags from recycled materials like fabric and old coffee sacks. When our mutual friend Sarah suggested I connect with her, I reached out over Instagram, and she agreed to meet up at a beach near her house.

When the day came, Kaley and I drove my Previa a few hours up to Malibu to surf and meet Anna.

"I hope we make it back to San Diego," Kaley said as we drove north, only half-kidding. "It still freaks me out that the engine is under your seat."

"Me too," I said with a slight laugh, trying not to think about it and freak myself out too.

It was a hot, sunny Southern California afternoon, and the waves were small and perfect. I surfed until my skin was pink and the sun began to set, turning the sky beautiful shades of lavender. When Anna arrived, she waved to us with one arm as she tucked her longboard under the other and jogged across the street to meet us.

Suddenly, I felt a burst of nerves. Anna was not only the first person I would talk to on my adventure—she was also about my age and already so many things that I longed to be, like an amazing surfer who traveled and advocated for a better and more sustainable world. What if I had to justify my project? What if she thought it was a dumb idea? What if I ran out of things to ask? How personal was too personal, and what was so impersonal that it felt shallow? Would she feel comfortable enough to answer? Suddenly, the realization that I didn't know her at all and that I didn't actually know how any of this project would go, set in.

Anna and her longboard at dusk.

"Kaley, I just got nervous," I whispered. "What if I say the wrong things, or she thinks this whole thing is lame? What if I'm lame?"

"She wouldn't be here if she thought you or your project were lame," Kaley said. "Don't worry. You're going to be great. I'm here too. I won't let it get awkward."

Before I had a chance to think more about it, Anna kicked off her handwoven sandals and gave me and Kaley a hug before we made our seats in the warm Malibu sand.

"If you're comfortable with it, Anna, I'd love to record our conversation," I said. "Mostly so I can be present now and still remember all the details later."

"Oh, no problem," she said, giving me permission to open the voice recording app on my phone and press start, setting it on the towel between us. I had so many things to ask that I barely knew where to begin, so I jumped into what seemed most approachable: her travels.

"Traveling taught me that the world isn't a place to be terrified of—and to trust myself," she said as we began talking. "Now I plan strange surf trips to destinations a lot of people don't have on their radars. I'll spend hours and hours on Google Earth, researching to find remote surf breaks."

I laughed. She's right—they are untraditional surf trips, like Alaska or Iceland. I became inspired scrolling through snapshots of crystal-blue water surrounded by white-capped mountains and snowy hillsides. Anna often wore the thickest wetsuit I'd ever seen, smiling with purple lips. Her adventures captured surfing in a whole new light, exposing more depth than the mainstream marketing of sun-kissed women in bikinis holding surfboards. Surfing felt more real and raw to me because of Anna.

"What I seek from travel has changed over the years," she said. "First, it was a selfish pursuit of surfing good waves, eating good food, and coming back tan. In retrospect, what I remember most from every trip is my connection with people. I remember a kid I met, or a Buddhist temple I stumbled across, or something I learned from people I shared a meal with. That's what's most moving to me; that's where I want to put more energy moving forward."

As she spoke, I noticed the reflection of the moon beginning to cast a white glow over the ocean ripples. The sand between my toes. The light breeze. The periwinkle horizon. We all paused, swept up in the moment.

"I'll go anywhere I can admire nature," Anna said, looking around. "She's the grand architect—the best artist I know of. And we're a part of nature. Yet someone going on a hike might think it's not okay to go off the path or touch the trees or walk in the grass. Why shouldn't we roll around in the dirt?" she questioned. "I wonder sometimes why I feel this way and others don't. I think it comes down to the way I was raised. I grew up in Topanga, not far from here, where the suburban areas aren't separate from nature. There aren't paved areas and sidewalks and gates and then nature. There are houses built out of wood under an oak tree next to a creek and a dirt lot and mountain lions. Humans feel like a part of nature there, which makes me feel like nature is my home and that I need to take care of it."

"As opposed to feeling like we're separate from nature, and we need to stay away from it," I offered. "That perspective probably translates easily to surfing too."

"Yes, exactly," Anna said, nodding.

"So, as an entrepreneur who has this beautiful perspective on nature and sees so much of the world, how do you think that plays out in your business?"

"I got horrible advice from somebody once," Anna said. "They told me, 'Don't try to save the world with your first business.' And it just ate away at me. It would kill me to know that I'm making a product that's degrading the earth. My business started when I was looking to buy a board bag, and I realized that everything was cheaply made and would probably fall apart within a year. So I thought, okay, I need to step up and do this. The bags I make repurpose scraps of fabric and coffee bean sacks from roasters around Los Angeles that import coffee from around the world. I try to use ones from fair-trade, organic coffee because I feel like that's a nice sentiment to put into the board bag."

Kaley, Anna, and I continued chatting about how beautiful it was to have things that are one of a kind—surfboard bags, travels, and friends.

"I like when I have travel friends who will do low-budget things with me and dirtbag around a bit," Anna said with a laugh.

"Kaley is my dirtbag travel friend," I chuckled, putting my hand on her knee so she knew it was with love.

"Yeah, we have the van to prove it," Kaley added.

"Those people are super special!" Anna said excitedly as she continued talking about the friends she often finds herself traveling with.

As we began talking about the impact Anna's friends and family have had on her, she shared something unexpected.

"You know, my dad passed away over a year ago, and in the beginning, I was sure it was the worst thing to ever happen to me," she said. "I bottled it up because if I didn't, I wouldn't be able to get through the day. Looking back, I think that was the worst thing I could have done."

Kaley, whose dad had passed in June, shared, "I see my dad more in nature than I ever could have imagined, so I'm more aware of nature now because I feel like that's where his spirit comes through to me. I've always loved being out in nature, but it has a different meaning to me now."

"If you think about it physically, humans become nature," Anna said. "I can only imagine the same is true spiritually. For me, I still feel like I'm chipping away at it. Every day I spend a good amount of time thinking about the kind of person he was, what he meant to me, what he taught me, and the things I'm going to miss as well as the things I'm going to learn. I'm learning to be more gentle with other people as well, with the understanding that everyone is going through something. It's funny," she continued, "going through something like losing a parent puts you in this club of people who have suffered and experienced extreme pain, and you get so much closer to people who have lost people they loved or been through trauma."

"I read a cool quote the other day, because obviously I've been reading a lot of books about grief," Kaley shared. "It said something along the lines of, 'I know when I see people now who have true joy; they've done the hard work and gone through something fucking huge'—to put it in my own words. And it put everything into perspective for me, because I know joy in a different way now than I did before my dad died."

"Yes!" Anna exclaimed. "I feel that too. It's like the bottom has dropped out, so the whole scale is extreme. And the lower you go, the more potential you have to go high. You just feel more. I was always the happy, positive one in my friend circles, and it became hard for me to learn how to ask for help from people when I needed it in order to find that joy again."

"I mean, when you're grieving a loss, everything is hard," Kaley said. "Ordering a coffee can feel brutal just because."

I hadn't known Anna had also lost her dad in a sudden way, similarly to Kaley. As I watched them talk about the experience of losing a father, my mind spun around the words "grief" and "loss." Perhaps I was a bit more like Anna than I'd realized—trying to maintain the optimistic disposition people recognized in me and not wanting to burden anyone with feelings of despair.

The conversation began drawing to a close along with the day. Snapping back to the present moment, I thanked Anna for sharing so much with us and asked what advice she would give to young people who want to do good in the world.

"I started my business because nobody else was doing it," Anna said. "So my message to anyone would be to start a creative venture or some hobby that is your own thing and pour all your energy into it. Everything is connected, and every skill set you acquire has a place in your life. Even if you don't get monetary value from it, it adds so much into your life. That in itself is valuable beyond measure."

I smiled. How many times had it seemed like the various things I loved were nothing more than a random collection of hobbies that operated in siloes: surfing, photography, writing, drawing, travel, and so on? Yet when they managed to overlap—like in this moment—it felt serendipitous.

Darkness triggered the streetlights to flicker on as we stood and brushed the sand off ourselves.

"Thank you so much," I told Anna. "It's wonderful to learn more about you and hear more of your story."

We hugged and headed toward our respective cars and cities. On the road back to San Diego, a small wave of relief and pride washed over me. The first interview was done. Even though there had been a few moments of anxiety on my end, the conversation had flowed naturally overall, and Anna had felt safe enough to open up, which was important to me. I'd finally put action behind something I had only been talking about up until this point, and it filled me with gratification. This was the trial run I needed to show myself that I could actually do this trip around the country. Maybe people wouldn't think my questions were dumb or that I was lame. Maybe they'd be like Anna: open and honest, vulnerable and reflective. Perhaps they'd even be happy to have someone to talk to.

3

*"And so the question is,
what am I going to do with that privilege?"*

AUGUST 2–NORTH HOLLYWOOD, CALIFORNIA
3 DAYS ON THE ROAD, 187 MILES

I left San Diego the next afternoon, arriving at my friend Shalem's North Hollywood apartment just as the sun was setting. They greeted me at the door with open arms. The home they shared with their wife, Avital, was like a hidden refuge in the overwhelm of Los Angeles. Bikes hung on the wall in between colorful, handmade art pieces that told stories of their families and cultures.

Avital removed leftover cake from the fridge and scooped a dollop of ice cream onto three small plates before serving us. When I offered to help, they politely declined, insisting we had too much to catch up on.

Shalem and I met while I worked at Mixte, and they were the transportation justice advocate at an environmental justice organization in San Diego and Tijuana. They shared data, resources, and stories describing the impact of community planning with me to turn into blogs, social media posts, press events, and news articles. When they left the organization, we remained close friends, bonded by our shared understanding of the power of storytelling to support grassroots change and our appreciation for meaningful conversations with like-minded people.

We stayed in touch over the years. When they proposed to Avital, I took their engagement photos. When Shalem and Avital got married, KC and I went to their wedding. When they moved to Los Angeles, I visited whenever I was in the city. One time, KC and I even took a trip up the coast, and all four of us spent the weekend riding bikes, going to the beach, and eating delicious food. When Shalem started their company, Pueblo Planning—a values-driven participatory planning and design firm that intentionally focuses on populations often left out of the planning process—I told them I would help with any communications they needed. To this day, I still joke that I'm their forever communications director.

Over the years, I'd seen Shalem work hard to balance the heaviness that comes with centering their work in justice with the lightness of things that bring them joy. In one conversation, they could go from breaking down something as complex as how racism has permeated and shaped the built environment, to sharing a personal story with raw emotion, to an infectious belly laugh complemented with a knee slap.

It made my heart simultaneously happy and a little bit sad to see Shalem, as memories of the times we spent with KC surfaced. I focused my attention on being as present as possible.

"We've known each other for so long," I said between bites of cake. "And you've always been an inspiration in my life, and in the lives of everyone who knows you. I'm hoping I can do you justice by sharing some of your story now, the same way you've empowered so many to share theirs over the years. Can you start by telling me a little about your work as a community planner and transportation justice advocate?"

I paused for a moment, unexpectedly verklempt. A knot rose in my throat. *Don't cry already—you haven't even started yet!*

"I can give you the traditional response about why freeways through neighborhoods aren't right," Shalem said plainly. "It's terrible for your health, air quality, the environment, etc. But from a justice lens, it's much deeper than that. It disconnects people. And to truly understand how injustice and racism are embedded in how neighborhoods are built and planned, we have to go back to the beginning."

With their signature patience and direct eye contact, Shalem explained how in the 1930s, the federal government came up with a color-coded map that led to housing segregation.

"Many people now know this as redlining," they said. "If you wanted to purchase a home with any skin color other than white, you couldn't buy in specific neighborhoods, based on this map.

"This is why you have environmental justice communities today—because people of color could only purchase a home in the government-regulated zones, even if they had money. When this happened, the people in the neighborhood were never listened to or consulted—particularly people of color who were, and are still, ignored and seen as not having the solutions to their own communities. This is discrimination. This is environmental racism. And this is not by accident."

Shalem looked calm in their black, thick-rimmed glasses, their right ankle resting on their left knee.

"One of the core elements of any justice work is understanding that the community has the answers," they continued. "They know what they want; they just don't always have the tools or the vocabulary to express what that is to the people making decisions."

"And part of what you do now is translate between community members and decision makers so they can be more involved in the process, right?" I asked.

"Pretty much," they said. "In order for urban planning to work for everyone, it must be done in a more thoughtful way. Planning has so much power to shape neighborhoods, and so many ripple effects—for better or for worse. For myself, planning is not innovative if it displaces people. It's not innovative if it puts a burden on one group of people over another. It's not innovative if it repeats these patterns of injustices and if the community wasn't consulted in a genuine way. My company,

Pueblo Planning, uses the tools that we as people are innately familiar with, such as storytelling or making art, and encourages them to play with those tools to illustrate their community vision. My job is to really listen and absorb what they're saying. Then I look at codes, precedents, policies, and practices to apply planning language to what they've described so that policymakers can understand what the community wants. City governments and agencies often hire me to do this work, to be the go-between for planning and community needs. But honestly, I'd like to live in a world in which my role would not be needed—a world where it's just common practice to engage the community in this way."

They paused, intentional about what they wanted to say next.

"My passion for this stems from my own experiences. I know what it feels like to be hit by a car, and I know what it feels like to be displaced from your home," Shalem said, their voice trailing off slightly, the way it does as you encounter an old memory.

"When I was eight, I got hit by a truck. I was crossing the street in front of my house, on my way to play basketball—which I had done a million times before. I don't remember the impact itself, but I remember most of what happened afterward—running home and collapsing on my living room floor, losing blood, my mom screaming, the police officer driving me to the hospital, the nurses scrubbing the asphalt out of my knees. It was horrible. I especially remember the guy who hit me. He was so distraught—sobbing and crying in my living room with my parents. His reaction has always stuck with me. He was just as much a victim of bad planning and poor infrastructure and lack of investment as I was.

"That place holds a lot of meaning for me," Shalem continued. "Three years later, when I was in fifth grade, that's the same home that my family was displaced from. We lived on the same block as a junior high school, and I'm guessing it was the school board that made the decision to expand the school by enacting something called 'eminent domain'—where you take property in the name of the 'public good.'" Shalem put "public good" in air quotes.

"Of course, my parents didn't have the means to contest an eminent domain notice, so we were forced to leave our home and move ten miles away. I didn't realize until years later when I went to planning school that certain planning tools, like eminent domain, are often used to displace Black, brown, and low-income communities in the name of the 'public good.' Later in life, this had me questioning the notion of 'public good,' what it truly means, and who defines it.

"It's been close to thirty years since that happened. To this day, all that's left where my house used to be is a vacant lot with a chain-link fence around it. To me, the message is loud and clear: a vacant lot is more of a public good than poor, brown people."

I shook my head and let out a long, slow exhale.

"As a child, these were just things that happened—things I was just trying to get through and survive. It wasn't until I was an adult studying planning that I was able to identify and process these experiences as actual traumas, intentionally inflicted by folks who sat around a table, similar to the tables that I sit at today, making decisions."

Their eyes watered, only slightly.

"The stories that people are experiencing in their own lives are being forged by outside forces, whether they know it or not," they said. "And that's an issue of justice."

I imagined how many other children like Shalem grew up to understand that their home could be taken away at any moment or that it wasn't safe to walk to the park. Children who noticed that their neighborhood looked and felt different from other neighborhoods without fully understanding why—eventually realizing that people in power chose to make it that way.

I put my hand on my friend's shoulder as they continued.

"So for me, this work comes with a deep sense of empathy," they said. "At the same time, I also acknowledge the privilege that my education, marriage, and job allow me. So the question is, what am I going to do with that privilege?"

As Shalem noticed Avital beginning to tidy up the kitchen and that we had been talking for hours (as usual), the conversation naturally drew to a close. Shalem refused my offer to sleep in my van as they walked me through the things I needed to know about their home—how to pull the couch out into a bed, where the extra blankets were, and the quirky lock on the bathroom door before we said goodnight with hugs and love-yous.

After pulling out the bed like Shalem showed me, I curled up in a loosely knit blanket under the window. Their last few words had me wide awake. *How would I use my privilege on this journey? How would I ensure that I was leveraging my tools, gifts, and circumstances to move in the direction of justice?* A big question after a long day of driving and too much cake, but also the right one.

I didn't have all the answers on the couch bed in my friend's LA apartment, but one thing was clear to me: storytelling. I would use what I had to tell stories of people like Shalem that needed to be heard.

The next morning, Shalem walked me out to my van to say goodbye. I popped the trunk and showed them the bed my friends had built and how I'd organized my Tupperware bins and my surfboard below it.

Shalem with a smile on their face.

They laughed. "I'm impressed," they said, "but I never doubted you."

Although I knew Shalem and I would be lifelong friends, I never knew when I would see them next—and they probably felt the same about me.

We hugged for a long time. A hug that said, "Thank you for being here, being who you are, and for sharing that with me." Then I turned on the engine, waved goodbye, and made my way toward Venice.

4

"And what happens if you do break? Maybe you can be fixed, maybe not. But chances are you will be fixed. And life will go on."

AUGUST 4–VENICE, CALIFORNIA
4 DAYS ON THE ROAD, 210 MILES

Skateboards slapped the concrete. It was Saturday morning in Venice, California, and the skate park had an ocean view, like most places in Venice do. As 59-year-old Tracie rolled up in her wheelchair, skaters from throughout the park greeted her with high fives, fist bumps, and hugs. She wrapped kids in hugs and talked to them like normal people, not the way a lot of kids are used to being talked to by adults.

When her fanbase returned to skating, Tracie turned her warmth toward me. This was our first time meeting in person, and I noticed my nerves, the same way I had with Anna. I had reached out on Instagram a few weeks ago to tell Tracie about my project and ask if she had any interest in meeting. She'd responded with the same enthusiasm she now exuded in person, sprinkling the words "magical," "joyful," and "fabulous" liberally into our conversation.

Tracie's lightness was like a dip in the ocean on a hot Southern California day—refreshing and reinvigorating for my spirit, which still slipped back to KC often. Since leaving San Diego, it seemed like I was straddling forging an adventure ahead and unpacking an unresolved relationship behind me.

Pulling myself into the present, I asked Tracie how often she came to the skate park and how she got to know everyone. She connected it all by telling me about the early stages of her multiple sclerosis (MS) when she wasn't in a wheelchair yet but walking with a cane.

"I went with some kids to a skate park like this one once, and I remember a woman explaining to me that a wheelchair is a tool. That's when I tried one for the first time, and from there, I was sold. I ordered my first chair, and once I got it, there was a lot less pain and a lot more joy," she said. "In life, your joys can change, and sometimes they have to change. Change has always been a very natural thing for me."

Your joys can change, and sometimes they have to change, felt like a profound perspective to apply to my own emotional state. Maybe I was just in between changing joys.

"Right now, I'm finding joy in skating as much as I can while I can. I love going around the curves and the thrill of having the wind in your face." She looked down and wrapped her hand around a silver piece of metal on her chair, explaining that this was her custom-made box chair.

"Your chair is like your legs," she said, rubbing her hands around the metal curves. "It's an extension of your body. It's part of you. As soon as a kid gets in a chair like this, the world becomes bigger.

"A lot of kids ask me what it's like," she said. "I tell them it's like being able to ride your bike or skateboard everywhere! When you think about it like that, how lucky am I? Having a wheelchair is pretty darn fabulous." She laughed, a ray of sunlight brighter than the summer California sun.

"Every time I go to a new skate park, people ask me if I'm going to be okay," Tracie said. "Usually I just laugh and say, 'Yeah, I think I'll be okay.' And usually, I am. But I'll admit, sometimes I can be overly independent."

"Have you always been like that?" I asked.

Tracie and Cookie Crumble geared up and ready to roll.

"Yes," she said, following with a more playful, "of course!"

"The thing is," she continued, "I know I'll need help someday because my MS will change and get worse. I don't want to ask for help from anybody until I actually need it, you know?"

She leaned back in her chair, as if she was sitting with what she had just said. "Until then, let me have my independence. Let me get places however I need to get there, even if that means making other people uneasy for a few minutes."

In my own way, I understood not wanting help until you actually needed it. I didn't talk to my parents about not wanting my swim coach around until years had gone by. I didn't go to therapy after my sexual assault. I didn't even think about quitting collegiate swimming until I was so depressed and anxious that my mom said, "You know you don't have to do this, right?" Somewhere along the way I had become so programmed to power through that asking for help felt a million miles away. I was slowly unlearning that while also recognizing that we live in a culture that idolizes independence and individualized success. As Shalem would say, "This is not by accident."

"Look, the world wasn't made for all of us," Tracie said. "We all struggle with different things, and there are many ways to get around. I'm lucky enough to be able to crawl and stand up, and I can walk with a cane—just very poorly. But I deserve to be treated like a person who can make her own decisions about her body."

Tracie's words brought me back to identical sentiments I'd heard from transgender activists about the right to gender-affirming care, as well as from pro-choice advocates around the right to reproductive justice decisions, including but not limited to abortion. We all have the right to make our own decisions about our own bodies.

"Do you think that's one of the reasons you love skating so much?" I asked, staying focused on Tracie. "The freedom and flow dictated solely by the person skating, carving a path entirely up to you?"

Tracie nodded. "Big time. It feels like flying. And it's so beautiful because everyone's got their own skating style. But I do wish there were more women skaters. When I try to get women to try, they often tell me they're not good enough or say something else to put themselves down. I see moms at the skate park watching their kids every day. I always urge them to pick up a board and skate with them, and they usually tell me they're afraid they might break.

"Here's the thing, though," she continued. "You might break while walking in the sand. You might break while driving your car. You might break doing anything any day. And what happens if you do break? Maybe you can be fixed, maybe not. But chances are you will be fixed. And life will go on. I promise you that."

I smiled—taking in Tracie's warmth felt like sunbathing.

"Do you want to go into the park?" Tracie asked. "You can get a few photos, and I can show you some things."

"I'd love that," I said, trailing behind her closely as she wove through skaters lingering on slabs of smooth concrete and looking at big dips and divots as if they saw something I didn't. I recognized that look: it was the way I looked at the ocean. To a lot of people, they're just waves. To me, they're blank canvases.

Tracie put on her gloves and helmet and rolled up confidently to an eight-foot drop into the biggest bowl at the park.

"I have this signature move I coined a few years ago at a contest," she told me over her shoulder. "I like to drop in with my hands up in the hair. I think it scares people, but I love it. Here, I'll show you."

I walked to the other side of the drained concrete pool and watched Tracie get as close to the edge as she could without going over. Around the park, people slowed what they were doing to watch as Tracie looked down at the drop just over the edge of her chair. I held my breath. With one push, Tracie thrust herself over the edge, her wheels not even touching the ground as she descended and simultaneously released her hands, throwing them up in the air as if she were on the biggest drop of a roller coaster.

This was what she meant by flying.

Seconds later, her wheels reconnected with the ground and she whipped into a cement curve, one wheel lifting and planting again as she came to an eventual stop.

"Tracie, that was incredible!" I gasped as she emerged from the bowl.

"Aw, thank you," she responded as she unstrapped the Velcro on her gloves. "But I'm only doing it to play. I play every day."

"I've never dropped in, even to a little baby bowl. It looks terrifying," I told her.

"Mia, we're going to have to change that," she said. "We'll get you hooked up with some skating lessons. I know lots of the folks down in San Diego, and there's all sorts of skating things you can go to. Let me tell you, when women get together and work together, it's pretty magical."

As Tracie did a few more runs around the skate park, I watched her and cheered. I didn't care how loud I was. That was my friend, an amazing person who believed everyone deserved to experience the joy of skating and did everything she could to make that possible. She was a true connector and encourager, even when it made other people uncomfortable.

When she finished, she rolled over to me to say goodbye and let me know she was going to hang out a while longer for a little more play.

"Any big plans for your sixtieth birthday this year?" I asked as I packed up my backpack.

"Well, hopefully, I'll still be here," she said with a smile. "And hopefully, I'll still be skating."

We hugged goodbye, and as I headed back to my van, parked nearly a mile away, I couldn't help but wish I had my skateboard.

5

"I wouldn't drive this thing anywhere."

AUGUST 6–PASADENA, CALIFORNIA
6 DAYS ON THE ROAD, 236 MILES

Leaving Venice felt like the right thing to do. The city was crowded, hot, and busy. Everything was rushed and scrunched too close together like there wasn't enough room to breathe or be with yourself. I clung to Tracie's joy as I pulled onto the road, where the mix of exhaust fumes and weed wafted in through my open windows.

After a few minutes on the I-10, I noticed the little red temperature gauge on my dashboard creeping up. At first, it was slow—and then it started climbing faster and faster.

My palms began to sweat as I clenched the steering wheel, glancing from the road to the gauge every few seconds. As quickly as it had begun, suddenly the red line approached the H at the top of the temperature gauge. I knew I had to stop driving, so I took the first exit I could, parked on the side of the road, and turned the car off with a sigh of relief. I couldn't drive anywhere like this, even if it was a few miles to Pasadena. I needed to find a mechanic and get it fixed.

Luckily, I found one within a few blocks (the perks of LA, I suppose). I passed time in the waiting room, reading old issues of *People* magazine, and the mechanic emerged like a hero, declaring it fixed. "A simple issue of coolant running low," he said.

I paid and left the shop feeling like I'd dodged a bullet. I'd already gotten the inevitable road trip car problem out of the way. Nice! That was bound to happen, and it wasn't so bad. *Should be smooth sailing from here*, I thought, getting back on the freeway.

Less than five minutes later, I watched the temperature gauge soar again and felt my panic do the same. This time, I got angry. I took the first exit I could find (again) and parked along a curb (again). I hit the steering wheel with both my hands, thinking about the time and money I spent getting the van ready for this trip that was meant to avoid exactly this situation. This time, I called a tow truck. The driver arrived an hour later, eyeing my van with skepticism as he loaded her onto the tow.

"I wouldn't drive this thing anywhere," he told me, shaking his head like a disapproving father.

I didn't have the capacity to respond to him, and I wasn't ready to face the reality of my situation, so I nodded without saying a word. What was it, day four of my several-month trip? And my van was undrivable? *I didn't even make it a week*, I thought. I knew my van was old and kind of a piece of shit, but I had put so much into ensuring it would at least be in decent condition. My mechanic in San Diego had assured me she was in good shape. Shouldn't it have gotten me further—out of the state, at least, more than a day's drive away from San Diego? How could I be stuck here, only three hours north?

Suddenly, all the people I'd been planning to meet and the places I'd imagined going seemed so far away. I turned toward the window and watched the setting sun in silence.

Eventually, the driver dropped me and my broken van off at another mechanic a few miles away from my sister Mercy's house in Pasadena. Mercy, or Mer, as I call her, told me she'd send a Lyft to pick me up. Despite my protests, her intervention arrived as the sky turned from navy to black, and I slid into the air-conditioned back seat, feeling defeated and grateful for her persistence.

At her house, I barely made it to the steps outside her door before I began to cry. It wasn't just the van; now it was the memories. Last time I was at Mer's house, I'd danced up these same stairs with KC in excitement. They had come to LA with me and were going to meet my sisters for the first time. I'd been so joyful, telling KC all about my family and our silly stories and what makes each of them an important character in my life. It was a very happy memory.

How different the same place can feel at two different moments in your life. How stuck you can feel in between joys.

I couldn't keep it in. Mer held me and stroked my hair as I curled my body around my legs on the stairs, making myself as small as I felt.

I slept until I couldn't sleep anymore, waking up in Mer's one-bedroom apartment with puffy eyes and tired bones. When I dragged myself into the kitchen, Mer was pouring hot water into a filter stacked on top of a Mason jar.

"How did you sleep?" she asked, glancing up from her pouring with a hopeful smile.

"I could have slept forever," I responded, flopping into a wooden chair at the edge of the table. "Mer, what should I do?"

"I don't know, my darling," she said calmly. "What do you want to do?" (My sister had always called me "my darling." It made me feel loved.)

"I have no idea. I put so much into this car already. I can't decide if that's reason enough to keep it and hope, or if I should call it quits now. I don't want to give up on this trip, but I also don't know how to keep going."

Mer nodded as she placed the kettle back on the stove and set the piping hot jar of coffee on the table between us.

"Whatever you decide will be the perfect decision," she said, putting her hands on mine. "And, you don't have to decide right now. You know you can stay here as long as you want to. Let this be your safe space as you sort this out."

I squeezed her hands, tearing up at the relief of not needing to figure out a place to stay as I needed to figure out everything else—my upended trip, my deteriorating car, my broken heart.

When Mer left for work, I opened Spotify, put "Hold On" by Dan Mills on repeat, and ran a hot bath. Soaking in the steamy water, I pulled out my phone and reread texts of encouragement from friends when I'd left San Diego only a few days ago.

> You got this!

> Have fun, be safe, and stay in touch.

> So inspired by you!

Not to mention the painfully ironic:

> Hope you make it past LA!

They all made me feel like a fraud. Too much to look at, I put my phone down and sank under the warm water, letting myself feel lost yet grateful for today's moments of slow healing and the space to figure out what to do next.

6

"Do you see how this is all connected?"

AUGUST 8–LOS ANGELES, CALIFORNIA
8 DAYS ON THE ROAD, 247 MILES

My interview with Chandra Anderson, CEO and founder of The Model Behavior (a nonprofit providing vulnerable women with menstrual products to help them live healthy, dignified lives) was a welcome reprieve from thinking about my van troubles. After the second mechanic assured me she was fixed, my van made it back to Mer's apartment without any problems, despite my paranoid glances at the dashboard.

Still feeling tense, I braved the drive to Chandra's apartment in downtown Los Angeles for our scheduled interview. As I circled her apartment building to find parking, I finally saw it: the cursed temperature gauge, again on the rise.

I sat at a red light in bumper-to-bumper LA traffic, panicked. *Turn green, turn green, turn green*, I thought, pulling against the first open curb I could find. I didn't care that it was yellow; there wasn't enough time to scan parking garages or look for open street parking.

I started sweating as I called my sister.

"Hi, my darling! What's up?"

"Mer. My car overheated again," I said, doing nothing to hide the disdain in my voice. "I'm on the corner of 3rd and Hope, parked against a yellow curb. I have to go to my interview with Chandra. I think I'm running late. I'm going to call the tow truck as I walk. Do you think you can meet me here?"

"I can't believe this is happening again," she said. "Yeah, I can be there in forty-five minutes or so. Text me the address. I'll call you when I'm there."

When I got the tow truck company on the phone, they told me it would be about two hours before they could meet me: just enough time for me to meet with Chandra and compartmentalize this nightmare.

I pulled up Google Maps on my phone and plugged in the address Chandra had emailed me. The pin dropped in the middle of a shopping center. Confused, I reminded myself it was LA, a densely populated city with apartments and living spaces anywhere they could fit. *I'll figure it out*, I thought. I walked around a small shopping center for at least fifteen minutes, still feeling a residual panic. Not only was I late for my interview with a person I didn't even know who was taking time out of her day to talk to me, but my car was likely permanently broken. Fuck.

I looked across the street and saw a glass building with a small entrance that looked like it could maybe be apartments. Inside the front doors, a woman sat at a big, black desk and asked how she could help me.

I need a lot of help, I thought.

"Yes, I'm looking for Chandra Anderson. Does she live here?"

The woman gestured toward the elevator and told me which floor to get out on. Inside, I closed my eyes and took three long, deep breaths before the elevator doors opened into a sparkling clean, modern hallway with a big gray door.

After one knock, I found myself greeted by a young, beautiful woman in a denim dress. Chandra welcomed me into her serene apartment, handing me a small Pellegrino from the fridge like I was a guest in a luxury hotel. I looked around the open space at the minimalist furniture, books, and floor-to-ceiling windows. From inside Chandra's living room, I could see the chaos of LA—cars honking, people quickly pacing the sidewalks and bolting across the street whenever there was a break in the traffic.

"I'm so sorry I'm late," I told her. "I've been having the worst time with my van. It's overheated three times in the last two days! I actually had to pull over off the exit and walk here while I called a tow truck driver, which took way longer than I thought it would. Also, my sister Mercy is on her way here so she can give me a ride home after we're done talking. Are you comfortable with her joining us when she gets here? Again, I'm so sorry, Chandra—this was definitely not how I wanted to meet you!"

While I was embarrassed at my messiness, I didn't see a way of hiding it. How could I ask her for her vulnerability and honesty without offering the same?

"Oh, no, that's terrible!" she said. "And yes, of course. Do you need anything?"

"Just a new car, I think," I said, feigning a laugh and trying to make light of the situation despite the growing pit in my stomach. "Thank you so much again for your flexibility."

"It's not a problem at all," Chandra said as she sat on the blue couch across from me. This was so far from how I imagined my interviews going, and the last thing I wanted her to think was that I wasn't appreciative of her or respectful of her time.

"I brought these for you," I said, taking a pack of maxi pads out of my bag that Mercy and I had gotten yesterday. I wanted to show up with something for Chandra, someone who leads efforts to collect menstrual products for women's shelters in her community.

She laughed, pulling me in for a hug. "Thank you so much. That's so kind of you!"

As we started talking, Chandra told me about her organization's initiatives to collect pads and tampons for neighborhood shelters through weekly donation drives, and how she delivers the donations to the Los

Angeles LGBTQIA+ Center, downtown women's centers, and other safe houses, shelters, and halfway houses right here in her own community.

"You know, in many countries and cultures, having your period is viewed as dirty or impure. There are places in the world where women are separated from society when they're on their period or not allowed to go to school during menstruation," Chandra told me. "So let's say you're one of these women, and you miss school one week every month because of your period. Then think about how far behind you are after a few school years. When you start adding that up, it becomes a very real educational disadvantage.

"From there, it becomes a matter of economics. If you're behind in school, you're less likely to graduate. And if you can't graduate, you have less of a chance of being able to provide for yourself or your family. This leads to all kinds of other disadvantages, making it a matter of justice. Do you see how this all is connected?"

One day, they're missing a few days of school, and the next, they're not graduating and forced into low-wage jobs, poverty, and other dire circumstances. Shalem's voice in my head. *This is not by accident.*

"It's inequitable from the start," I said.

"Exactly," she responded. "Now imagine you're a woman in this country. You have enough money to either eat or buy menstrual products, but not both. What do you do? If faced with that choice, many women will, of course, choose food, and use whatever they can in place of pads and tampons because they can't afford them. Maybe it's a napkin from Starbucks or toilet paper wrapped around panties. Perhaps it's a paper bag. Even paper towels are a privilege."

She took a deep breath, and a small grimace crossed her face. She put her palms together under her chin. "It makes my heart want to jump out of my chest."

"Mine too," I said, putting my hands on my chest instinctively.

"You know, I used to always use the word 'women,'" Chandra continued. "I always talked about women, women, women in relation to the work we do. But at the last Women's March I went to, a transgender woman got up and said, 'Not all women have vaginas!' It hit me that I was excluding people without even knowing it. Now I try to say, 'anyone menstruating.'"

Up until this point, very rarely had I heard nongendered terms when it came to menstruation. Much like Chandra mentioned, it was always girls, young women, women, females, lady problems, or something else along those lines. Hearing Chandra use the phrase "anyone menstruating" was a reminder to be mindful of my own language to not exclude transgender men who may menstruate, transgender women who may not, and nonbinary people who experience menstruation.

"Language is just the tip of the iceberg," Chandra said as if she could hear inside my brain. "It's essential to educate, elevate, and create a safe space that's nurturing toward all women and all the issues we face, from immigration to LGBTQIA+ rights, to education access, to targeted violence, to equal pay for equal work. It's not just about pads and tampons. There is intersectionality here that we can't ignore."

Chandra told me she used to work in architecture but left because it was a toxic, male-dominated industry. Now, as the CEO and founder of The Model Behavior, she faces more subtle discrimination.

"Sometimes I'll present on our organization and people will come up to me afterward to tell me they loved what I said—and then ask me who wrote it. That's when I say, 'I wrote that.'"

Really, people? We're still doing this?

"Those types of questions make me feel so discredited," she said, taking a sip of her Pellegrino. "Unfortunately, as a Black woman, this type of criticism is expected. Unacceptable, yet still expected."

"I'm so sorry that happens to you," I responded. "The work you're doing is incredible—and important."

"Thank you. And you know, at some point I realized I was supportive of all my friends and everyone, but my inner dialogue sucked. I wasn't nice to myself! So I started working on being my own best friend," Chandra said, smiling. "It's not somewhere you get one day—you just try, every day. It's something we all continuously work at as living, hopefully growing, individuals."

You don't get there one day. You just try every day. The idea that we don't have to reach any final destination, that we don't have to get anywhere fast, felt like a cool balm on an angry cut. It was too much pressure to constantly be making progress. But showing up and trying every day? That was doable. Manageable. Hell, that was all I was doing: taking it one hour—one minute—at a time. Trying to make the best out of an adventure that appeared to keep ending before it could begin. Fuck the destination. Sometimes showing up is the only tool we have—and it is always enough.

Chandra proudly representing The Model Behavior.

Mer arrived like my sisterly knight in shining armor, eventually sweeping me away from the serenity of talking with Chandra and back into the hectic world outside. As we left, I felt my shoulders tighten and slide up toward my ears.

Walking back to my car with Mer, I told her about what Chandra had said about being supportive of yourself. I started to wonder: How many kind words had I said to myself on this journey so far? What love had I shown myself as I recovered from a breakup and navigated the van situation and set out on this entirely new adventure so far outside of my comfort zone?

Hardly any, I thought. I was more focused on getting there, wherever there was. Out of San Diego. Far away. Into myself again.

If someone I knew were in my shoes, I'd remind them to give themselves grace as they figured it all out. To let getting from one moment to the next be enough right now. But I said none of these things to myself. Maybe I needed to reserve some of the compassion I was extending to the people I was interviewing for me. Maybe I needed to work on being my own best friend now too.

Thinking this way about the relationship I had with myself made me feel just an ounce lighter. Perhaps it was releasing my own high standards. Or the pressure to have it all figured out. Or the heaviness that accompanied the idea that my worth was measured by my output.

Just show up. It's always enough.

Back at the van with Mer, the tow truck driver had arrived. A familiar routine unfolded as he loaded my Toyota Previa onto the large metal platform, chained her down, and whisked her away to another mechanic somewhere in LA.

This time, I didn't follow them there.

"Let's go home," I said to Mercy.

7

"I'm tired of loving things that are broken."

AUGUST 9–PASADENA, CALIFORNIA
9 DAYS ON THE ROAD, 258 MILES

Morning light streamed through the wispy curtains in Mercy's room, waking me from a long, deep sleep. Stirring under the covers, my body felt heavy, like someone had poured lead in my limbs overnight. As I sat up slowly and shifted my four-hundred-pound legs off the side of the bed, a clear thought appeared: I need to know exactly what it will take to save my van.

Just as I propelled myself up to standing, my phone rang. An unknown LA number appeared, and I answered to the owner of the third mechanic shop, the one my van had been towed to last night.

"It's the head gasket," he told me over the phone. "It's bound to happen at some point with all old vans. Unfortunately, there's no way you can see it coming. One day it's fine, and the next, it's kaput."

"How much does it cost to fix?" I asked, trying to wrap my head around the new vocabulary words.

"About seven thousand dollars," the voice on the phone told me, hurling me into shock.

I thanked him and told him I would call him back before dialing the only mechanic I trusted: Gilbert. Gilbert and his team worked on my van in San Diego before I left. Over the course of a few weeks, they put thousands of dollars' worth of work into her, which I justified to myself as a critical investment.

Gilbert ran a small neighborhood auto shop, and I could tell that he and his team took deep pride in their work. When I bought the van, he didn't judge me or tell me it was a piece of shit, even though he probably should have. Instead, he talked to me at length about my plans, listening and making recommendations on routes and repairs to ensure the van was reliable and ready. I never felt like he was upselling me or trying to scheme me into anything unnecessary, which was why I continued to go back to him. I always believed Gilbert had my best interests at heart, and it felt good to trust the person working on the van that I had hoped would take me around the country.

He knew my car better than anyone. And after three mechanic bills and zero improvement, calling Gilbert seemed like the only thing that made sense.

"Mission Hills Auto," the familiar voice answered.

"Hey, Gilbert, it's Mia. You worked on my Toyota Previa a few weeks ago."

"Heeeey, Mia! How's it going? How's she holding up?"

"Oh, not good," I answered honestly. As I summarized the past few debacles, my muscles tensed.

"This morning, the last shop told me the head gasket's completely gone," I told Gilbert, now on the brink of tears. "I think what I need to know is, is she worth fixing?"

"I'm so sorry to hear about all of this, Mia. Really, I am," he said slowly and sincerely. "I need to think about that a little bit and do some research before giving you an answer. Can I call you back in a few hours?"

"Of course," I said, even though I didn't want to wait another second. My body felt clenched, and I needed his answer to release it.

As long as I can remember, people have said I always see the best in others. They say it with equal parts admiration and condolences, like I'm doomed for disappointment because I expect the good—for people to be good, for situations to be good, for things to generally work out. Perhaps it was my disposition, perhaps a coping mechanism, perhaps a choice.

In this moment though, I didn't know what to expect at all.

Regardless of what Gilbert says, I want to keep this van, I thought, my faithful optimism surfacing once again. *He may call me back to tell me she is unreliable, untrustworthy, uncertain, and an unnecessary source of anxiety, and it would all be true. He may say she is an unpredictable drain on my money, security, time, and well-being, to which I would likely say, "It's worth it. I love her."*

But why? I questioned. *Why do I love her?*

The answer surfaced almost immediately: She reminds me of KC.

KC had loved this van. KC had lived in a van themselves. Living in my own van now made me feel alive and adventurous, just like my relationship with KC had initially. With both, I confused anxiety in my gut with butterflies in my stomach and chose excitement at the expense of feeling safe. As time passed, I became increasingly uneasy and full of questions like, *Is today going to be the day KC breaks up with me again? Is today going to be the day my engine overheats again?* They were my ticking time bombs, and deep down I knew it.

Amidst this train of thought, Gilbert called me back. As I answered the phone, my stomach planted itself firmly in my throat, making it difficult to speak.

Cautiously, he told me he couldn't in good faith recommend doing what it would take to salvage my van.

"There's no guarantee that more things won't break," he said, his voice slow and earnest. He explained his rationale and apologized multiple times, even though it wasn't his fault. By this point, Mercy had come outside, watching me to gauge what Gilbert was saying.

When we hung up, I threw my hat onto the steps in exasperation and shouted, "I'm tired of loving things that are broken!" before burrowing my face in my hands.

I immediately felt Mercy's big blue eyes on me as we reckoned with what I had just said. We both knew I wasn't talking about only the van anymore, the same way I hadn't been crying about only the van on the steps a few days earlier.

What came next finally sank in.

Gilbert was right. I could pour all my money, time, energy, and love into this van, and I would still know, despite how much I convinced myself otherwise, that I would only be prolonging the inevitable. The more I invested in her would only raise my expectations that everything would run smoothly, but it would never guarantee a thing. Even when we had good moments, they had all come with fear about how long the good would last before it turned bad. And when it did turn bad—which I always knew it would—it would hurt more because my intuition knew it was coming all along.

I wanted a companion I could trust. I wanted a companion that was reliable. I wanted a companion that I wasn't always trying to repair. I loved my van, and I loved KC, but I knew how they would both end. I could empty myself into them, and they would never be what I wanted them to be. How much of myself was I willing to sacrifice figuring that out?

And so, right there outside that Pasadena apartment, I decided to let them both go.

8

"Oh, my darling, I'm so happy I could be here for you like this."

AUGUST 11–BURBANK, CALIFORNIA
11 DAYS ON THE ROAD, 543 MILES

I booked the appointment with CarMax to trade in my Previa without hesitation, running on the adrenaline and relief of having finally made a choice. The call with Gilbert had been hard to hear, but it did propel me toward a choice. I could work with a choice. I could take another step forward with a choice. I wasn't stuck with a choice.

This time, when I called the tow truck, I was eager to get the show on the road. CarMax gave me $300 for my old van, which gave me a good laugh. I happily accepted the money as a comical *au revoir* to the end of a bittersweet chapter.

CarMax employees kindly helped me move my wooden bed with its memory foam pad from the Previa into my new (used) steel-blue 2008 Toyota Sienna as they joked about it being the most unusual day they'd had in a while. They removed the front row of seats to make room for the bed, carefully stacking them inside.

After a test drive and my signature on a stack of papers, I drove away from CarMax feeling like it was the best decision I'd made in a long time. I rolled down the windows and let the warm LA air wash over my face and through my hair as I headed toward San Diego to store the extra seats in Kaley's garage so I wouldn't have to lug them around the entire country.

On the three-hour drive from LA to San Diego, something inside me shifted. Mia driving her new van understood—finally—that you can't always fix things. Sometimes you have to just let go. The realization felt like freedom. I caught a glimpse of myself smiling in the side mirror, watching the wind whip my hair in every direction. I let it go wild.

Being back at Kaley's house was both surreal and familiar. Kaley has always been like family to me, and it brought my heart joy to see her again. We transferred the seats from my van into a corner of the garage where they could stay for the next few months, and then I was off again, as quickly as I came.

Parting with San Diego a few weeks before was an arduous undoing, like that dramatic movie scene where one person drives away slowly and the other person stands in the driveway, both of them waving and crying for way too long until the audience is like, "Okay, we get it. You're sad. Let's move on." Being back again brought a familiar rush of feelings: the ache of saying goodbye to people I loved (again), the nostalgia of driving familiar streets (again), and the underlying sting of knowing I'd outgrown a place that shaped me as I learned to let go.

By the time I got back to Mer's apartment in LA, the sun had called it a day, and I was ready to do the same. The dip back into my former life had left me exhausted and simultaneously lighter and more prepared to move forward.

"So, how do you feel having a new car?" she asked as I walked in.

"Relieved," I answered. "I don't think I realized how on edge I was, driving the Previa around and wondering if she would make it from one road to the next."

"I'm so glad it happened while you were here with me. I'm so happy

I could be here for you like this," she said.

I reached across the table and hugged her tight before tucking myself into bed for the last night. Her cat, Winston, purred and nestled between my legs.

Closing my eyes, all I could think of was what would come next. Nearly a week after I first got to LA, my new van and I would continue up the West Coast, stopping in Ventura in the morning and ending the day in San Francisco. Finally, I would be able to continue. Finally, I would actually make it past LA. Finally, forward.

As my heart and mind began buzzing with a mix of nerves and excitement, something deeper inside me settled into a sense of calm. I gave into the luring pull of sleep, eager for tomorrow.

9

"Things are harder when you're more."

AUGUST 13–VENTURA, CALIFORNIA
13 DAYS ON THE ROAD, 614 MILES

I left Los Angeles with giddiness bubbling up in my chest. I got the same feeling after I caught a good wave surfing or tried something new for the first time. Headed toward Ventura, I felt momentum I hadn't felt up until this point. I wasn't going far, but at least I was going somewhere. And this somewhere was my friend Beth's house.

Beth and I first met many years ago at a surf contest in Malibu, California, where she was making a video. I knew right away that I liked her—a small, blonde girl with funky sunglasses, running around on the beach, saying hi to everyone and laughing loudly. We fell into friendship naturally. We never lived close enough to each other to do everyday friend things together, but we stayed in touch and supported each other's projects, which always intersected at the crux of photography and videography, women and the ocean. For years, we often found ourselves in the same place at the same time. I'd show up for a film screening she was doing; she'd appear at a project launch of mine. We became each other's long-term cheerleaders.

Arriving at her Ventura home, Beth swept me into the biggest hug. Her dog, Bob, an Australian cattle dog, greeted me with equal excitement. In her mid-forties, Beth wore a tattered white T-shirt and thick, clear-rimmed glasses with a pair of colorful, beachy shorts and no shoes. Her short, blonde hair always looked like she had just stepped out of the ocean.

Beth and her pup on an easy Ventura morning.

In her kitchen, she poured me a mug of strong coffee and pushed a plate of fresh orange slices across the counter toward me.

"Do you want to go to the beach?" she asked.

"Always," I said.

We skipped downstairs, and I kicked off my shoes by the front door. At the end of her driveway, we walked to the right about a hundred yards before we hit sand dunes—and beyond that, the beach and the Pacific Ocean. We dug our toes into the cool sand as we watched her neighbors making the best of windy waves and intercepting dogs on their morning walks.

"Beth, I admire you so much. As long as I've known you, you've done so many different things," I started. "You've always got your hand in some amazing project or something creative to showcase untold stories. How do you describe what you do to people who don't know you yet?"

"I've been trying to figure out how to describe myself for a long time," she said with a laugh. "I guess I'm a little bit of a lot of things. I see myself as a filmmaker, but I also went to art school. I'm a creative, and I make stuff, but I don't want to say I'm a maker, because that term has completely run its course. I appreciate and value humility because we are, after all, a small part of a much larger miracle."

I related so much to that. Even growing up, my friends were all from different parts of my life. As I've gotten older, I've realized that American capitalism isn't designed for people who feel like they're a little bit of a lot of things. Our culture celebrates expertise in one industry or field, clearly defined spaces that are predictable and palatable, and linear paths. (Which, of course, doesn't just apply to careers, but to race and gender identity and sexuality and so much more.) Things are harder when you're more.

As she sipped her coffee, Beth told me about her filmmaking with SeaLevel TV.

"All the documentary films that I make with Jeff, my filmmaking partner at SeaLevel TV, try to uncover the hero's journey," she shared. "Stories of heroes always revolve around a lesson, and the lesson is usually about someone coming face-to-face with something everyone fears and overcoming it. That's what we try to do with our films. Sometimes you see films along the lines of, 'I care about the ocean, I love the ocean. Don't pollute the ocean.' This sends a message and creates awareness, which is good. But what is the emotional connection?"

Beth traced her fingers in the sand as she continued.

"Now imagine that I sit down with you, and I tell you a story about something that dramatically changed me forever. The authentic emotion contained in the telling has the power to stick with you, on a human-to-human level. We are innately programmed to pick up on the struggle and identify with somebody who's lived life, been knocked on their ass a couple of times, and gotten back up to do things for the right reasons. That, as Joseph Campbell says, is the power of the mythical hero."

She was totally right. I always longed to know people in a deeper way, and I wanted people to know the deeper me. (Hence, this whole trip.) We struggle. We doubt. We fail. We're confused and lost and lonely. Our vans break. So do our hearts. We try again. And when someone shares that vulnerability, an emotional connection is built, and trust, empathy, and understanding begin to bloom.

Beth's latest film, *Timeless Areas*, exposed this side of skateboarding legend Elissa Steamer. "Some people are just driven from a deeper place," Beth said, reflecting on her time with Elissa. "It's not about fame, it's not about recognition, and it's not about Instagram followers. It's because they need to go skating every day, or they need to be in the ocean every day—not because they're a mermaid or a salty soul. Couldn't that be just more exclusionary jargon?

"When I think about all those Instagram-curated terms, I wonder if they actually strip us of our individuality," Beth continued. "In some ways, it identifies us as a powerful group. But it also marginalizes the people who may not be a 'mermaid' or a 'merman.' It's a convenient fabrication aimed at an ideal that not many can achieve—an idealized marketing fantasy. How about just being someone who loves to be in the ocean?"

How we self-identify transitioned us into talking about women in filmmaking.

"We haven't been exposed to enough films and media coming from women, especially women of color," Beth said. "I know that for every story I do on a woman, there's going to be a hundred on a bunch of guys. For this reason, I tend to put the lens on women." Beth and I shared the goal of using whatever storytelling tools and skills we had to show women as the protagonists and heroes of their own stories. We both believed we could paint a more inclusive picture of what it means to be a woman, one story at a time.

According to "Indie Women: Behind-the-Scenes Employment of Women in Independent Film 2019–2020,"[3] the number of women directors, writers, producers, executive producers, cinematographers, and editors on independent films has continued to grow—accounting for 32 percent in 2018–2019 and 34 percent in 2019–2020—yet independent films still employ more than twice as many men as women. Similarly, the Annenberg School for Communication and Journalism at the University of Southern California published a paper titled "Race & Ethnicity in Independent Films: Prevalence of Underrepresented Directors and the Barriers They Face,"[4] which found that the ratio of white directors to directors of color is just shy of four to one, and that underrepresented males remain more than three times more likely than underrepresented females to direct US narrative and documentary films. In short: women of color are the least likely demographic to create and produce independent films.

Her eyes locked on the surfers, Beth turned the conversation from women in film to herself.

"I was born and raised in Boston by second- and third-generation immigrants from Poland and Ireland. It was hard knocks, and I got used to that. I played sports as a kid, so I pretty much have always been in male circles. At some point, I started to realize I was the only woman in a lot of situations. I don't know if that hyperawareness of being a woman in a male-dominated space helps or hinders us," Beth wondered.

"Coming to California allowed me to feel freer to explore and not be constrained by some of the tight, tough, super-judgmental structures

---

3   Martha M. Lauzen, "Indie Women: Behind-the-Scenes Employment of Women in Independent Film, 2019-20," San Diego: Center for the Study of Women in Television and Film at San Diego State University, 2020, https://womenintvfilm.sdsu.edu/wp-content/uploads/2020/10/2019-2020_Indie_Women_Report.pdf.

4   Katherine M. Pieper, PhD, Marc Choueiti, and Stacy L. Smith, PhD, "Race & Ethnicity in Independent Films: Prevalence of Underrepresented Directors and the Barriers They Face," Los Angeles: Annenberg School for Communication & Journalism, University of Southern California, https://www.arts.gov/sites/default/files/Research-Art-Works-Sundance.pdf.

that I grew up with. Now I've been so far out of my comfort zone for so long that I feel like I'm just in a different realm of my life. I don't know where it's going to take me, and that's unconventional and scary as shit for a woman in her late forties. But I'm afraid if I lived any other way, I would feel miserable."

Her honesty hung in the salty air, reminding me of how I felt just before leaving San Diego. When faced with known and stagnant versus the unknown and possible, fear wasn't enough to keep me from leaving my comfort zone, either.

"Part of the problem for me—and I say this knowing I'm not the only one in the world to deal with this—is that I'm overly sensitive," Beth shared. "I feel lonely a lot. I think a lot of people feel alone because we're all seeking, and in seeking there can be times of great loneliness. We're all trying to find that perfect spot. We're all seeking what's comfortable, but life isn't that comfortable most of the time. This is it, and there's no playbook for it."

I connected Beth's reflections on being a perpetual seeker back to her earlier comment about being a little bit of a lot of things and being "more." They felt intertwined and bubbled up into a question: Could we accept ourselves as seekers living this way, and in that build a certain tolerance for the times of loneliness and fear—or even learn to appreciate them?

"Hey, do you want to go surfing while you're here?" Beth suddenly asked, turning to me with excitement.

I did, with my whole heart.

Back at her house, Beth loaded two longboards into her white Volkswagen Vanagon, and I finagled a wetsuit out of the Tupperware in my van. She drove us to her local break with the windows down, her arm stretched out to feel the air. I did the same, relishing the moment. Being with Beth made me feel understood because she reminded me that nothing is black and white, and life isn't something to figure out but something to experience and share.

In the water, everyone said hi to Beth, and Beth said hi to everyone. I watched her catch a few waves, admiring her style and how she moved along the face of the wave with ease, acknowledging her friends with a "Woo hoo!" as she passed them. When one of us got a good wave, the other called out with excitement. We took party waves and traded boards. It was so silly and supportive, no different from how we'd been since the beginning of our friendship.

And just as we always did, when one of us fell, we came up laughing and paddled back out to do it again.

10

"Joy can be found anywhere."

AUGUST 14–PALO ALTO, CALIFORNIA
14 DAYS ON THE ROAD, 685 MILES

The drive from Ventura to my sister Grace's apartment in Palo Alto was three hundred miles on a stick-straight highway that runs north to south through California.

"Continue straight on I-5 for 298 miles," the British voice of Google Maps reminded me. The highway was busy this afternoon as I passed through small towns with gas stations and restaurants, brown farmland in between.

In the absence of new scenery and directions to follow, my mind slowed, and subsequent emotions finally had room to sink in. First, I thought about Mercy, and my heart felt bigger in my chest. If self-doubt, disappointment, and financial burdens were unavoidable, I'm glad it happened with her by my side. I thought of Beth, and how we'd spent the morning with no agenda, talking and watching the waves. How free I'd felt! Not more than a few months earlier, I'd spent my days in a flurry of working instead of surfing and trying to figure out how to love someone who couldn't love me back. It had been about two months since KC and I had broken up—and for an instant, I thought about calling them and telling them what I'd been doing and the people I'd met so far. I imagined how excited and proud they'd be, and how, in turn, I would feel excited and proud of myself. I imagined showing them the adventurous and brave version of me that I so badly wanted to be.

Realizing a few days before that I was ready to let them go had felt like an immediate weight lifted—and at the same time, the act of letting go was a process. I found myself turning the years we had known each other over in my mind the way I savored dark chocolate—letting it slowly melt on my tongue and doing my best to ignore the bitterness.

Suddenly, I felt unexpectedly lonely—with 170 miles left to go.

As thoughts of Mercy, Beth, and KC swirled, I barely noticed my sweating palms gripping the steering wheel so hard that my knuckles turned white. I stole nervous glances at the dashboard's temperature gauge, watching for the slightest wobble of the little red indicator, but it never budged. The numbers on the dash and radio lit up in neon green and white as the sky darkened. When I finally got to Grace's neighborhood in Palo Alto, every tendon and muscle in my arms throbbed. I lugged my body and a bag up the steps and spilled into her living room. No introduction. No hug. Just a dramatic flop onto the couch and an equally dramatic statement: "I think my arms are broken."

Grace emerged from the kitchen, unfazed, in leggings and a tank top. She is ten years older than me, but I've always felt like we were the same age.

"Hi, babe! What? Okay, let me see," she said, sitting next to me.

As she started to knead her thumbs into my right bicep, I felt the tight knots under my skin and winced.

"Ow!" I yelped, pulling my arm away. Her eyebrows arched in surprise.

"What's going on?" she said with a concerned laugh. "Weren't you just driving up from Ventura?"

Her laugh made me laugh. "Yes! And I was worried the whole time that my car would overheat! I think I have PTSD from shitty vans."

My acupuncturist sister diagnosed me with bilateral bicep strain (which felt even more dramatic than my entrance) and treated me with a handful of needles, three episodes of *Shameless*, and a heavy dose of teasing the way only siblings can. Slowly, my arms began to come back to life.

"This arrived a few days ago for you from Erin," she said, handing me a small brown package.

My needled arms carefully maneuvered to open the surprise. The card, which came tumbling out first, read:

Sweet Mia—
Googly eyes to remind you that joy can be found anywhere.
Hope you're enjoying the adventure so far!
Love, Erin

My life coach sent me googly eyes!?

Sure enough, a small plastic container of thousands of googly eyes fell out of the brown envelope. I moved around Grace's apartment, assessing what could come alive with two simple stickers. I stuck two eyes on the fridge. Two eyes on every candle. Even two eyes on the bathroom trashcan, which made me laugh as I pressed my foot on the pedal, lifting the lid. With the googly eyes, it now looked like a mouth opening.

"Put trash in me," I said in a low, rough voice as I moved the lid up and down like a ventriloquist. It was so terrible, and I was so exhausted, that it was hilarious. Grace came into the bathroom to see what was funny, and when I showed her, she had the same reaction. Soon, we were both crumpled on the floor, laughing partly at the googly eyes and partly at how hard we were laughing.

This was standard behavior for Grace and me. All our siblings were silly, but we were the two who amped each other the most; egging each other on until someone did something that made us laugh so hard that one of us peed our pants.

When was the last time I felt this light, this playful? I thought. Aside from surfing with Beth this morning, I didn't know, which told me everything I needed to know. On the bathroom floor with Grace, I promised myself to find more pockets of play, like Tracie. *Don't get so caught up in figuring it out that you forget to have fun along the way.*

With noodle arms and a mind far too sleepy to think about much I turned off the lights and wrapped myself in a blanket on Grace's couch. Tomorrow, I'd head to San Francisco to talk with my friend, Ava. We hadn't seen each other in years, so it felt like meeting someone new all over again, only with the edge taken off. I admired Ava's righteousness and unwavering commitment to justice, and I was always more nervous meeting people I admired.

But tonight, after a day of hanging out with Beth, surfing, driving, and laughing on the floor, not even my anxiety could keep me awake. It took all of three minutes for me to fall asleep on the couch in the warmth of Grace's home, leaving feelings about tomorrow for tomorrow.

11

*"And when you're out there fighting the good fight,
don't forget that you are not alone."*

**AUGUST 16–SAN FRANCISCO, CALIFORNIA
16 DAYS ON THE ROAD, 705 MILES**

Waking up in Grace's home was peaceful. Plants dangled off cabinets and shelves were adorned with books, salt lamps, candles, and crystals. The sheer, floor-length curtains softened the morning sunlight. Parting them, I noticed we were surrounded by redwood trees.

Grace emerged from her room in her pajamas and slippers, smiling. "I. Can't. Believe. You're. Here!" she said, swinging her head from side to side with each word. "Yessssss!"

Sitting at her kitchen table surrounded by miniature Buddhas, figurines, and flowers in small vases, we talked about everything that had happened since we last saw each other the year before. She updated me on boyfriends and dating; I updated her on breakups and breakdowns. We laughed and drank coffee and ate breakfast and lunch. At two o'clock, I left to meet Ava in Bayview-Hunters Point.

When I arrived at Open Windows Cooperative, the old industrial building hadn't changed a bit. The massive, echoey hallways. The warehouse windows. I'd been here once before for the launch of an art project, and I remembered it the way you remember a dream—mostly blurry, with pops of vividness. Now, the afternoon sun poured in through the enormous windows, creating boxes of light and small rainbows on the floor. Soft music filled the space.

Ava looked just like I remembered, only her black hair was shorter now, strands peeking out from beneath her yellow beanie. She still had both her nose rings. Her pale pink sweater donned a pin of a small rain cloud, which she said looked like, "a weird strawberry." I assumed she was in her late twenties, like me. She sat behind a drawing table on a stool, leaning forward onto the tabletop with her elbows and clasping her hands together in front of her.

"Since I last saw you, I'm up one dog and down one boyfriend," she said with a laugh, motioning to her pup, Iggy, who lay sprawled out on the floor.

"Funny how much can change, and at the same time, stay exactly the same," I said. "It's so good to see you again."

Ava thoughtfully answering my questions at Open Windows Cooperative.

As we started talking, I asked Ava to tell me more about Open Windows Cooperative. She explained that it's not a white wall gallery in the sense that it's not based on capitalism and showing art to sell it and make a profit.

"I can never afford art at galleries, and I don't like going anyway because they're stuffy and pretentious. Why can't art galleries feel homey? Why can't art shows be fun? Why can't art exhibitions be a little rough around the edges? It doesn't actually matter, you know?" She paused, and a smile crossed her face. "We try to make things more accessible here. When we have an art show, we make it a fundraiser for something. We do auctions and price the art really low. My role is focused on facilitating community and collaboration. I see our space as an opportunity for people to get together in a city where everyone works their asses off to survive."

The surrounding windows gave us a front row seat to a sky that changed from orange and pink to a deep lavender as the squares on the floor faded. I asked Ava what it was like to run an art collective.

"On any given week, there may be individuals coming in to work on their own projects. A few photographers joined recently, so there's been a lot of photoshoots. There's a woman who does performance and dance, and we have strangers that rent the space, cycling through. Sometimes we light candles for Shabbat. Whatever you can think of, we probably do it here," she said with a laugh.

"That must feel special, to hold space for whatever people need, whatever form of expression or creativity that takes, not attached to an outcome," I said, thinking of Beth.

"You know, as kids, we often get to play just for the sake of play, regardless of outcome. As we grow up, art begins to be seen as extra—this privilege or perk you get to enjoy if you have extra time or money. Over time, it falls by the wayside in adulthood," she said, a hint of remorse in her voice.

I remembered the googly eyes, laughing on the bathroom floor with Grace, and my promise to play more. I understood exactly what

Ava meant about growing up and letting this sense of joy for the sake of joy become a luxury.

"I feel like this misconception of art speaks ultimately to personal wellness and our inability to value it as a culture," she said. "If we did value art, we'd be doing shit like this our whole lives. But careers and money become 'more important,' so we stop. We feel like we don't deserve to do nice things for ourselves just because, so we don't. And to be honest, it's been even harder to do this in the two years since the 2016 presidential election. I'll find myself going about my day, and then I'll have a moment of despair, thinking, 'What the fuck is this world that we live in?'"

"Ironically, this is probably the time you need to engage your creative side the most," I added, reflecting on how the last presidential election left so many of us asking ourselves the same question.

"But you know, I am so impressed by young people. They're strong and informed and ready to kick patriarchy's ass," she said. "So my best advice is to find your people and start working together. Start small. Notice something in your daily life that needs some love that you have the power to affect. Find what fills you up and make a practice of it. Then, start thinking bigger. And when you're out there fighting the good fight, don't forget you are not alone."

Ava smiled again. I found myself enchanted with her perspective on community and the role of art in finding hope and connection.

"I love the metaphor of the flock of geese," she continued. "That no one goose can be at the front of the V cutting the head winds for the whole journey. When one goose gets tired, it falls back, and another goose takes its place. Have solidarity with your flock, and you've got a sustainable movement."

Trust that you will get further together than you will alone. What a beautiful reminder of what we can accomplish collectively—especially without ego.

As we said goodbye, Ava sent me off with some art—a poem by Nayyirah Waheed printed on a small piece of parchment, and a pin,

16 DAYS ON THE ROAD, 705 MILES 77

made in collaboration with Alexandra Williams and Mia Christopher, that reads: LISTEN TO WOMEN.

"Thank you," I said as we parted ways. "See you again soon, my friend."

12

"This is just how I am, and I'm not perfect. And at the same time, we're all not perfect. Everyone's not perfect. Together."

AUGUST 20–FREMONT, CALIFORNIA
20 DAYS ON THE ROAD, 771 MILES

In the few days between my interviews in the Bay Area, I cherished being part of Grace's everyday life. We ended each day together and began each day the same way. Most days she woke up earlier than me to make coffee and egg-and-bacon burritos. The sizzle would draw me to the kitchen table, where we had our best conversations, where I noticed myself wanting to talk less and listen more. This special time with my sister made it initially difficult to leave for my interview with Kim.

A few years ago, a mutual friend introduced Kim to me as an icon and advocate for women and gender nonconforming people in action sports. This made sense, considering that Kim had cofounded MAHFIA. TV and the Women's Skate Alliance (WSA) before her current role running the Bay Area chapter of Skate Like a Girl, a 501(c)(3) nonprofit dedicated to creating an inclusive skateboarding community.

Kim was in her early thirties and lived in a quiet suburb of the Bay Area. When I arrived, I parked outside her house and walked up to the front door. She answered in a black hoodie, black pants, and lavender sneakers and invited me in as she collected her things for our trip to the skate park.

As Kim disappeared into her house, I marveled at the eleven skateboard decks hanging in a row against a turquoise wall in her dining room. One said QUIT YOUR DAY JOB, one had a handwritten autograph, and two said VANESSA TORRES, surrounded by cats. I recognized these; they were from a brand called Meow Skateboards that was known for sponsoring women and gender nonconforming skateboarders.

As we got into Kim's car, I told her how much I loved the skateboards on her wall, especially the Vanessa Torres ones. I had long admired Vanessa's smooth and classic skateboarding style, as well as the role she played in paving the way for a more inclusive skateboarding industry. She had been one of the first professional female skateboarders—not to mention queer skateboarders—in a sport historically dominated by heteronormativity and men.

Research confirms the grip (pun intended) men have long had on skateboarding. The Public Skatepark Development Guide[5] shows that 77 to 83 percent of skateboarders are male. Go to any skate park to see for yourself how little representation there is for gender diversity, BIPOC, and the LGBTQIA+ community. When Skate Like a Girl was founded, more people than ever were calling out and challenging this exclusionary culture. Skate Like a Girl and similar organizations worked to prove that skateboarding had a far larger and radically more diverse community than most people realized. All this was leading up to skateboarding's first-ever Olympic debut in Tokyo in 2020—a historic leap for skateboarding on an international stage.

Inside the park, Kim picked up her board and dropped into a bowl with ease. I watched her feet shift in her lavender sneakers as the board obeyed. A group of young kids congregated a few yards away, watching

---

5 "Who Are Skateboarders?" Public Skatepark Development Guide, accessed July 23, 2024, https://publicskateparkguide.org/vision/who-are-skateboarders/.

Kim at her local skate park.

her before she kicked out and pushed over to talk to them. Much like Tracie, Kim wanted the joy of action sports, especially skateboarding, to be available to everyone, and for everyone to feel like they belong.

After chatting with the kids, Kim and I found a partially shady spot to sit as she began to tell me about MAHFIA.TV—her first venture into the industry of action sports.

"When I was growing up in the Bay Area, I was lucky enough to have access to *SG Magazine*. It started as *Surfer Girl*, then became *SG Skate, Snow, and Surf*. Back then, there was no YouTube or FUEL TV or anything like that, so this print magazine became my one way to access the action sports community," Kim said. "At the time, there was no one creating action sports content for anyone besides men, as this was before we had iPhones and GoPros. So my friend Johnny and I decided to tell the stories within this community we loved and launched MAHFIA Productions. For a long time, we presented ourselves as the go-to content media production company in the realm of girls' action sports, specifically skateboarding."

Kim explained that for a little while, the excitement of being an entrepreneur was fun. It also felt like a never-ending race that ended in exhaustion and defeat, particularly when the companies who wouldn't pay MAHFIA for content ended up using their footage anyway. That was when Kim let MAHFIA go and moved back home to the Bay Area.

"It took a lot for me to accept that MAHFIA was done, and it wasn't easy to let go," Kim told me. "I had this awful story I told myself about how I was a failure, I wasn't cut out to be an entrepreneur, and everything would be easier if I fell in line with an existing corporate structure."

"I'm familiar with the awful stories we tell ourselves about ourselves," I said with a smile. "We know cognitively that it's not true, but inside we still feel it. And we're always the hardest on ourselves." Her words reminded me of Chandra, and how she had to decide to be her own best friend. Before leaving San Diego, I wrestled with my own impostor syndrome and negative self-talk that got close to keeping me from trying something new. I had a hard time believing I was the person to do it. There had to be someone better suited to do this, I'd thought. For myself, and many of the people I'd interviewed so far, these fear-based stories we told ourselves were part of our journeys.

"Exactly," Kim responded. "Anyone who's driven knows it's hard to get out of your own tunnel vision sometimes. Especially if you put everything into one thing, it's hard to see it not work out. We're so good at creating and analyzing all these scenarios in our heads, but fear is just a feeling and an emotion, not a tangible thing. It's healthy to have a little fear, but for me, after MAHFIA ended, it became limiting. Plus, there was an additional layer of context because of my family's history."

Kim's energy shifted from the excitement of describing her entrepreneurial endeavors to a more reflective place.

"When Japan invaded China in the late 1930s, my grandfather randomly chose to go to Taiwan with one of his brothers while seven of their other brothers stayed. They thought they'd go for a few months because shit was hitting the fan in China. But after they left, all the borders were shut down, and no one could come back into the country.

They never got to go back. As a result, he was stuck in Taiwan. He worked extremely hard to build a business there before moving to America for more opportunity."

"So when you let MAHFIA go, you felt like you had let down your entire family," I said.

"Yes, until my perspective changed. One day, I realized that maybe the reason my family worked that hard was so I didn't have to claw my way to the top. Maybe they worked that hard so I didn't have to prove myself—so I could contribute to others in a way that was meaningful to me. Once I looked at it from that perspective, everything changed," she said. "I realized my contribution would be using what I had to help kids who have never seen the beach, don't have money to buy a skateboard, or can't access a place to snowboard."

The liveliness returned to her voice as she talked about these realizations, and I remembered Shalem, questioning how to use their privilege.

"The key for me was recognizing that I could still do what I wanted to do with MAHFIA, which was empower women and gender nonconforming people in action sports, just that it would look different than I thought it would."

"Funny how that happens sometimes," I said, thinking about my own journey so far. I was still doing what I set out to do, but it definitely didn't look the way I thought it would. It felt freeing to hear Kim put words to the reconciliation between trusting our *why* while being open to the unpredictability of the how.

"I had worked with Skate Like a Girl through MAHFIA, and I knew there was a chapter in the Bay Area that was real grassroots, but it was put on hiatus because there wasn't anyone available to run it," Kim continued. "Meanwhile, the chapters in Portland and Seattle were growing and hosting after-school programming, free programming to underserved communities, youth camps, ladies' nights, and more. I got to the point where I was like, 'There's no one else doing this. I can't wait around for someone else. I'm inspired to take this on, so I'm going to do it.'"

Here it is again, I thought. The common thread that I had first noticed with Anna: "No one else is doing this, so I will."

"Skate Like a Girl's Executive Director Kristen offered to guide me through the process of resurrecting the San Francisco chapter," Kim explained. "Shortly after, I met my co-director, Ashley Masters, and things just started to fall into place. Now we have eighteen people volunteering with us in the Bay Area to host adult and youth summer camps, after-school programs, and free skate clinics for the community." She smiled proudly.

Kim pulled her skateboard out from under herself and sat on the grass.

"When all your friends skate, surf, and snowboard, you build this collective experience of falling and getting back up," Kim said. "So when you encounter a challenge in life, on some level you have the tools to get through it. We've learned resilience, and we know falling is not the end. I wish every person in the world could have that, instead of being worried about what other people think and about looking good. There's so much freedom in just being able to be like, 'This is just how I am, and I'm not perfect.' And at the same time, we're all not perfect. Everyone's not perfect. Together." She paused, looking around at the park. "I'm going to do a quick lap!" she shouted and dropped into a bowl a few yards away.

I leaned back on the small patch of grass onto my elbows, thinking about what she had shared. Everyone's not perfect, together. How can we release the pressure on ourselves to be what we perceive as perfect or to have a perfect outcome? How can we trust the process and focus on something more meaningful, like the impact we want to make or the community we want to build? How could I release pressure on myself to be the perfect person to do this and to have the perfect trip, and instead find joy in the journey?

Back at Kim's house, we said goodbye with a hug and a promise to stay in touch. As I drove across the Dumbarton Bridge, the sunset turned the water a silky yellowish-orange. I could easily stay in California, but I was starting to feel the pull to explore beyond the comfort of this state and the familiarity of people I knew and loved.

Tomorrow, I would continue north.

13

"It's a funny process, the process of returning to yourself."

AUGUST 22–MOUNT SHASTA, CALIFORNIA
22 DAYS ON THE ROAD, 1,095 MILES

Leaving the Bay Area felt like my first venture into wilderness. High-rises faded into modest homes with yards. Crowded freeways with cement medians became winding, two-lane roads without guardrails. Bay Area smog became Northern California wildfire smoke.

The recent string of wildfires through this part of the country had me on high alert driving into Mount Shasta. I could smell the smoke through my windows as the roads got emptier and emptier, and dusty shades of gray clouded everything except the vibrant turquoise water of Lake Shasta. I hadn't been to a mountain town before, so I wasn't sure if it was usually uncrowded or if this was abnormal. I started to wonder if it was safe to be here—if everyone else had gotten the evacuation memo except me. The only other option to spend the night was a town a few hours away in southern Oregon, and I already felt exhaustion creeping in. I decided to stay.

I parked my van at a local campground and looked around. No one was there—not even at the front desk. Just one night, I promised myself, settling into a secluded campsite surrounded by the tallest trees I'd ever seen. They made me feel small. This remoteness was actually what I imagined my adventure would be—evenings spent outside with the trees and stars, time spent away from screens and the opportunity to settle into being alone with myself. So far, I'd been extremely social, juggling interviews, family members, friends, and, of course, expensive car mechanics. Beneath all of that, whatever energy I had left went to holding my tender heart.

Taking my camping stove out for the first time, I fumbled with it until small blue flames appeared, and I placed a full kettle on top and waited for the water inside to boil. With satisfaction, I poured steaming water into my mug and sank the lemon green tea bag into it. The tea warmed my insides and brought a new sense of peace with it—as if I'd been waiting to take a sip of tea in the middle of the woods alone for a long time.

It's a funny process, the process of returning to yourself. It's made up of simple, small moments of comfort—like a couch to sleep on, or a surfboard to borrow, or orange slices for breakfast, or a conversation with someone new that makes you realize you understand each other. Sipping my tea, all parts of me were finally slowing down, and in the slowness, they began to inch their way back together.

Weeks ago, Anna had said she did what she did because no one else was doing it. That's what Shalem had done—they'd seen the necessity of including community voices in the planning process, so they created a company to do that. Tracie saw the opportunity to get more kids and women into skating. Beth told the stories that were often left out. Ava wanted a place that made art feel accessible again, so she created it. Kim wanted a local chapter for Skate Like a Girl, so she started it.

Isn't that also what you've done? my mind wondered. *You wanted stories of people living unconventionally and didn't see enough of them, so you went out to find them.*

Unlike with the folks I had interviewed, I wasn't used to seeing myself as courageous yet. For the past year, I'd felt like someone recovering from a life in which I'd become entangled. I saw myself as someone licking her wounds while my family and friends had referred to me as adventurous and brave. The thought of myself as courageous, like the people I was meeting, came as a stark departure from my own tired narrative.

Considering for a moment that I was similar to Anna, Shalem, Tracie, Beth, Ava, and Kim, a small piece of me cracked open to make space for a new story. In the middle of the smoke and the stillness of the mountains, I felt myself exhale.

14

"I feel like I've known you for so long."

AUGUST 23 – PORTLAND, OREGON
23 DAYS ON THE ROAD, 1,455 MILES

The next morning, the lingering smoke had lifted, and the daylight seemed to breathe life into the quirky mountain. En route to Portland, the magnificence of the Pacific Northwest began revealing itself. Deep green, sky-high pine trees lined the highway as I took slow, deep breaths, rolling down the windows and filling up my lungs with the crisp, cold air.

Since I had begun talking to Erin, I had learned it was all about joy and play (read: googly eyes). She saw life as the grandest adventure, the ultimate opportunity to play, without toxic positivity. She knew we needed to experience hard things. Erin was helping me find joy, not in spite of hard things, but because of them. There was never pressure to show up in one particular way to our weekly calls. I could be on cloud nine, an absolute mess, or anywhere in between, and she held space for all of it.

Turns out that Erin was house-and-dog-sitting for her friends in Portland at the same time I would be there, and she offered me the extra bedroom for as long as I wanted to stay. My excitement grew, knowing I would finally have the opportunity to spend time with a person who had come to mean so much to me—as well as Kaley, who also happened to be in Portland!

Kaley had been one of the hardest people to say goodbye to when I left San Diego (both times). We lived together and spent nearly all our time together. She was the friend who would go on a spontaneous trip to Death Valley National Park and the friend who would watch the Twilight saga on the couch with me all afternoon, eating pizza and feeling sick afterward together. We talked about everything, laughed about nothing, and loved each other so much that she felt like a sister. After Kaley's dad passed away in June, I did everything I could to make her days just a little bit more bearable—whether that meant loading up the car to go surfing and rolling the windows down, or listening as she described her favorite memories of him.

Kaley and I had plans to go to Alaska together six days after her dad passed. (What was it with preplanned trips to Alaska and healing?)

"We don't have to go," I told her the day before the trip. "I can easily cancel. We can take this trip any other time."

"I actually want to go," she said. "I think it's right."

We spent the next week driving through Alaskan towns from Anchorage to Seward to Homer. The trip was slow and steady—we weren't in a rush to be anywhere or do anything. We let ourselves feel small surrounded by Alaskan wilderness and be in every moment, whatever that moment was, completely. If she wanted to talk about her dad and count eagles in the sky that reminded us of him, I'd listen and count. If she wanted to immerse herself in the grandeur of nature, I'd find the grandest place. If she wanted to listen to music and look out the window, I'd drive and find the playlist. If she wanted to cry, I'd hug her and let her salty tears melt into my jacket. We took our time driving the long, curvy roads and letting ourselves feel everything, the way you do among mountains and the ocean. By the end of the trip, we had counted thirty-one eagles.

Now, at the northernmost part of Portland in the St. Johns neighborhood, I met Kaley and some friends at a brewery. They sat outside at a long, wooden picnic table, surrounded by sandwiches, fries, and beers. Kaley leapt up to envelop me in a hug before introducing me to her friends, Regan and Kaleigh, who both lived there. They invited me to sit down and join them, but I suddenly felt extremely anxious.

How do I decline without looking like an asshole? I wondered. The thought of sitting inside with a beer and my laptop felt like what I needed in this moment, which took me by surprise. Normally, I loved meeting new people. *Why don't you want to sit with them and have a beer? They seem so nice.*

I'd been so busy in LA and San Francisco with my van, my sisters, and my interviews that I had forgotten to slow down and spend time planning for cities where I didn't have these preexisting relationships. *What if I can't find anyone to talk to, or what if I can, but they don't have time for a few weeks?* My thoughts spun into an all-encompassing feeling of being "behind" and an impending sense of urgency. Logically, I knew I was the one making the timeline, but emotionally, I felt like I'd dropped the ball on planning for Portland. Every worry now began to surface as my stomach proceeded to tie itself in knots.

"Thank you so much, but I think I need to get organized after the long drive," I said, well-aware of how lame I sounded.

Inside, I ordered a hazy IPA and tucked myself into a booth to focus on where to go from here. As I began to research women and gender nonconforming entrepreneurs, and deep dive into social media rabbit holes with the hashtags #ShopLocalPDX, I realized just how much work this would be. I had to find the people I wanted to interview, then go through the process of reaching out to them (either on social media, website contact forms, or—if I was lucky enough to find it— through email). I would then introduce myself and my project before asking them if they'd be interested in talking with me. Even if I managed to get in touch with someone and convince them to talk to me, then came the scheduling, which was made infinitely more complicated by the fact that I would only be in each city for a few days.

When Kaley's friends left, she came inside to find me hunched over my laptop. "I'm stressing out," I told her. "I have no idea who I'm going to talk to here, and I'm worried that I won't have enough time. I waited too long to set all of this up. I was feeling so good on the drive up here and then almost immediately, I started panicking that none of this is going to work out. Also, do your friends think I'm an asshole?"

"What? Not at all," she said, laughing and sliding into the booth next to me. "Everything is going to work out. This city is full of amazing people." She leaned over my shoulder and looked at the list I was compiling on my computer. "Look, there's so many options!" she said.

Her words made me the tiniest bit calmer. My belly stopped churning for a moment. She lovingly reminded me about the spreadsheet conversation we'd had before I even left on this trip: "Stop overplanning. You're doing this because you want to make sure everything will work out, which it will when you trust the process." Kim's words surfaced in my mind: "Know your why and let go of the how."

"Did you know Erin is in Portland?" I asked Kaley, changing the subject.

"What?"

"Yeah, she's house-sitting for a friend. I'm going to stay with her while I'm here as I figure out who I want to interview. I'm sure she wouldn't mind if you wanted to stay too. She said it's a big house."

"Well, I was planning to sleep on a friend's couch . . . but that sounds better! If she doesn't mind, I'd love to stay with the two of you."

Maybe it was the beer. Maybe it was Kaley. Maybe it was the promise of a warm bed in an actual house. Regardless, I was relieved to feel some of the anxiety fall away.

When we got to the house, a short woman with chin-length, white-blonde hair answered the door. Erin was smaller than I'd imagined, about five-foot-one with round, bright red glasses that framed her crystal-blue eyes. I knew she was in her early fifties, but now seeing her in person, I didn't believe it. She reminded me of a pixie or a fairy, a mix between Zooey Deschanel and a modern-day Tinkerbell, with the most exuberant energy.

"So, you're sweet Erin!" I said. "I can't believe we're just now meeting in person."

"I'm sweet Erin!" she responded, throwing her arms out for a long overdue hug. "I know. I feel like I've known you for so long."

The next morning, we emerged into a dining room with floor-to-ceiling windows overlooking the tops of pine trees in a lush forest. It was dreary but not sad—as if the world was giving us permission to stay inside, get cozy, and prepare a massive pot of fragrant vegetable soup.

The Lumineers drifted through the house softly as Kaley read a book and Erin wrote in her journal. Resuming my research from the night before, the fear that I was an impostor of some kind resurfaced. In coaching sessions prior to this trip, Erin and I had talked about acknowledging difficult emotions when they come up and lovingly telling them they're not in control versus ignoring them, which makes them scarier. I understood now that fear would be an inevitable part of my journey, but I didn't want to be driven by it.

Oh, you again, I said silently to my familiar friend. *I see you. You have a place here, but you're not in the driver's seat.*

Fear present and quieted, I began researching and reached out to schedule a few interviews. Portland had so many one-of-a-kind diverse businesses that it didn't take me more than a few hours to introduce myself and ask if they'd be interested and available to speak with me. I even reached out to a few folks in Washington, including the owner of an LGBTQIA+ and feminist auto repair shop called Repair Revolution (surely they would understand my van woes!).

A few days later, it came time to drive Kaley to the airport for her flight back to San Diego. We made the best of another goodbye with big hugs and lots of I-miss-you-alreadys. Watching her walk through the turning glass door and into the airport, I choked up. She felt like a trusted part of me, and I wanted her to stay. And, at the same time, I remembered Beth's words: "In seeking, there is loneliness."

My seeking was something I had to do on my own.

15

"I felt alive."

AUGUST 25–PORTLAND, OREGON
25 DAYS ON THE ROAD, 1,464 MILES

The sky was blue, and the weather was warm on this late-August Portland day. I took the morning in slowly as I walked down a quaint street known for its small restaurants, cafés, and quirky shops. A place with outdoor seating caught my eye, compelling me to order a coffee, take a seat in the sunshine, and reflect on my trip so far.

Every person I'd spoken to had left my spirit replenished and renewed. They each had brought such transparency and vulnerability to our conversations, giving us the opportunity to connect over our humanity. There's something so profound about sitting across a table from someone and talking about the truth of what's going on in our lives.

With this in my mind and heart, it felt painful to pull open my planner and look at my list of things to do:

- Call the auto insurance company
- Pay rent in San Diego
- Back up all my audio files and photographs from the interviews

These were not hard tasks. I had done them a thousand times before. And yet, they seemed so arduous in this moment. Everything inside me was buzzing for something that would make me feel alive, which brought one thing to mind: surfing.

It had been humming in the background of my mind since paddling out with Beth, and I decided to finally stop ignoring it. I closed my planner and headed for the coast. A four-lane freeway wove me under bridges and past tall, shiny buildings. As I drove out of the city, the road began to ascend into Tillamook State Forest, where it weaved up, down, and around for nearly an hour through a sea of trees that reached for the sky. Eventually, I intersected with Highway 101, the well-known road that runs along the West Coast. I took the Seaside exit, pulling into a surf shop to get wax and hopefully some local tips on where to find waves.

The girl at the counter didn't look up when I walked in, and as I wandered around, she didn't seem to notice me at all. I had secretly hoped she would greet me and we'd get to chatting so I could casually tell her I had no idea where I was or where I should go.

"Hi, how are you?" I finally said. "Could you point me to a good place to surf around here?"

She looked up, clearly disinterested in me, before responding. "Drive fifteen minutes, turn into the park, follow the road to the beach."

I'd take it.

Repeating her directions to myself, I eventually noticed a wooden state park sign. I followed it to find myself on a winding, narrow road swallowed in mossy, towering trees that made it feel like I was in a rainforest. I started to feel skeptical. As my doubt peaked, the jungle-esque road opened up into a small parking lot that seemed instinctually familiar. Longboards were stacked on top of cars and sticking out of truck beds. Half-dressed people lingered against cars with open trunks. Beach chairs were propped up facing the ocean, and wetsuits dangled on side mirrors and over open doors to dry. Approaching the end of the road, I saw cliffs of jagged, brown rocks surrounding a cove. People played on the beach, and a handful of silhouettes frolicked and splashed in the afternoon waves with their jeans cuffed up to their knees.

Everything that came next was habit: parking my car, putting on my wetsuit, hop-skipping down to the beach with my board and plunging myself into the ice-cold ocean. Going under my first wave, the frigid salt water knocked the wind out of me. I resurfaced with tingling hands, feet, and lungs. It was freezing—and I felt alive.

Once I got past the breaking waves and my muscles warmed up, I paused to take in the scenery. I clocked a smattering of colossal rocks with dark blue waves crashing into them with a dramatic splash and birds swirling overhead. Four older men joined me in the lineup, all of us focused on the horizon. A place like this in San Diego would be at least ten times as crowded. Maybe the cold kept people away. Maybe here, you just had to want it more.

A few waves appeared, and I found myself perfectly in position to take one, riding it in to the shore and paddling back out to do it all again. I was enjoying myself wholeheartedly until I realized the tingling in my feet had started to hurt. When I couldn't feel my hand on my foot, I decided it was a good time to get out. Now I understood why everyone else wore neoprene hoods, booties, and gloves. They knew what they were getting into—literally. I'd barely made it twenty minutes before feeling like my extremities were going to freeze and break off.

On shore, I set my board down and flopped next to it, lying on my back with my hair in the wet sand. My feet tingled as the blood flowed back into my toes.

While going for a spontaneous surf wasn't something new, not having to hurry back to something else was. Surfing felt different with the absence of external pressures—less like something squeezed into my life and more like something I prioritized. It was an entirely new, more intentional connection with the ocean and with myself.

I cherished the sticky skin and salty hair I'd earned the whole drive back to Portland.

16

"We need to hear more of these stories because when we don't, we feel like we're alone."

AUGUST 27–PORTLAND, OREGON
27 DAYS ON THE ROAD, 1,479 MILES

The next morning, I found myself in a semi-industrial Portland neighborhood. Sunlight streamed through a rolled-up garage door as two pups, Hazel and Rizzo, greeted me. Two women, Dana and Sara, followed, introducing themselves as the cofounders of Spooltown and inviting me in.

A few days before, as I was doing research for my Portland interviews, Erin had connected me to a friend of hers whose wife cofounded this manufacturing company in town called Spooltown—a small, women and queer-owned sewing factory specializing in handbags and accessories. Their website read:

We believe in visible, ethical American manufacturing. We believe that people should see the process of making because it's hard. And amazing. And worthwhile. We believe that social change starts with the small decisions, and we're committed to helping build infrastructure for the new economy of makers.

After introducing myself over text, Dana responded to propose a date and time.

Now I found myself standing in the Spooltown workshop at nine o'clock in the morning, leaning against a table that looked like it was used for cutting large pieces of fabric. Dana and Sara joked with each other as a handful of machines punched in the background, and people moved around us carrying fabric and tools I didn't understand. Neatly stacked bins with scraps of leather, cloth, and other materials, all clearly labeled, surrounded us. It wasn't glamorous, but it felt real—like a perfectly functioning ecosystem.

"When we started this in 2011, it felt like the beginning of the 'maker wave,'" Sara said, using air quotes in a way that reminded me of Beth, refusing to call herself a maker. "People were becoming interested in the values and stories behind the products they bought. This aligned strongly with our philosophy, which has always been to buy less stuff, but buy something you give a shit about.

"People don't see the ups and downs of how things are made anymore. They only see the Instagram-curated post of one sewing machine and one person happily crafting along in a hipstery way," Sara said. "Our shop is what it actually looks like to make things all the time."

"The prettier the feed, the more suspicious I am," Dana chimed in. "Always."

"We don't do any apparel," Sara explained. "It's what we call sewn soft goods: bags, home goods, linens, pillows, and accessories. We use heavy leathers, waxed canvases, and denim, as well as a couple of things that are incredibly lightweight. For example, we're the sole manufacturer for GladRags, which is a local company for . . . menstrual pads."

Chandra immediately sprang to mind; I bet she would have loved this!

"At the end of the day, I'm proud of what we've created here," Dana continued. "And the reality is that we don't have a lot of time for Instagram because we prioritize the manufacturing itself." She paused and turned to face me. "Eventually, you realize you can't do it all. You have to choose what you're good at and find other people to help you with the things you're not."

When I asked Sara and Dana what they're good at, the answer came easily: ethical manufacturing. To Spooltown, that means sustainable, humane practices and transparent processes.

"It's been vital to us from the beginning to show that manufacturing can be done small, locally, and visibly," Dana said. "Every single person here is a full-time employee. Everybody gets benefits. Everybody gets paid by the hour, not by how many pieces they make. The companies we work with understand that our price point is always going to be higher because we refuse to compromise our working conditions. We're never going to be the cheapest shop, but at least everybody is taken care of."

Sara nodded in silent support of her business partner. They didn't talk over each other or speak for each other. They just seemed in sync.

"It's gotten more natural to say no over time, but it never gets less weird to say no to business. I thought it would, but it hasn't," Dana continued. "It takes strength to know what your limitations are and courage to say no to something because it's not a fit. I still think, 'Hope I didn't fuck that up by saying no.' But it's more comfortable with two of us because we're each other's gut check in those moments." She paused

Dana (left) and Sarah (right) joking with each other at Spooltown.

and glanced over at Sara, who was smiling contently and leaning against the wall behind her.

"You two have such good rapport—and such a good sense of humor about everything," I said.

"You have to, or you'll lose your fucking mind," Dana said, and the three of us laughed together. "Somebody asked me recently, 'What do you and Sara do all day?' And I told her we argue lightly."

At that, Sara laughed out loud. "Totally," she said. "That's about right."

"In all seriousness, I do think it's the partnership that's made us last," Dana said.

"Well, I'm sure a lot of people admire what you've both built here. What advice do you have for the younger people still figuring it out—who don't have the same experience, partnership, or resources?"

"Look, we're in a town full of designers, and that can be a wonderful thing," Sara started. "A lot of people have an idea for something that they don't know how to make yet. So when those people ask me for advice, this is what I tell them: Buy a sewing machine, and sit down and make things. It will give you respect for the process. It will make you understand what works about your product and what doesn't work. It will provide you with skills that you didn't have otherwise.'" She shrugged and smiled. "I know it seems crazy that, as a manufacturer, I would tell people to invest in a sewing machine and learn how to use it, but that's truly my best advice. That will teach you way more about manufacturing than anything you're going to learn talking to a manufacturer. Once you've made things yourself, you'll understand how things work. You'll ask better questions, you'll get better answers, and you'll earn more respect from others in your industry."

As we talked, Dana and Sara gave me a tour of their shop and let me take photos. Dana opened the neatly organized bins to reveal perfectly cut pieces of leather, holding them in her hand and explaining how they were cut using the tools around us. Sara explained what certain machines did and introduced me to some of their team members, who stopped to chat with us for a few minutes as they moved about the space with piles of fabric or racks full of material. I thanked them for their time and told them they'd shared so much more than I could have hoped for.

"I'll walk you out," Dana said as we headed toward the rolled-up door. Outside, she asked me where I was headed next and what I was planning to do with the interviews.

"I think I'm going to stay in Portland for another day or two before heading up to Washington," I told her. "From there . . . I don't know yet, actually. And I think I'm going to turn the interviews into blogs or social media posts for now." I paused, feeling incomplete. Blogs and social media posts suddenly seemed wholly inadequate compared to the depth of the conversations I had been having.

"But I'm actually toying with the idea of turning all of this into a book," I added.

WHAT? You are? my subconscious shouted at me. It was the first time I'd said the B-word out loud. *What made me want to say it now? Should I have said it at all? Was I biting off more than I could chew?*

"I'm going to get on my soapbox for a second," Dana said.

"Okay," I said, suddenly nervous. Had I offended her?

"You have to turn this into a book," she told me. "There's not nearly enough women and gender nonconforming folks, much less who are entrepreneurs, much less who are queer, whose stories are accessible. We're a community, and yet we don't know each other. We need to hear more of these stories because when we don't, we feel like we're alone. So please, write the book."

For the first time, I silenced my doubt entirely and responded with what was in my heart.

"Okay, Dana. I will."

As I said the words, my body settled into an unexpected calm, as if the initial fear only existed inside me until I made the decision and verbalized it. My shoulders melted down. The fear took a seat. A sense of knowing washed over me, even though I only knew three things:

1. These stories would live on in a book.
2. That book could be a source of community for people like Dana.
3. My "why" appeared to matter to more people than just me, after all.

17

*"More diversity, more open minds,
more futures without fronteras."*

AUGUST 28–PORTLAND, OREGON
28 DAYS ON THE ROAD, 1,490 MILES

Portland was starting to feel natural. Erin and I had settled into a comfortable routine over the last few days: I made coffee and went to interviews while she made tea and worked from home. In the evenings, we walked in the woods and talked about our days. I knew I could easily spend the rest of my trip here, just as I had felt with my sisters in California. At the same time, I had too much more to see to stay. I wanted to find the right pace for my journey—one that allowed me to take a place in and experience it while also maintaining momentum.

My last interview in Portland was with one of the owners of Letra Chueca Press. I found the traditional print shop on Instagram and became instantly captivated by the posters, cards, signs, and pop-ups featuring big, colorful block letters spelling out messages of justice. The words wove between English and Spanish together beautifully, like ANTIPATRIARCHY BEGINS EN LA CASA and RAISE FEMINISTAS. When I arrived at the studio, Camila was laying greeting cards with these phrases on a table.

"Your art is beautiful," I told her, gesturing to the cards.

"Thank you! We usually come up with the phrases together, Daniela and I," Camila responded.

Camila and Daniela cofounded Letra Chueca Press—an independent, sustainable, multicultural space using traditional printing presses and techniques to empower underrepresented communities. I wanted to learn more about how they honored their families, heritage, cultures, and communities with design that courageously confronted racism, violence, capitalism, and colonization. They weren't just about design; they were about "decolonizing design" and reclaiming language, words, and art for change.

We took a seat on two metal stools across from each other, cards on the table between us. Camila was from Chile, and she'd been in the United States for almost nine years. Camila shared that her business partner, Daniela, was from Nashville, and coincidentally, Daniela's grandmother was also from Chile. Daniela also happened to be the apprentice of another letterpress printer. Daniela and Camila met in a collective studio, and that's when they started to make things together.

"The way we met is super funny because, to me, it's very hard to find Chileans here in Portland," Camila said. "They heard my accent and were like, 'Are you from Chile?' It was awesome to meet another person like me."

It was awesome to meet another person like me. Camila's words brought me back to my conversation with Dana—how she urged me to write a book so she could know other people like her. We all want to feel like we belong. Without it, it's easy to fall into the illusion that we're on our own.

From the way Camila talked about Daniela, I got the sense that their relationship was loving and deep—more like sisters than friends, like what I had felt with Kaley or Jamie. Since leaving San Diego, they had been the two I called on the long drives in between places, sharing with them what cities I'd seen, how the interviews had been coming along, and how I was feeling throughout it all. They were the constant that never wavered, even when things were hard.

"I'm sorry Daniela isn't here," Camila said. "They got busy this morning with something else."

"No sorrys at all," I told her. "I'm grateful to meet you and that you had a little bit of time this morning. Tell Daniela I say hi and that we missed them."

It didn't take long for me to inquire about the Letra Chueca workspace. Two desks covered with prints of various sizes were nestled under small windows. There were old maps with the words, THIS IS AMERICA, A STOLEN AND PLUNDERED LAND, and THOU SHALL NOT STEAL, printed on top. A large piece of white paper with bright pink letters read BAE LINGUAL and rested on a window frame.

On the opposite side of the room was a letterpress, a print holder, and a cabinet full of small wooden shelves. Camila walked me through her space, pointing out the stories behind each object, like the letterpress they'd had to fix several times and the letterset her mother bought.

Camila and a piece of Letra Chueca art.
(English translation: No saints, no whores, only women.)

"I can't lie; finding the right space has been one of our biggest challenges through this journey," Camila told me. She described how they'd shared previous spaces with white, cisgender men, and how difficult it had been. "Sometimes they'd make fun of me when I made mistakes with language, since my first language is Spanish, and I can't always find the right words in English. In Daniela's case, being a strong, Latine queer person made noise with them too. Being accepted for who we are and finding a safe space where we don't need to put our energy and emotional work into them to *empatizar con nosotres* has been very hard. Craft fairs have also been a challenge," Camila said. "I've been talking to Daniela about not going to craft fairs where we have to do a lot of emotional labor. I don't want to be in places where people aren't going to get what we're doing. I want to reach those people, of course, but why do I have to do so much work and explaining?"

Camila brought up something I'd been wary of on this journey—not asking folks disproportionately impacted by injustice to educate me. Before showing up, I'd research their website, Instagram, and any interviews they'd done prior to our conversation to be informed and prepared with thoughtful questions.

On a larger scale, to me, this looks like understanding our country's history and reading books like *How To Be AntiRacist*, by Ibram X. Kendi; *White Fragility*, by Robin DiAngelo; and *Hood Feminism*, by Mikki Kendall. It means educating myself about the issues that don't impact me directly, while decentering myself and learning how to be an advocate. It means that my education, awareness, and willingness to be uncomfortable are critical.

"I'm saying this because, in my experience, when I came to the United States, I had to unlearn what I thought was okay in the Chilean culture without knowing the experience of others crossing *las montañas*," Camila shared. "For example, I referred to a friend as *negra* or *negrita*, and my white friends would be angry at me. I was like, 'I don't understand, because in all the other countries of Central and South America, we use that word often and not with a bad connotation.' This is how I understood that it was my responsibility to get to know the real history of this country—not from white people. It's also not up to people of color to explain to me their history. It's my labor to get to know that, not theirs.

"When I moved here, I also learned a lot about becoming independent from my mom and dad and not being another economic heaviness in their life. I started doing design work for a mainly male agency because I needed the money," she said. "The only thing they asked me to create were advertisements with skinny women's bodies. I tried to change that and work around it, sharing ideas that could sell a product differently. Always, they refused. They wanted to see the skinny body because that's what sells, so I said, 'I'm done.' I don't want to design things I don't believe in for people who don't understand the privilege it is to put words and images into the world."

I loved the way Camila identified the privilege it is to put words and images into the world. I promised myself to remember this as I was writing my own book and to use it to make something that, like Camila, I believed in.

"Recently, Daniela and I did a project in downtown Portland called WE HAVE NAMES + THESE ARE OUR DREAMS, in support of Power to the Dreamers, which is a local volunteer organization led by undocumented folks. We wanted to do something that would personalize the language the media was using to talk about real human beings," she said. "People who came to see the first part of the show were asked if they wanted to share their names and dreams. Then, Daniela and I spent the whole night printing those names and dreams for the show. I never worked so hard printing that much," she said, her eyebrows pinched together. "It was so inspiring to see that wall full of prints the next day, taking up so much space. The media was looking at Dreamers as numbers and dollar signs, but they're humans like us, and they have the same feelings and hopes in this life."

"Art has so much power and potential in that way," I said, thinking of Ava. "The way you and Daniela humanize people and issues through your work makes me realize how much more of this I wish there was in the world—or, at least, how much more of it I wish everyone saw."

"Yeah, the media is not giving anyone anything," Camila said, putting some cards into a drawer. "It's saturated by things we shouldn't be caring about, and the people who run it have so much power. They should be giving real information, not showing us things that don't matter or that are designed to confuse and divide."

"So, what can people who are making art—or who do have some type of influence or platform—do to disrupt this?" I asked Camila.

"Every artist and every maker should add some kind of activism or human part to their work. Their job should be trying to give to the world what not everybody can. We want to inspire people to ask their own questions, seek their own answers, create their own media, and build more diversity, more open minds, more futures without fronteras. Having this printing press, we have the power and the privilege to be able to print words that are truth," she said.

I didn't want to leave without supporting their work, so I bought a few cards and the BAE LINGUAL poster as we wrapped up. We both expressed a kind of gratitude for each other that felt deeper than a thank-you-for-the-art gratitude: Thank you for understanding. Thank you for caring. Thank you for standing with me.

As I stepped out of the studio, the afternoon sunshine snuck through the trees and lit up leaf-shaped shadows on the sidewalk. I stopped and closed my eyes, allowing the cool breeze to consume me. In San Diego, in my old life, I often sprinted from one thing to the next without giving myself the opportunity to feel or respond. It was exhausting, but I couldn't see that before. It seemed like now I wanted to feel everything. I wanted to notice my perspective shift and be attuned to my gratitude. I felt compelled to move slowly and allow the conversations I was having to seep into my bones. My mind returned to the other day on the Oregon coast—lying in the sand and letting the waves tickle my tingling toes as the feeling returned to my frozen body. I suppose I'd gone numb for a little while. Standing on this Portland sidewalk, I finally started to get the feeling back.

18

"You can forgive someone, miss someone, even love someone, and still not want them back."

AUGUST 29–PORTLAND, OREGON
29 DAYS ON THE ROAD, 1,502 MILES

I woke up in a cold sweat from a weird dream. I had been crawling through an air vent – a shiny silver maze with no distinct beginning or end– looking for KC. I moved on hands and knees, cold and lost, until I reached the end of the vent, which opened up into a musty dive bar with low lights and dirty yellow walls. A few men with greasy hair played pool, and a single bartender chatted with the regulars. I wandered over to a rickety, wooden table and took a seat.

Suddenly, KC appeared (the way people do in dreams) and sat at my table. I didn't face them, but I knew they were there. Even though I had just been searching for them, I kept my back turned when they sat down. It was as if I wanted to find them, but once I had, I didn't actually want to be near them at all. I didn't say a word, and eventually, they got up and left.

Then I woke up.

As dreams sometimes do, this one left me in a funk that even a good cup of Portland coffee couldn't shake. Now three months after our breakup, KC had come to mind less and less since I'd left LA. When they did, I could usually muster up a way to be grateful for some part of our story. On my best days, I could see they had shown me what love looks like, and in turn, what it does not.

Some days, though, like today, I still felt the hurt and confusion of it all. And on those days, I tried to remember that you can forgive someone, miss someone, even love someone, and still not want them back.

19

"How far from lonely I had felt around them all."

AUGUST 30–ORCAS ISLAND, WASHINGTON
30 DAYS ON THE ROAD, 1,827 MILES

Finally, the time had come for me to leave Portland. *I could stay in this city for a long time,* I thought, packing my stuff from the guest bedroom and moving it back into my van. *I could spend my time interviewing the seemingly countless extraordinary folks who live here and then driving to the coast for a surf. It doesn't sound bad at all.*

Still, I was pulled forward, compelled to finish the journey—something I hadn't always felt with projects in the past. I had a habit of getting bored and, like a puppy, turning my attention to the next new and interesting thing. This time was different. It wasn't like learning ukulele or guitar or skateboarding or Spanish, where I was only accountable to myself. This journey impacted more people than just me.

Plus, now I had said "book" out loud, so there was that. Like Camila had said, the power of art and words is profound, and it's a privilege. Shalem again: "What am I going to do with that privilege?"

I wanted to do justice to everyone who had shared their stories with me—and the people they could potentially reach.

This project just became so much bigger than me, I thought.

❋

Upstairs, I ran into Erin in the kitchen, cup of tea in hand. "I just got back from Powell's!" she said, holding up a small canvas tote bag.

"Powell's?" I asked.

"The big bookstore that Portland is known for," she said, chipper as always. "And I got you something!" She pulled out a thick paperback book with a black cover and gold writing and handed it to me.

"*Women Who Run with the Wolves*, by Dr. Clarissa Pinkola Estés," I read out loud.

"It's the perfect book for you while you're on this adventure because it's all about brave women," she said. "Like you."

I hugged her, moved by how much she believed in me. I felt like I was just learning how to believe in myself.

She walked me out to my van, and as I pulled out of the driveway for the last time, she stood at the door waving to me. It was time, but that didn't make it any less sad to say goodbye.

My last stop in this beautiful city was a coffee shop called The Great North. I had plans to meet a girl named Devin, to whom I'd been introduced by my friend Lee from San Diego.

"I think you'd really like her," Lee told me one night over dinner before I left.

"Oh, yeah?" I said, amused. "Why's that?"

"I don't know, Mia," he said, stabbing his plate. "She likes *Pride and Prejudice* and shit."

"What does that even mean?" I asked him, laughing. I had never read or seen *Pride and Prejudice*; I only knew it was a book by Jane Austen and that Keira Knightley was in the movie.

When I was in LA, Devin reached out over Instagram to introduce herself and offered to get coffee with me when I made it to Portland. Excited about meeting new people on my trip, I agreed, and we set the date just before my van broke down. Cue my unpredicted emotional crisis and upended plans.

When she began sharing Instagram photos of camping near the ocean and cooking over a campfire on the beach, I asked her where she was. She told me she went to Canada to learn how to surf—something she'd always wanted to do. Her last day there was my last day in Portland, so it didn't look like we'd meet after all. *Wasn't meant to be*, I thought.

Still, as two people doing something outside our comfort zones on our own, we found comfort in talking to each other. Over text, we asked how each other's trips were going. She told me about the waves; I told her about the book and the interviews. We began revealing pieces of ourselves, sharing stories and learning more about each other. This went on for about a week until she told me she was coming back from Canada a day early. "I'm over camping and soup, and it's so damn cold here," she said.

Coincidentally, she'd be back in town the morning I was planning to leave. We would have a three-hour overlap in Portland.

I pulled up to The Great North to find her sitting at a small, red table outside. She wore a dark green zip-up hoodie, light blue jeans, and black shoes with Velcro straps. Her curly, brown hair was tousled and short.

"Hi!" she said with excitement.

"Hi!" I responded. "Welcome back to Portland."

"Yeah, that drive was ridiculously long," she said as I noticed her green eyes. "Should we get some coffee?"

At the little red table, the conversation flowed comfortably. She laughed a lot, which made me do the same—the kind of laughs that make your cheeks and belly hurt in a good way.

"What made you want to go to Canada?" I asked her.

"It's kind of a long story," she said. "My whole life, I'd always wanted to learn how to surf. My parents weren't surfers—my mom was a beach person but not an ocean person if that makes sense. Then I dated a girl for a long time who basically told me it was a stupid idea, and I was too old to learn how to surf." Devin paused before adding, "She was not a surfer, by the way.

"When we broke up in January, I realized I needed to learn how to be alone with myself and not be dependent on anyone else." She took a sip of coffee. "Then a mix of things happened with plans falling through, and I ended up with eleven days off. So I decided to go camping in Tofino and learn how to surf and write a book. They were both things on my bucket list, and I was in this space of radical self-growth, appreciative and excited about all of this freedom I was giving myself to do the things I'd always wanted to do."

Sounds outrageously familiar, I thought.

"I'd also heard that there were no sharks in Tofino—which I discovered was a lie after I got back to Portland," she said, with a dash of humor to cut the seriousness. "There are, in fact, sharks in the ocean. But I'm glad I thought there were no sharks while I was there."

"Wow," I said, amazed at her courageousness and how strikingly similar our stories felt. "Tell me everything. What has this newfound self-growth been like for you? How are you noticing yourself show up differently in the world? What is your book about? Oh, also, how were the waves in Tofino?"

She laughed, scrunching her eyes and putting her hands together in her lap. "Am I being interviewed? Is this what it's like?"

"No!" I said, feeling my face flush with embarrassment. "Sorry, I just like hearing real conversations like this. I like talking about what people care about, and what they love."

"That's admirable," she said, taking another sip of her coffee. "I don't think a lot of people do. Or maybe they say they do, but they don't really."

She summarized her story the way people who don't want to talk much about themselves do—by giving the broad strokes and opening up only when I asked for more. "Well, I'm from San Francisco. It's a small town," she said with another laugh. "It is, though."

"How is that possible?" I asked.

"Everyone who's from San Francisco knows everyone," she told me. "My family has been there for generations."

"What's your family like?"

Stop interviewing her!

"How much time do you have?" she joked. "I've got two siblings. My little sister lives in Los Angeles—she's a production assistant. And my brother does . . . something in Oakland. My dad also does something." She laughed. "I have a complicated relationship with my mom, like most of us do. She's a public defender in San Francisco. A real bleeding heart, if you will."

I didn't ask more about her family, trying to be less "interviewy." Instead, I asked about Devin—what she did for work and outside of work.

"Right now, I'm an emergency room tech at St. Vincent's, which is a hospital in Portland, and I'm taking classes to get my prerequisites for physician assistant school." She seemed shy as she said this, uncomfortable to be talking about herself so much. I noticed pink in her cheeks underneath her freckles. "When I'm not working, I'm in school, and when I'm not in school, I'm working. Full-time work, full-time school. It's so much fun," she said sarcastically, before adding more seriously, "I've worked in healthcare for a long time. I know medicine is where I want to be, but I want to be more of a provider and member of the team that helps decide care, create whole-patient plans, and make a difference."

"Do you think working in healthcare for so long makes you more or less compassionate?" I asked.

She let out an instinctual laugh-snort combo and immediately covered her mouth.

"That's an excellent question," she said, still sort of laughing. "In some ways, it makes me feel less compassionate because our healthcare system is a for-profit system that gets manipulated for money. It's hard to watch patients come in and not get what they need, and us as healthcare workers not be able to give them what they need. It feels really backward. We have a lot of work to do."

"Is that what your book is about?" I asked her.

"No, not at all," she responded. "It's fiction, sort of. I guess if I had to describe it, I'd say it's a dark comedy about a family carting around their dead grandmother in a coffin in Ireland." She smiled. "When you look deeper, it's also about boundaries and self-growth and falling in love. I'll give you a copy."

"My trip has included a lot of that so far, except Ireland and coffins," I told her as we both laughed. I shared how my van had broken down in Los Angeles and how it had felt like a moment to let go of a lot that was weighing me down, including a past relationship I also needed to heal from. It seemed Devin and I were both focused on being in a better relationship with ourselves.

We talked about our lives, similar experiences and perspectives on growth until I jumped to my feet, realizing it had been three hours.

"Oh, shit," I said. "I have to go. If I don't leave now, I won't make it to Bellingham in time to pick up my friends from the airport."

Devin walked me across the street so I could show her my van—the bed my friends had helped me build, the surfboard tucked underneath, and the neatly organized Tupperware drawers stuffed with everything else. I felt proud of it, my little home on wheels. I gave her a piece of art Ava had given me, a poem by Nayyirah Waheed printed in light pink letters:

be softer with you.
you are a breathing thing.
a memory to someone.
a home to a life.

"Are you sure?!" she said. "I don't want to take your art—"

"I'm sure," I responded. It felt right for her to have it.

As we said goodbye, she strapped the piece of art down onto her bicycle using bungee cords, put on her hoodie, and buckled her helmet. Her Velcro shoes launched her forward before she turned to wave goodbye. I waved back from the front seat, leaning out the window as her bicycle disappeared down the street, around the corner, and out of sight. After a few seconds, I turned on my car and headed toward the freeway for a six-hour drive north. Perfect. I needed time to process what had just happened.

Heading into Washington, my mind replayed every detail of the person I'd just met. She was so funny! So kind! So smart! Vulnerable and insightful too. Had she actually been ready to come home from Canada, or had she come back early for me? Also, how did Lee know?

For the first time since saying goodbye to KC, I felt a tiny spark for somebody new. How ironic that we would meet right now, right after we both admitted that we were actively focused on healing ourselves and relishing this sense of freedom. I wasn't looking for this. This wasn't in my plan. I didn't know where to go from here or how to navigate whatever this was. I was on a road trip across the freaking country!

Arrival signs at Bellingham International Airport snapped me back into the moment. The airport was small—only one story tall with wooden beams that made it look like an oversized cabin, not an international travel hub. Pulling up to the curb, I saw the familiar duo waiting with their suitcases. My heart swelled as I rolled down the window and shouted, "Well, look who it is!"

Andy was the executive director of a bike organization in San Diego and one of Mixte's first-ever clients. He liked bikes, beer, baseball, and spending time with people who liked the same. We used to have our meetings at local breweries around town, both of us showing up on bikes for a beer before pedaling home. Not the safest, I know. But it's what we did.

Sandy was Andy's opposite in almost every way. When I met her early in my career, also as a Mixte client, I was intimidated by her no-bullshit demeanor. As time passed, I came to appreciate her directness and the way it prompted me to have more confidence and conviction in myself.

Now, Andy and Sandy were like family. I'd spent holidays at their house, gone on trips with them, turned to them during hard times, and asked for their advice more times than I could count. Seeing them now felt like home—what with Andy's chuckle and Sandy's big hug. She climbed into the passenger seat while Andy climbed into the back and sat on top of my cooler, back against the bed frame.

"Okay, so," Sandy began. "We're going to head to Anacortes to catch a ferry for the San Juan Islands, where we'll stay with our friends Chris and David!"

"Beautiful place," Andy chimed in, looking out the window. "Beautiful bike-riding. And great breweries, for an island."

"Yes, we know what you care about, Andy," Sandy said as she looked at me and winked. They'd been married for twenty-five years, and their playful dynamic made me laugh every time.

Anacortes was a small town at the end of a long road about an hour south of Bellingham, well-known for its boating and ferries to and from the San Juan Islands. We could see the ice-blue water from almost everywhere. At the ferry dock, we parked in a designated lot, and I stuffed what I figured I would need for a day or two into a backpack, leaving the rest in my van. It was strange leaving her, knowing so much of my life was inside. *I hope you're here when I get back.*

On the ferry, Andy, Sandy, and I found a booth by the window. It was getting dark outside, but I could barely make out the outline of snowy mountains in the distance across a long stretch of calm water.

"When are we going to push off?" I said after a while. "We've been docked for like an hour."

Andy smiled. "We've been moving this whole time," he said calmly. "Pretty cool, huh?"

"What?!" I said. I hadn't felt a single jolt or seasick moment that told me we might be in motion, and it was now pitch black outside our window.

"Want to go see?" Andy asked.

On the deck, there was no question we were moving. The wind stung my face, sending my hair in every direction. Our hands tucked into the pockets of our jackets, Andy and I silently watched the cars roll off the ferry and onto the islands at each stop: Lopez, Shaw, and then our stop, Orcas Island. Getting off, we met Sandy's friend Chris at the end of the dock. She seemed jubilant and warm, running toward Sandy with open arms.

"This is our friend, Mia, the one I told you about," Sandy said to Chris as she motioned toward me.

"Hi, Chris, it's so nice to meet you! Thank you for letting me crash Andy and Sandy's vacation," I said, feeling slightly awkward.

She smiled and paid no mind to my apology. "We're so happy you're here!"

Her husband, David, helped us load our bags into the small black sedan. When we arrived at their house, I stepped through the front door and saw a fire in the fireplace and a premade bed for me on the couch.

"Mia, this is where you'll sleep," Chris said. "I'm sorry it's the couch—we didn't have any more beds!"

"This is wonderful," I said, touched by her generosity. "Thank you so much, Chris. This is so thoughtful of you."

"Any friend of Sandy and Andy is a friend of ours," she said, putting her hand on my arm and giving it a little squeeze.

It didn't take long for everyone to disperse for the evening; it was past all our bedtimes. I took my shoes off at the front door, set my bag next to the couch, and snuggled under the comforter Chris had laid out for me.

When I began this trip, I felt alone—alone in San Diego, alone in my community, alone within myself. As I left, people kept asking who was coming with me.

"Oh, I'm going by myself," I would say.

Then they'd ask some variation of "Aren't you afraid to be alone for so long?" or "Won't you get lonely?"

"I don't think so," I'd say. The truth was I already felt alone, and I was surrounded by people all the time. That seemed far lonelier than simply spending time by myself.

I hadn't considered that I actually wouldn't feel alone on this trip at all. I hadn't expected to meet so many people who would make me feel not only less alone, but truly cared for. The kindness and accommodation of people astonished me. Chris, Shalem, Chandra, my sisters, and even Erin had opened their homes to me. Dana and Sara, Ava, and Camila had opened their businesses and workshops. Anna, Tracie, Beth, and Kim had shown me their favorite places. Even Devin had shared so much of herself with me. How far from lonely I had felt around them.

As everyone dispersed, I closed my eyes with a sense of fullness and let it pull me into a warm, deep sleep.

20

"Just sit there and be you."

SEPTEMBER 1–ORCAS ISLAND, WASHINGTON
32 DAYS ON THE ROAD, 1,831 MILES

I woke up with Devin on my mind. My eyes closed, I saw her sitting across from me at the red table, playing with her hoodie strings and drinking coffee, laughing. I liked the idea of spending more mornings with her. *I wonder what she's doing right now*, I thought.

As I sat up, I heard Andy in the kitchen making coffee. He reached over the top of the couch and handed me a mug, and I followed him to the patio overlooking the Eastsound, a bright blue, pristine bed of water surrounded on three sides by fir trees reflected in the water. We sat without saying a word as everyone else trickled upstairs and conversation began to fill the cozy kitchen.

"Would you like to check the crab traps with me this morning?" David asked us. My Maryland-born heart perked up as he said we could have fresh crab for dinner, depending on the haul. Everyone agreed except for Chris, who drove the four of us to a small dock, where we boarded David's seventeen-foot boat.

At about six-foot-three, David towered over us with dark blue eyes, white hair, a sarcastic sense of humor, and a big smile. His humor reminded me of Devin, and I found myself curious about his life.

"Have you always lived on Orcas Island?" I asked him as he scanned the water's surface, looking for the crab traps he set yesterday.

"Oh, no," he said, eyes fixed on the water as one hand steered the boat. "But now I try to avoid going to America as much as possible."

"As in, leaving the island?"

"Exactly," David said, glancing over at me with a smile.

"Got it," I said with a laugh.

"I was drafted into the army after high school, but I never went to war," he said. "After that, I fought forest fires with the US Forest Service for, oh, about forty years before we moved here. Aha!"

Spotting a crab trap, David headed toward it, and as he began to haul them up, asked Sandy and me if we'd like to try. Andy was seated, not eager to participate. But it was the first time I'd ever done something like this, and I excitedly agreed to give it a go. Sandy and I took turns pulling the rope and checking the cages. We threw a few crabs back because they were too small to legally keep, ending up with three that David said would be great for dinner. Everything about engaging with the open water this way was exciting to me—I had always been someone who loved the water.

Maybe David could tell I loved it, because he offered to let me steer the boat back to harbor. I accepted, and with a little bit of his help, we made it to the dock in one piece.

Back on dry land and still with plenty of day ahead of us, Andy and I asked David and Sandy to drop us off at the local bike shop; we wanted to go for a ride. Much like the way this trip started, I didn't know where we were going or what the plan was, but I was in.

We wasted no time renting two bikes and setting off on the winding two-lane roads through sunny hills and dense forests. As the forest got thicker, we entered Moran State Park and eventually got to Buck Bay. We pulled up to an old shack-turned-oyster-bar as people meandered around, standing and sitting in clusters, enjoying oysters and sunshine.

Excited and trying not to crash the boat.

Andy and I wasted no time picking and shucking fresh oysters and planting ourselves at a tall wooden table overlooking the shimmering water as we enjoyed our refreshing, delicious oysters—perfectly salty and tart after we squeezed lemon on them. We were both content to enjoy the food and view, which was one of my favorite things about Andy. We had an unspoken understanding of what mattered to us, and we enjoyed doing those things together without the need to talk a whole lot about it. I'd ask him a few questions, and he'd give me a few answers. We'd laugh and make fun of each other a bit. Then we'd both silently understand that today was just a good day.

Reluctant to leave this beautiful place, we got back on our bikes and kept riding until our final stop, Doe Bay. Inside the general store, we bought dark chocolate, sea salt and vinegar chips, and a can of beer each. As we checked out, a rack of ninety-nine-cent postcards caught my eye. I picked up one that read DOE BAY on the front and decided to send it to Devin.

With an indulgent few hours behind us, the ride back home was painful—and somehow more hilly than I remembered, but Andy waited for me at the top of every climb with high fives. When we finally made it back to the bike shop, I was sweaty and could barely feel my legs, but also in a state of bliss, too happy to care. The day spent outside, getting our blood flowing in such a beautiful place with an old friend made the exhaustion worth it.

Back at David and Chris's house, the sun set behind the trees outside as we enjoyed an appetizer of fresh crab covered in melted butter, followed by marinated veggies, beans, and roasted corn in soft tortillas. Everyone laughed as we passed food around, talking about our day and learning more about each other. They asked about my trip, and I asked about their lives. Eating and drinking around the table with the four of them, I felt tired, full, drunk, and happy.

Overcome with the urge to tell someone about the day, I excused myself to text Devin:

> Have you ever had one of those days that you just KNOW you'll remember for a long time?
>
> But instead of realizing it after the fact, you know it's that kind of day while you're in it?
>
> It's like, realizing these are the good old days—right now.
>
> Has that ever happened to you?

She responded right away.

> Yes, absolutely.
>
> Those are the best days.
>
> Are you having one?

>> Yes. I'll tell you about it later.
>>
>> Gotta go be present!

> Enjoy every second lil lady!

Then I tucked my phone away, returning to the table for as many helpings of this moment as I could get.

The next morning was bittersweet, as it was time for me to leave. When I woke up, I noticed David in the kitchen, standing over the stove.

"Do you want huevos rancheros?" he asked, glancing over at me.

"That would be great, if you're making them," I said, rubbing my eyes and sleepily nodding my head. "What can I do to help?"

"Just sit there and be you," he responded.

I untucked myself from the blankets and joined him in the kitchen.

"So, you fought forest fires for forty years?" I asked him, propping myself up onto a stool at the kitchen island. "Did you ever work with any women?"

"I did, but not many," he said, stirring a pan over the stove. "I was always a big advocate for getting women into the fire service because it got rid of the masculine, macho stupidity in the industry. But in my time there, there were very few. You know, there's a big smokejumper base in Missoula, Montana. You should see if there's anyone over there you can interview."

"What's a smokejumper?" I asked.

"They're some of the most elite firefighters," he said, eyes bright. "They parachute in to fight wildfires in extremely remote areas."

Sitting in the kitchen with David, I noticed a pattern developing: people learning about my project and wanting to help me meet folks to interview. And in this case, the person helping me was a man. I sat with that for a moment, processing how tender that felt and why it mattered. I knew that women and gender nonconforming folks couldn't be the only ones advocating for gender equity; men had to too. And we all had the responsibility to ensure those rights included people of all races, incomes, abilities, religions, sexual orientations, and more. I wanted to see people not directly impacted by harmful gender roles—especially cisgender white men—care about stories of other women and gender nonconforming folks pushing boundaries and rewriting narratives. And that was happening in this kitchen.

As the huevos rancheros finished cooking, everyone emerged, still in their pajamas, and congregated in the kitchen. Chris poured steaming, black coffee into mugs and passed them out as the laughing and talking picked up like the night before had never ended. Before long it was time to say goodbye. I wrapped Chris and Sandy in big hugs and an outpouring of gratitude and headed toward the ferry with Andy and David.

On the scenic drive, I counted dozens of goats, cows, and horses dispersed along the grassy hills, distracting myself from my fast-approaching goodbyes. Was it silly that I felt so attached to these four people, even the two I'd only just met?

At the ferry, we got out of the car and exchanged hugs. When David bent down, he swept me up into what felt like a dad hug. "It's been like having a long-lost daughter visit," he said quietly. "You're more than welcome to come back to our home anytime."

My emotions caught me off guard as I realized how kind David had been, and how much it made me miss my own dad. I'd talked to him a handful of times since my trip began but not enough. I missed being near him and doing everyday things with him, like making breakfast and driving in the car. Like David, he loved to teach me new things too.

Turning toward the ferry, I became both deeply touched and overcome by a sudden ache in my chest. I was leaving behind four people I felt safe with and a cozy, comforting home, exchanging it for solitude in my van, in unfamiliar places, which was exciting and daunting at the same time. Similar to how I felt at Grace's house, I recognized how much easier it would be and how much happier I would feel if I just stayed here, with people who loved me.

Yet again, something deep inside me compelled me to continue on, even when that meant leaving what felt the most comforting behind.

I didn't look back. I climbed the ramp to the ferry and sensed what was about to happen. I found a seat alone next to the window, did a quick scan to make sure no one was around, and then, as the ferry started its slow, almost unnoticeable surge "toward America," I put my head in my hands and cried.

21

"Forget the rules you made for yourself."

SEPTEMBER 2–BELLINGHAM, WASHINGTON
33 DAYS ON THE ROAD, 1,893 MILES

> I've got a few days off in three weeks and I'll pretty much meet you anywhere in the country.

> Or Canada.

> Or Mexico.

> I figure, if I'm willing to drive 12 hours to have coffee with you once, why not twice?

These texts from Devin came as I sat in my sister Mercy's room once again—this time in Bellingham, Washington. As a full-time caretaker for a wealthy family with homes in both Bellingham and Los Angeles, Mer's job required her to split her time between the two cities. When I got off the ferry from Orcas Island, it was a short, thirty-minute jaunt north to Bellingham to be in the company of my older sister once again.

Of course, one of the first things I told her about was meeting Devin, the three-hour coffee, and how we'd texted every day since I left Portland. Mercy, always an attentive listener, folded clothes as I monologued.

"And look what she just sent me," I exclaimed, holding my phone out. Her eyes scanned the screen, and she smiled.

"Okay, now," she said in a goofy voice. "She liiiikes you!"

"This is wild," I said in shock. "Anywhere in the country? In Canada or Mexico?"

It was one thing to have a road trip crush. It was another thing entirely to have a person I connected with, who wanted to stay in touch and hear about my day and casually come and visit me wherever I might be on the continent. Devin's texts were refreshing, in stark contrast to people I'd liked before who seemed ingenuine or tried to play it cool. Even KC sent me cryptic texts that I felt like I needed to decipher and overanalyze. But this whole trip so far was hinged on vulnerability. I didn't want to act unfazed or shy away. Prioritizing the possibility felt right in my gut, so I told her I'd love that. Perhaps it was my budding feelings for Devin, seeing my sister again, or the spontaneity of this whole trip, but I wasn't overthinking the text exchange with Devin. In fact, for the first time in a long time, it felt like I wasn't overthinking much at all.

Here with Mer, all I could think was, *I'm so glad I listened to Kaley. What would have happened if I had booked myself solid for the first month or more?* I was almost positive I wouldn't have bought a different van, met Devin, or gone to Orcas Island with Andy and Sandy.

I stepped out onto the wooden deck, feeling proud of myself for letting go. I pulled a pen and the postcard I'd bought in Doe Bay out of my backpack. In block letters, I wrote, THE BIG 2-8! and surrounded it with a few short sentences about how she would have loved Doe Bay and that I hoped she had a happy birthday.

Just as I finished, sweet Erin called me for our weekly coaching session. "How have your interviews been going?" she asked me.

"Amazing," I said. "I'm in Bellingham right now with my sister, and part of me feels guilty that I don't have any interviews planned here—like simply enjoying a place isn't enough. Shouldn't that be enough?"

She listened actively with "mmhmms" as I spoke.

"What if you forgot the rules you made for yourself?" she asked. "What feels right, right now?"

"Allowing myself to enjoy the journey without judgment," I said without hesitation.

"Ah . . . allowing yourself," she said. "You are the only one who can do that."

"You're right," I said. "I'm still connecting my self-worth to my output and productivity. I need to give myself permission to just be."

"How can you do that?"

"Be present," I said. "And I guess recognize that I'm still unlearning some old patterns. Have more compassion for myself."

"Try that," she said, "and see where it gets you."

The next day, it came time for me to leave Mer (again) and head south toward Seattle.

"You know, if you want to get another condo somewhere else in the country, I'll happily stay with you there too," I said jokingly to Mer. "Want to keep this cross-country sister tour going?"

She smiled mischievously and said, "I'll see what I can do."

23

"As we look forward, we must also look back."

SEPTEMBER 5—SEATTLE, WASHINGTON
36 DAYS ON THE ROAD, 1,989 MILES

It was dark when I pulled into the campground outside Seattle. Relief swept over me as I realized it wasn't ultra-remote; this one had a little more infrastructure, like lights and bathrooms with plumbing.

I curled into the bed in my van earnestly. I hadn't slept in my van since Mount Shasta, and I felt cozy tucked between the foam pad felt and quilted duvet from my grandmother. Like usual, I slept with my head toward the windshield instead of toward the trunk, giving myself more room to move around when I woke up.

Seven hours later, it was hot inside the van, which meant the sun must have been up for a while. I reached for the pile of clothes I'd left between the bed and the front seats—intentionally within reach so I didn't have to move around in my underwear a lot inside—especially since it wasn't tall enough for me to stand up. The windshield blockers provided some much-needed privacy as I shimmied into a pair of black leggings and a blue crewneck sweatshirt before sliding open the door and letting the cold Washington air rush inside.

A few young kids played in the campsite next to mine, chasing each other and laughing. It was ten o'clock, a late start, so I skipped making coffee and headed directly into Seattle, eager for the day ahead. I'd decided I wasn't going to interview anyone today. Instead, I was going to learn more about the history of the movement for women's rights and the ongoing struggle for gender equality, an idea that came from a few places—Camila's point about the responsibility we all have to self-educate, Ava's use of art to navigate complex sociopolitical movements, and the realization I knew surprisingly little about the history of the community that blazed the trail, despite my current mission to share these stories of challenging gender norms. How could I do any of the people I spoke with, or myself, justice without honoring the ones who came before?

The Seattle Public Library was a magnificent triangular glass building in downtown Seattle. I wandered around the ninth floor, letting my curiosity lead me and stacking books in my arms. One such book was *The Feminist Revolution: The Struggle for Women's Liberation*, which featured a foreword from Roxane Gay. Fittingly, she'd written, "As we look forward, we must also look back."

I found a seat by one of the many beautiful windows to spend the next few hours immersed in photographs, essays, timelines, and narratives detailing the struggles for affordable childcare, birth control, access to abortions, equal pay, education, job opportunities, the right to take up public space, and more. I read about how intertwined racial and gender equality have always been, although white cisgender women have almost exclusively advocated for the rights of white cis women, largely leaving women of color and trans women behind.

After a few hours of reading, bittersweet emotions swirled within me—gratitude for a movement that had accomplished so much to allow me to do things I take for granted, like vote, open a bank account, access birth control, and drive a car, and anguish that this same movement had only accomplished so much for some women. As a white woman, my stomach churned, thinking about the mountains we could have moved if we cared about everyone's liberation instead of only our own. Knowing that my despair changed nothing, I acknowledged the importance of what I had done today to understand history and promised myself to use what I had to do what I could.

Heading back to my campsite, I felt heavy. I considered calling Devin for the first time, knowing that would invite in some much-needed levity, but I was nervous. Would we have the same easy conversation that we did over coffee?

When she picked up, I got a sudden jolt of energy. It turned out, we both had quite a lot to say, which eradicated any awkwardness right away. I told her about my day in the library and the things I'd learned.

"For me, gender equality is less of a thing you do and more of a lens through which you see your life experiences," she shared. "Like putting on a pair of glasses that you can't take off."

As we talked, Devin opened up more about her moments of doubt in the movement for gender equality as an LGBTQIA+ woman.

"I never let myself get attached to the idea that I would be able to get married. I knew I was queer since I was young, and for a long time, marriage wasn't a possibility for me," she said matter-of-factly. "For as long as I could remember, it was a part of life that seemed unattainable because of who I am. I remember being part of a peaceful protest against Proposition 8 [legislation that, in June 2008, made gay marriage in the state of California illegal] in front of city hall in San Francisco. I watched my first girlfriend get arrested right after she told me she loved me for the first time. It was very, very gay," Devin said with a laugh. "Could not be gayer."

I laughed too, appreciating the layers of her I was discovering.

"Hey, did you happen to check the mail today?" I asked her.

"I diiiid," she said slowly. "There was this postcard in there from a girl I like wishing me a happy twenty-eighth birthday." I smiled into the phone, feeling proud of myself. "Which is funny, because I'm only turning twenty-seven."

"What—are you serious?"

She let out a big laugh, and I imagined her cheeks flushing. "Yes," she said. "I think it's hilarious and also so thoughtful. Thank you."

"Well, what do you want from the next year of your life?" I asked.

"That's a good question," she said. "I hope this year is full of growth and learning."

I smiled into the phone and told her I hoped it would be too.

24

"Because of who I am as a person and the way I am in the world, I have now filled this work with social justice."

SEPTEMBER 9–SEATTLE, WASHINGTON
40 DAYS ON THE ROAD, 2,031 MILES

When my Toyota Sienna and I rolled into Repair Revolution, Eli greeted us with a sideways baseball cap and a huge smile.

"So, this is the van that broke down in LA?" they said, referencing my initial email to them and putting their hand on the hood.

"No, that was the Toyota Previa," I said. "This is the van that replaced her."

"Ah, that makes more sense. Toyotas are usually pretty reliable when they're not too old. Looks like you've got a good one here." Eli took their hand off the hood and smiled. "Welcome to Repair Revolution! Would you like the tour?"

I followed Eli into the auto repair shop dedicated to empowering customers, especially folks who identify as LGBTQIA+, BIPOC, or women, and revolutionizing the automotive industry through radical transparency. The outside of the brick building had a mural of a fist holding a wrench and punching up into the air, surrounded by the words REPAIR REVOLUTION. Inside, six people worked on cars next to a small waiting room with a few couches for customers. Outside the waiting room was a hallway of framed photos of what looked like the Repair Revolution team with happy customers, family members, friends, and each other.

Up a narrow set of stairs, we emerged into Eli's office. I sat on a brown leather couch, and they swiveled in their office chair across from me.

"Eli, this place is amazing," I told them. "How did you realize this was something you wanted to bring into the world?"

"Everything I do in life is informed by my personal experience and the experiences of the people I love," Eli said, leaning forward in their chair. "I come from a low-income background. I watched my family struggle in different ways, and I was homeless for a period of time when I was a teenager. I used to work at a nonprofit with young kids who only ate at school, chemically dependent parents, and families just trying to survive. I felt heartbroken on a daily basis, and we didn't have the resources we needed to deal with the crises affecting the people we served. Eventually, I realized I wasn't able to effect change there anymore."

Eli paused and took a deep breath. "I mean, with cars, it's just fucking metal. You fix it, and it's better. You can fix cars in a way that you can't fix humans."

"Wouldn't that be nice, though?" I offered.

"Yeah." Eli laughed. "It really fucking would."

After leaving the nonprofit, Eli began their journey into the automotive world, which they described as a "total culture shock."

"I should never walk into an auto repair shop for a job and have somebody tell me they don't have any receptionist positions open, but it happened all the time," they recalled, shaking their head.

Eli finally got a job at a dealership instead of an auto repair shop, but because of the daily sexism, homophobia, and toxic masculinity, they felt more wrecked coming home from that job than ever before.

"There was a part of me that was like, 'You like to fix cars. So you gotta put your head down, fix cars, learn as much as you can, and tough it out,'" they recalled, twisting in their chair. "I tried to talk myself out of it not being okay, telling myself I was being too sensitive."

I wondered what Eli might have felt if they'd seen other people who looked like them, doing what they did. Would they have spent so much time believing there was something wrong with them, or that they were the one who needed to change? *Telling these stories matters*, I thought.

Eli eventually realized that they had to get out of the dealership and open their own shop to do everything radically differently. When they left, they tapped every resource to find someone who was willing to fund their business plan for Repair Revolution.

"I got rejected a lot, but I was used to rejection by that point," Eli said, one corner of their mouth turning up. "I got denied for six business loans before I finally found a nonprofit that was willing to take a chance on me. If you're a no-name startup business, it's tough to get anyone to take you seriously. But I made it fucking happen. And do you want to know something hilarious? I remember thinking, 'I'm going to fix cars, and it's going to be this non-complicated thing. I'm going to leave social justice out of it.' Ha!" Eli laughed joyously, hands over their torso, lifting their legs off the ground. "Now here we are. Because of who I am as a person and the way I am in the world, I have now filled this work with social justice."

Pointing out how both of their very opposite careers centered on building a place for people who had historically been left behind made Eli laugh one of those funny-how-it-all-works-out laughs. I knew those laughs. I loved those laughs. They brought levity to the long, multi-generational work of systemic change.

In my own way, I understood reinventing everything about your life only to realize you're just living your same values in a different way. I'd left a communications job, where I advocated alongside community leaders for change, to drive around the country and talk to women and gender nonconforming folks who were leaders creating change in their communities. It looked completely different on the outside, but the inside was still the same. I suppose those are our North Stars—the

Eli in their happy place.

pieces that remain when you strip the outside away. And when you know your North Star, can you ever be truly lost?

When Repair Revolution started, Eli only wanted to hire people who understood why this shop would be different, people who understood their North Star.

"Now, every person here is inspired to do this work for similar reasons," Eli said. "I just hired someone who has thirty years of experience in the industry but couldn't find work for the past year. For a thirty-year-experienced technician to not find work for a year in an industry desperate for technicians is fucking weird." Eli shook their head. "She would get called in for interviews based on her resume; then they would see her and not hire her because she didn't fit the mold of what they wanted. Now, the thing preventing her from getting a job at all these other jobs is what's going to make people feel safe when they walk into our shop."

"How do you describe your shop to people?" I asked, wondering how to put all of this into words.

Eli shrugged and threw their hands up before letting them plop in their lap. "I wish I knew," they said with a laugh. "It feels weird to say that we're woman-owned or LGBTQIA+-owned because my gender presentation is complicated. But here's what I do know: 85 percent of my clients are LGBTQIA+, and 100 percent of my staff are. We're all feminists because that's a requirement to work here. My crew is invested in the work we do because our shop was built on the vision that we will do our part to work toward gender equality and create an empowered experience for customers who share that vision."

Eli explained that they also do everything they can to educate Repair Revolution customers about their cars, because having the knowledge to make informed decisions is where empowerment comes from. I thought of Gilbert and all the extra time he spent with me before this trip. How he patiently answered my questions transparently and never pressured me into making expensive repairs.

"Our whole philosophy is that we want all people to make informed decisions about their cars, and for this to be a place of trust and community," Eli shared. "We spend all sorts of extra time with our customers. When we can, we'll take them out to their car and show them what we see and explain it. We'll let them know if it's a safety issue or how much time the component has left before replacement is truly needed. Then they can decide. I want the person who is struggling to afford rent to not pay a hundred extra dollars for something they don't need."

They told me that Repair Revolution offers hands-on workshops once a month, designing the curriculum around what the community wanted. Eli and their team would even ask folks to bring in their cars to work on so they know how to do it when they go home.

"I'm hoping to do more of the workshops because it's something I genuinely enjoy, and we're in a place where we can offer them free, which is essential to me," Eli said.

"What you've built here feels so . . . full of heart," I said. "You mentioned feeling heartache in your past jobs. Do you feel that here?"

"Not at all," they said confidently. "I feel more true to myself in this job than ever because I get to be myself and share that with my staff and customers. I get to see them come out of their shells and be silly and really fucking gay, and it's absolutely fine," they said. "Actually, it's more than fine. It's great."

Then, with enthusiasm, Eli shared that their crew was going to start a motorcycle club called The Pansies.

"Pansies are the toughest flower," they explained. "They survive all sorts of harsh conditions and live all year-round, even through the winter. They're like the heartiest, strongest flower there is."

Merriam-Webster defines the word "pansy" as a term of "abuse or disparagement," and I had always known it as an insult to imply weakness. But that was far from the meaning Eli had, and I loved the reclamation of pansy as a symbol of strength and resilience. Eli and their crew had survived harsh winters. All of the people I'd met had.

I left Repair Revolution hoping that we were all just pansies—tenacious and eager for the spring.

25

"I care way too much about the story."

SEPTEMBER 10–PORTLAND, OREGON
41 DAYS ON THE ROAD, 2,430 MILES

I knew it was time to leave Seattle because the antsy feeling was back—the same antsy feeling I'd had in Los Angeles and in the Bay Area. The pull had returned, nudging me forward.

The drive from Seattle to the US-Canada border included a beautiful three hours of sunshine, blue skies, and tall, green grass all around. I stole frequent glances at the snowy peak of Mount Ranier out the window until tall flagpoles topped with American and Canadian flags told me I'd reached my destination. Pulling up to the small booth standing between me and Canada, I rolled down my window.

"Hi," I said excitedly, reaching out the window to hand her my passport.

"Where are your license plates?" she asked, not looking at my passport.

"Oh, I don't have them yet," I told her. "I bought this car a few weeks ago, which is why I still have the CarMax tags. They told me they'd mail me the actual plates, so these are my temporary ones for now."

"But they don't have any identification on them," she said, emotionless.

"They just say 'CarMax.'"

"I know," I said, not understanding the problem. Isn't this what happens when you buy new cars?

"You can't come in with those," she said, like she was talking about me taking off my shoes outside. "You'll get towed. If something were to happen, we wouldn't know how to identify the vehicle."

"Okay . . . and, how likely is it that I would get towed?" I inquired.

"It's 100 percent likely," she said, expressionless. "You will 100 percent get towed immediately—by that truck right there." She pointed to a truck a few yards beyond her booth. "Please turn around."

I took my passport back, drove just past her booth, and made eye contact with the guy in the truck before making a U-turn to reenter the United States. Thirty seconds later, US Border Patrol told me to roll down my window.

"What were you doing in Canada?" the agent asked me without looking up from her clipboard.

"Literally nothing," I said with a smile she didn't see. "I turned around after that booth right there because I don't have plates on my car yet. I didn't even get out of my car."

She looked up at me and then past me, peering into the back of my van. "Is that a bed in your car?" she asked.

"Yes," I said. "My friends and I built it becau—"

"Secondary," she said, pointing to a large parking lot with a metal roof. "Leave it unlocked with your keys in the ignition."

For fuck's sake.

I pulled into the parking lot and, as instructed, left my van unlocked with my keys dangling in the ignition. Frustrated, I walked into a crowded waiting room with a handful of kiosks, a piece of glass separating us from people with very serious expressions, typing away. It was the kind of quiet that dripped with tension. If I felt confusion and helplessness as an American citizen reentering America of my own free will, what must it feel like to immigrate from another country or seek refuge from violence and danger?

Living in San Diego, I heard horror stories from the US/Mexico border all the time—in the news, in conversations, on social media. I'd spent many hours in line to get back into the US from Mexico, and I was aware of the inhumane treatment so many people faced at that border in particular. Sitting in the uncomfortably quiet room, I considered all the opportunities Customs and Border Patrol has to be the first touch point of safety for so many people. I also considered the painful irony of America's history of colonizing lands and displacing native people, only to turn around and brutalize anyone seeking safety or a better life on land that has never been ours. Camila's decolonizing designs moved through my mind.

I don't know how much time passed before an older white man called me. "Bolton, you're done."

My car was in the same spot I'd left it, keys still in the ignition. A few things were tussled, like my grandmother's comforter and some of the Tupperware that was now tilted onto its side. I didn't waste any time getting back onto the highway, nowhere to go but south. After this four-hour excursion—which would be a seven-hour excursion if I headed back to Seattle—I didn't have any energy to research a new town to explore or somewhere new to camp. I had one idea, and before I gave myself the chance to doubt it, I called Devin.

"Hello?"

"Hey! So, long story, but Canada wouldn't let me in. Can I spend the weekend with you in Portland?"

"What! Yes, I'd love that," she said. "And please, tell me the long story."

The next morning, I drove to Portland with butterflies in my stomach. Devin would be at work when I got there, so I made plans with our mutual friend Catherine (aka Cat). I hadn't seen her since before Devin and I had met. We had so much more to talk about now.

Cat had suggested a place called PlayDate PDX so her young son could entertain himself in the indoor jungle gym while we talked over a glass of wine. Inside, she was standing by the jungle gym, watching Max go down the slide and catching him at the bottom. I walked over and gave her a big hug, happy to see a familiar face.

"Thanks for meeting me here," Cat said, gesturing to the maze of ball pits and slides in front of us. "It's harder than you'd think to find a place when you have a kid with you."

"I believe you," I told her as we walked over to the bar and her son disappeared into a ball pit.

Cat ordered a bottle of rosé on ice, and we found a seat on the patio. The afternoon sun peeked between the buildings of downtown Portland, and we took full advantage of being able to still sit outside.

"It won't stay this way much longer, so we have to enjoy it while we can," she said, opening the bottle and pouring us each a full glass.

I technically knew Catherine already, because I had met her once before. I knew she dated Lee. Were they still dating? I wasn't sure. I also knew she was Devin's good friend, which made me feel cautious and curious at the same time. What had Devin said about me? What did Catherine know? How could I subtly pry without looking like I was prying? Would she want to get to know me as a person, or was she just scoping me out to see if I was good enough for her friend?

I soon realized my anxiety had been misplaced. The conversation was casual and easy as we talked about our jobs, our lives, and eventually our romances. By the second bottle of rosé, I was fully into my not-so-subtle prying about Devin.

"So, what's going on with you and Devin?" she asked me. "I mean, I've heard amazing things. It's so funny how things work out." She leaned one arm over the patio fence, tilting her head back to tip the remaining rosé from the glass.

"Oh, yeah?" I asked, a little drunk and losing my ability to self-regulate.

"She likes you," she said simply. "It's not my place to share much, but I will say she thinks you're wonderful and hasn't stopped talking about you since you had coffee together."

I blushed, taking a well-timed sip of my rosé. "Well, I don't fully understand what's going on," I said honestly. "But we've been talking a lot, and I want to spend more time with her."

As Catherine and I finished our second bottle, Devin let me know she was on her way.

"Devin's en route!" I blurted out, more to myself than to Catherine.

"What are you two lovebirds doing tonight?" she asked with a smirk.

Lovebirds?

"Um, I think we're going to a play?" I said, realizing how little information I had. Devin had asked me if I wanted to go to a play yesterday when we were on the phone. I had said yes. Sure, we'd met once and had a long, great conversation. Sure, we'd texted and talked on the phone since I was in Portland last. But what does any of that even mean when you're on a cross-country road trip? When so much of your conversation hinged on the self discovery and personal growth you're both experiencing? Much like I felt pulled from city to city, I also felt pulled to Devin. So, despite being afraid, and all of my inner chaos about some nonexistent plan I felt bound to, I leaned in. The more time we spent doing normal things like texting, talking on the phone, and going to a play, the more she went from being someone I met in a city to being a real human being I knew and cared about, and that scared me. It wasn't part of the plan.

Then again . . . what plan?

Catherine began to smile as I heard footsteps behind me. Devin ascended the patio stairs in brown Blundstone boots, blue jeans, and a maroon cardigan over a white T-shirt. She took her sunglasses off and barely had time to tuck them into the collar of her shirt before I got up and threw my arms around her, which caught both of us by surprise.

When we got to the theater, I linked my arm with Devin's as she told me about the play.

"I promised my friend Kelly I'd come tonight. Her boyfriend is in the show, and she didn't want to watch it alone."

"That's sweet," I said. "I'm excited to see it!"

Inside the theater, the show had already begun. Most of the seats were empty, so it was easy to spot Kelly. Not until we sat did I realize how tipsy I actually was—and how impossible it felt to use my indoor voice.

"What is this play about again?" I asked Devin, attempting a whisper.

"Shhh," she said, putting her finger up to her lips and stifling her laughter. "I don't know; I just got here too, remember?"

It quickly became clear that the theater was too small and too quiet for my current state. I tried to pay attention to the show, but I wanted to talk to Devin.

"I don't think I get it," I said a few minutes later, looking at Devin and hoping she could read my mind. *I'm in no shape to be at a small neighborhood play*, I said with my eyes. *Help.*

She snickered and buried her face into her knees, muffling her giggles. This made me giggle too, except I felt unable to be quiet. Knowing we were not supposed to laugh only made us want to laugh more—like teenagers in detention.

When the curtain closed, I burst into the hallway. "Okay, I'm ready to go," I told her with all the seriousness I could muster.

She buckled at the waist again, laughing and bracing herself on her knees. "It's only intermission!" she said. "We barely made it twenty minutes in there."

"I still think it's time to go," I said, giggling again. "I don't think I can do this."

Somehow, she convinced me to stay—and somehow, everyone else in the audience allowed it. I spent the rest of the show holding her hand. At no point did I understand what was happening onstage. When the play ended, Devin said goodbye to her friends, and we headed outside arm in arm.

When we got to my van, I realized Devin and I were standing really close to each other. As we whispered in our own little private bubble, my pulse started to pick up. Then she leaned down and kissed me—a kiss that didn't feel like a first kiss. It was soft and easy, like we had kissed a thousand times before.

"Do you want to come back to my house?" she asked, smiling. "I don't want you driving—or sleeping in your van here."

I agreed, and she drove us to an old, pink house with an upstairs, screened-in porch in North Portland. I followed her inside and up a creaky set of wooden stairs to a room with hardwood floors and two windows, one of which was propped open by a hardcover, tattered textbook titled *Gray's Anatomy*. Her bed was tucked between both windows, and a pile of books collected under her windowsill. Behind her door was a small table that also doubled as a bar, with a few bottles of expensive whiskey and an empty brown bottle with dried lavender sprouting from the top.

You're in her room. At night. You're in her room at night.

Standing in the center of her space, it seemed like the world was spinning around us. She kissed me again—this time a little firmer. Putting my hands on her shoulders, I could feel her muscles clearly defined under her T-shirt.

"Hey, I have to tell you something," she said, pulling back slightly. "I just want you to know that I had a breast reduction a few years ago, and I have scars around my breasts. I just didn't want you to be surprised."

"I had a breast reduction too!" I told her, shocked. "Look!" I lifted my shirt to show her the scars on the underside of each breast and up the center to my nipples.

"What!" she said, reciprocating my shock.

"They're handcrafted," I said, making us both explode in giggles again.

The next morning, I woke up slowly, savoring every detail of her morningness: her dark brown ringlet curls. Her freckles. Her gray sweatshirt. Her adorable glasses. When she went downstairs to make breakfast, I stayed in bed with the duvet pulled up to my chin, wondering if this was real.

Eventually, we left the house with no destination in mind. We held hands as we walked by the coffee shop with the red chairs. In the week and a half that I'd been away, the trees had begun to turn yellow, orange, red, and every color in between. I pulled my beanie down over my ears, reminded of how much I loved fall.

We laughed and kissed and laughed more like those people in every romantic comedy that makes you want to throw up a little. There was a time not that long ago when watching people in love had given me a visceral, dry-heaving reaction. Now here I was, feeling bubbly inside.

We ended our stroll at a place I recognized. "Hey, I've been here before!" I exclaimed. It was the same brewery where I'd met Kaley and her friends, and where I'd sat inside and had a mild anxiety attack. This time, Devin and I ordered two beers, and instead of sitting inside with my laptop, alone, we sat outside and talked until the stars came out.

The following morning was luxurious—sleeping in until we were wakened by the morning light with cold gusts of air coming in through the window. The comforters were so warm, and so was the person next to me. I finally admitted it to myself—I was smitten. My weekend in Portland was beginning to feel like one magical, mesmerizing blur. For something so unexpected, I was surprisingly calm and at ease.

When Devin woke up, we turned to face each other, heads resting on her pillows and knees touching.

"What do you want to do today?" I asked her playfully.

"I was actually thinking we could go to the coast," she said, tucking my hair behind my ear.

On the drive, she held the steering wheel with one hand and my hand with the other. We talked the whole time, stopping in Cannon Beach to get breakfast on this dreary day before continuing into the familiar Ecola State Park. Devin parked the car where we could watch the waves.

"So, you grew up in San Francisco, where you became an EMT," I repeated back to her. "You moved to Portland with your ex-girlfriend, and you broke up in January because she's the worst."

"Basically, yes," Devin said, looking up from her bagel.

"And now you're on your summer break from classes?"

"Yep. I have three more weeks until I go back to school," she responded. "I technically already have my degree. I'm just taking extra classes to raise my GPA because I need at least a 3.2 cumulative GPA to even be considered for PA school, and I was a little asshole in college, so I'm behind." She paused, wiping the cream cheese off her face. "I was homeless for a short period of time when I was in college. Plus, I partied too much when I was nineteen. Now I'm making up for it, one class at a time."

In a 2018 survey of eighty-six thousand college students,[6] the Hope Center for College, Community, and Justice found that 56 percent of respondents had been housing-insecure, and 17 percent of respondents had experienced homelessness in the last year. The report also found that, across all races, the majority of students experiencing basic needs insecurity were women. My heart broke a little for Devin as I imagined her as a nineteen-year-old girl. Of course, she didn't have a high GPA. She didn't even have a place to live.

"How are your grades now that you have a patio outside your bedroom?" I asked.

"All As," she said with a laugh. "And I study on that patio all the time, by the way. But honestly, my grades now only matter because I need to meet the minimum GPA requirements on paper."

"It's such a bad way to evaluate someone," I said. "There's so much more to what someone's capable of besides one cumulative number. It's completely blind to people's personal circumstances, challenges, what they've overcome, or what they're capable of."

"Oh, I know," she said, her green eyes flashing. "But I'm almost there. And all I have to do is meet the minimum and then get in the

---

6 Sara Goldrick-Rab, Christine Baker-Smith, Vanessa Coca, Elizabeth Looker, and Tiffani Williams, "College and University Basic Needs Insecurity: A National #RealCollege Survey Report," The Hope Center, 2019, https://hope.temple.edu/sites/hope/files/media/document/HOPE_realcollege_National_report_digital.pdf.

room. Then my chances are much higher. I'm a people person, not a paper person."

I thought about all of the people I'd met up until this point—how much would I have missed if I'd only read their resumes or a list of their accomplishments? I never would've understood them or had the opportunity to hear their stories, appreciate where they came from and what they'd experienced to shape them into who they are. It's the stories that matter—the numbers on paper are more a sign of privilege than ability.

"I don't think I would make a good school administrator," I said, shaking my head and taking another bite of my bagel. "I care way too much about the story."

"Yeah, you're right," Devin responded. "You wouldn't be any good at that."

Devin on a misty Oregon morning.

Rain pattered on the windshield. Messy, white-capped waves crashed onto the shore, and a foggy mist hung low, clouding the rocky peaks surrounding the cove. Even the tips of the trees melted into the fog. It was completely different from when I'd been here a few weeks before—definitely not a day that made me want to get into the ocean.

Eventually, we started making our way back to Portland. As we headed east, Devin asked me if I'd like to read her book.

"It's a little dark because it's based on my own trauma. You definitely don't have t—"

"Yep," I said before she could try to talk me out of it. "I'd love to read your fictional nonfiction story."

"Okay, I'll give you a copy." As she focused on the road ahead, I watched the corners of her mouth turn up slightly.

26

"I want to learn how to trust more and fear less."

SEPTEMBER 12–SPOKANE, WASHINGTON
43 DAYS ON THE ROAD, 2,781 MILES

Waking up next to Devin had begun to feel natural. I'd gotten used to the gray mornings, breakfasts in bed (spoiled me, right?), and slow walks with hot coffees and fall colors. We spent our time watching movies, cooking, listening to music, and talking about whatever was on our mind. Suddenly, it was the night before I planned to leave Portland, and I had to remind myself I was on a cross-country road trip.

Devin came into her room wearing a matching pajama set—gray with green dinosaurs—when the words tumbled out of her mouth.

"So, let's call this what it is," she said, so direct it startled both of us. "Do you want to be in an actual relationship with me?"

Before I could respond, I watched a wave of pure panic wash over her face. Her eyes got big, and her cheeks immediately got red as she dove face-first into bed.

"OR, YOU KNOW, WE DON'T HAVE TO TALK ABOUT IT RIGHT NOW," she shouted, her voice muffled by the pillow.

Did she just ask me to be her girlfriend?

I wasn't going to stop my trip. I was about to leave Portland. Didn't she want to wait a little longer—at least until I got back? That would have made more sense. Did this make sense?

I looked at her, her face buried so far into the pillows all I could see were her red ears and her messy curls. The ridiculous moment made me laugh, which helped distill the initial flurry of thoughts into one question: *Did I want to be her girlfriend?*

Without all the worries about how it would work or why she was asking, my body was calm. The answer seemed clear.

I touched her arm, coaxing her out from the comforters and looking at her wide eyes. "Yes, I think I would like to be in an actual relationship with you," I said. Much like when I told Dana I would write the book, once I made a decision and said the words out loud, any lingering fear dissipated.

"Really?" she said, surprised and giddy.

"Really," I said, smiling. "I didn't expect any of this, and we have a lot to figure out, but I want to."

In her dinosaur jammies, Devin tackled me into the bed, smothering me in kisses. *This is worth trying*, I thought. It's one of the strangest feelings—to have so little figured out yet feel so unafraid.

As Devin got ready for work the next morning, I packed my bag with all the things I'd scattered around her room over the last four days and headed outside to my van. Just as I threw my bag inside and shut the trunk, she emerged from the pink house with wet hair, blue scrubs, and my sweatshirt on top. I softened as I watched her walk across the yard and up to me.

"Hey, remember that time you asked me to be in an actual relationship with you while you were wearing dinosaur jams?" I said.

"Oh my god, so embarrassing," she said with a laugh, putting her head into her hands. "But I have no regrets."

"Me neither."

"Oh, hey, I have something for you," she said, running back into the house and emerging with a large manila envelope. "It's my book, if you still want to read it."

"YES, I do! Thank you!" The envelope was thick and heavy, the name MIA written on the front in blue pen. *What a remarkable way to learn more about someone*, I thought.

"All right, I have to go now or else I'll never leave," she said, giving me a kiss on the forehead. "I'll call you later."

As she got into her car and drove down the street, I smiled and leaned back on my van, feeling grateful for the way the past four days had unfolded. I took a deep breath and looked up at the big, pink house. So much had happened here in the last four days. It was like everything had changed—my mindset, my trip, my relationship. My relationship. I was in a relationship.

I turned on my car for the first time in four days, listening to the cold engine warming up. My mind slowly began to shift away from Devin and back to my trip. Where should I go next? I'd been so consumed by this dreamy time in Portland that I hadn't even thought about this.

I remembered David's mention of smokejumpers, so I sent a Facebook message to the Smokejumper Visitor Center in Missoula, Montana.

> Hi friends! My name is Mia, and I'm traveling around the country to speak with courageous women. A friend who was a firefighter for 40 years recommended I visit the Missoula center on my way through this upcoming week to see if there are any women smokejumpers who would be willing to chat with me. I'm hoping you can help connect me or perhaps point me in the right direction. Thank you for any guidance you can give!
> With gratitude, Mia

A few seconds later, I got a response.

> I think we could probably arrange that. When will you be in Missoula?

Sitting in my car in Portland, we coordinated an interview a few days from now because Google Maps told me it was a nine-ish hour route through Spokane, Washington, and Coeur d'Alene, Idaho, before arriving in Missoula, Montana. With that, I set off for the next leg of my drive; heading east of Portland meant driving along the Washington-Oregon state line (the Columbia River) and through the Columbia River Gorge, where massive rock cliffs formed to my right as the dark blue river ran to my left.

Similarly to leaving Portland last time, I was eager for the long stretch of driving ahead of me—time to process all the newness. When my phone signal became consistent, I called Erin for a little help with the processing.

When she answered the phone and said she had time to talk, I blurted out, "I have a girlfriend now."

She laughed and said, "Okay! Tell me more," and I described the joy of spending time with Devin as well as some low-level anxiety and guilt that I didn't fully understand.

"Everything's going so well, and it's been so fun. But there's this undercurrent of guilt. It almost feels like—like things have been so good, and I don't deserve it," I said.

"Can you think of any other times you've felt this way before?" Erin prompted me.

This was one of my favorite things about coaching. The coach's role was to be curious, ask thoughtful questions, and use tools to help the other person realize the answers. The fundamental understanding in life coaching is that the client has all the answers within them. The coach's role is to help them see what they already know.

"I think I had this feeling when I moved to San Diego," I told her. "And when I bought a van. And when I left Mixte. Yeah . . . I felt guilty when I left Mixte."

"What about those situations made you feel guilty?" she inquired patiently.

"In each of those situations, I felt like I was doing something good for myself, being brave with my life, choosing things that made me happy. They were moments where I took big steps toward choosing myself. Still, the question of, 'Do I deserve to be this happy?' was always there, often accompanied by a sense that when things were good, the other shoe was about to drop."

My answer surprised me and felt deeply true at the same time.

For starting out so talkative, I had suddenly fallen quiet. Perhaps noticing I was lost in thought, Erin asked if she could share an observation.

"We live in a society that commonly labels women who are indulging themselves or putting themselves first as selfish and wrong. Gender-based expectations still urge us to be selfless, and anything other than that is seen as self-centered. It makes sense, then, that prioritizing our own quality of life can come with conflicting feelings. And, by staying alert and prepared for the worst, your body is just trying to protect you. It's a natural, biological response we developed to keep us safe from predators."

This realization was both comforting—after all, it made sense—and uncomfortable, realizing I still had a nagging sense of unworthiness about my right to my own happiness. I was unsettled. I didn't want to be selfless. I wanted to be selfish and not feel guilty about it. I wanted to go all in on what brought me joy. Why couldn't it be as simple as enjoying when things are good? There would always be the unknown, but I didn't want to live my life looking out of the corner of my eye.

"I want to learn how to trust more and fear less so that I don't move through my life feeling unable to enjoy it. Can you help me with that?"

"We will work through it together," Erin said. "Like with everything, awareness is the first step."

Talking with Erin, I hardly noticed the Columbia River Gorge had become rolling, golden hills against a bright blue sky. Gray clouds and dark green trees had become tall, yellow grass bending in the wind, and I could see the two-lane road ahead carving a paved path through it all. By the time I got into Spokane, Washington, I was exhausted. I pulled into the first campsite I could find in Riverside State Park as the sky turned a deep navy. I rolled down the windows just enough to let the sound of the rushing Spokane River lull my worried mind to sleep.

27

"I don't think anyone should be afraid to try."

SEPTEMBER 14—MISSOULA, MONTANA
45 DAYS ON THE ROAD, 2979 MILES

No landscape had taken my breath away so far quite the way the Coeur d'Alene Lake did in northern Idaho. It was pristine—like a sheet of glass reflecting the colorful fall tree line surrounding it. Big gray rocks lined the riverbank up to a paved walking path around the lake's perimeter. Driving by didn't feel like an option.

Pulling over, I got out to walk along the path, climb down onto the gray rocks, and lightly dip my fingers into the icy water, watching the ripples multiply outward infinitely. Unhurried, I sat on a rock, listening to the birds chirping overhead. I closed my eyes and took long, slow breaths. *There is no rush*, I reminded myself.

Less than three hours later, I was in Missoula, Montana, pulling off the main highway toward the Missoula Smokejumper Visitor Center. Inside I met a kind older man named Ben, who let me know he was the one I'd talked with over Facebook Messenger.

"Thank you so much for setting all this up," I said.

"Yeah, you got it," he responded, coming out from behind the counter. "Follow me. I'll get you squared away with Emma."

I followed Ben out of the visitor center to the smokejumper base. Tall, green-and-yellow mountains poked into the sky all around us—there were no restaurants, hotels, or tourism of any kind in sight. Just hills, mountains, the Missoula Smokejumper Visitor Center and Base, and one long, paved runway.

Outside of the base, two men and one young woman sat talking at a table. When Ben and I walked up, they quieted and turned their attention to us.

"This is Mia, the girl here to interview you, Emma," Ben said.

Emma swung her leg around the bench she was sitting on and stood. She was tall. Her dark hair was woven into a braid that rested on her shoulder underneath a worn, forest-green hat, and her sunglasses dangled by a lanyard around her neck. Emma was one of very few female smokejumpers.[7] The rigorous training and intense work made it a male-dominated field, but that was changing.

"Hi," I said. "It's great to meet you. Thanks so much for making the time."

"No problem," she said. "Would you like a tour?"

"Of course I would!"

I followed Emma through the front doors of the smokejumper base. The first room was at least thirty feet high, with parachutes pulled open at various heights and strings falling all the way down to the floor around us. Emma called this room "the tower."

"Those are cargo chutes," she told me. "Anytime a parachute gets dropped with para cargo, we bring it in here and string it up to inspect for tears or holes. We look everything over to make sure no damages occurred in the jump, and if they did, we fix them ourselves."

"You fix them yourselves?" I asked her, surprised.

---

7   Danielle Knight, "Women in fire: Blazing through barriers," U.S. Department of Agriculture, Forest Service, March 18, 2024, https://www.fs.usda.gov/about-agency/features/women-fire-blazing-through-barriers.

"Yeah. Here, I'll show you," she said, leading me to another room full of sewing machines. "Last year, I was so nervous to get on the sewing machines."

"You jump out of planes! Why are you nervous about sewing machines?"

"I know," Emma said with a timid chuckle. "But the pedal just takes off and puts thread in the material and it's nerve-racking to me!"

She led us to another room, this one bigger and more open. Items were stapled to the wall, including at least five bags of freeze-dried meals, two Clif Bars, one can of Spam, one can of sardines, instant roasted garlic potatoes, four packs of instant oatmeal, one bag of roasted nuts, one package of ramen, a pack of Reese's Cups, three bags of Lipton tea, three packs of instant Folgers coffee, and a plastic container of water. Next to it was a backpack packed with a parachute, chainsaw, and an axe.

"This display is the actual contents of our cargo packs. It's enough food to feed one person for three days," Emma said, gesturing toward the wall. "This is everything that we jump with, except the chainsaw, which they drop as para cargo depending on how many we need. At the lightest, a pack like this is eighty-five pounds. Mine is heavier."

"It takes minimalism to a whole new level," I said.

"Yeah, for sure," Emma said, walking toward the locker room. "It's all about not packing more than we need."

"Do you ever go backpacking in your personal life?" I asked her jokingly.

"Not anymore," she said, cracking a smile. "I used to. Now I do it too much for my job."

Emma headed toward one locker in particular and opened it, pulling out a big bag that had one word on it: HAWN. Inside the locker, she showed me all the gear she wore—heavy, durable brown jackets and pants—as well as a handful of binders, notebooks, and backpacks she used in her downtime and training.

After the tour of the base, we found a seat outside to talk more. In case Emma's more reserved nature was a result of my behavior, I felt compelled to ensure that she believed our conversation was a safe space and that I was there only for whatever she wanted to share. I told her a little more about my journey, why I was on this adventure, and about my friend David, who had introduced me to smokejumpers. As I opened up, she made more eye contact and seemed to relax into the conversation a bit more, making me think she might just be more of an introverted person.

Emma began by telling me she'd always dreamed of being a hotshot but never thought she was strong enough or physically fit enough to do it.

"What's a hotshot?" I asked.

"Hotshots are twenty-person national resource fire crews that are based out of one spot but can be dispatched anywhere in the country that needs them," Emma said. "I eventually ended up getting hired as one for three seasons. Around the same time, I was also going to business school. I think that's when I realized that I'm just not a businessperson. I'm not into dressing up in nice clothes every day and sitting in an office. I was enjoying fighting fire, and I got to be outside—why not keep doing that?"

Eventually, Emma's friends had started telling her to apply to become a smokejumper. Well-aware of how physically and mentally demanding the job was, she kept saying she wasn't ready until finally, after much encouragement, she applied and got hired.

"In the few months before I got there, I trained as much as I could," Emma told me, starting to become a bit more energetic. "I did two workouts a day from January through April, and I was in the best physical shape I've ever been in. When I got to rookie training, I realized I would have never made it if I hadn't done that. The expectations were high, the days were long, and the hours were grueling. Every day, I thought, *This is it. Today's the day I'm going to be sent home.* But also I told myself that if I were going home, someone else would have to take me out. I wouldn't do it myself," she said.

"How did you feel when you finished rookie training?" I asked.

"Relieved," she said with a sigh. "Thankful and proud too, I guess."

"I bet!" I said. "What's the day-to-day like now?"

Emma explained that being a smokejumper is extremely formulaic. Every fire is different and out of human control, so they have everything within their control down to a science. When there's a fire, the alarm sounds throughout the base, followed by an announcement of where the fire is and who is in the first load—which is everyone who gets to go on the call.

"That's when we run to our locker, get dressed, and within five minutes, we're on the plane and taxiing down the runway," she said. "It's pretty exciting—everybody stops what they're doing and comes to help you and cheer you on if you're on the list."

Emma explained that there are two guys on the plane known as spotters. When the plane takes off, they're the two who figure out where the fire is and talk with dispatch and the pilot to size up the fire and the best place to jump. From up in the air, the spotters throw streamers to gauge how long it would take for them to reach the ground, how much wind there is, and other factors that would impact the jump. Based on what they see, the jumpers in the plane plan accordingly.

"Contrary to popular belief, we don't jump right into the fire," Emma said. "We jump into whatever spot is safest and closest to the fire, which sometimes means we hike a long way, and other times, we're pretty close. After we land, they send the para cargo down with all that stuff you saw on the wall. That's when it becomes clear why we train so rigorously."

I could practically feel my jaw on the floor. Emma let out a small laugh when she saw my reaction.

"Is it like that all year-round?" I asked in disbelief.

"Fire season is only six months out of the year, actually. But as a smokejumper, you can work all year-round if you want to," Emma responded. "In the winter, sometimes people go to the southeastern part of the United States to do prescribed burning—which involves intentionally laying fire down to clear out invasive species and built-up brush, giving forests a renewed chance to grow. And because they make and fix almost all of their own gear—including jumpsuits, harnesses, bags, and more—smokejumpers spend a lot of time in the winter manufacturing."

"How many of the smokejumpers here are women?" I asked.

"There's about seventy total jumpers here, and I'm one of five women," Emma said. "I think there's only about fifteen female smokejumpers in the nation right now. I've never had any problems working in a mostly male environment—but I know it isn't always that way for women in this field."

I told her a little bit about my conversation with David in Orcas Island, who shared his experience of being an ally for women in the Forest Service. Emma nodded. "If you're doing a good job and holding your own here, nobody says anything. Nobody is easy on you because you're a girl, and no one is hard on you because you're a girl. You're just a person held to the same standards as everyone else. If women want to do this, they should at least try. I don't think anyone should be afraid to try."

While I agreed that no one should be afraid to try, part of me longed for Emma to acknowledge how inaccessible smokejumping had historically been for women. My gut told me there was more to uncover, but I didn't want to push it. This was her experience, and I was grateful she was sharing it with me at all.

Emma at the entrance of a smokejumper plane.

At the end of our conversation, she generously offered one last stop on the tour—the plane. Winding through the base again, I followed her out the back doors and onto a long, black runway surrounded by the mountains in the late afternoon light. Emma propped herself up to sit in the doorway of a small plane parked near the back of the building, her legs dangling off the edge. Inside the plane, the cabin had one long bench lining each side. An assortment of tools and resources were organized below the seats and in boxes, keeping the plane ready to go at all times.

Emma was smiling consistently as she sat on one of the seats and leaned back, looking around. She was in her comfort zone now, in her own world. As we sat in silence for a few moments, I got the sense that we were finally at the part of the interview that was most comfortable to her.

As we hopped out of the plane, I thanked Emma for spending so much time with me.

"It's not a big deal," she said humbly.

We parted ways as the sun set behind the mountains, and I headed into town to find a place to sleep. *Thank you, David*, I thought.

I pulled into a suburban neighborhood in Missoula just as the sun set and found a quiet, well-lit street with other cars parked on it so I wouldn't stand out. I went through my normal routine: window reflectors on the dashboard; clothes in a pile on the floor within arm's reach; belongings hidden under the bed or in the glove box; car locked from the inside out and keys tucked under the pillow; alarm set for sunrise; phone plugged into the Goal Zero portable battery; and a call to Devin to say good night.

By the time it was dark outside, I was sound asleep.

28

"Everything you see will one day be gone. It will all change."

SEPTEMBER 16–GARDINER, MONTANA
47 DAYS ON THE ROAD, 3,278 MILES

Nights where I slept in my car on residential streets—also known as "urban camping"—often meant the morning would go a very specific way. First, I would always wake up with the sun, before people began milling around their neighborhoods, walking their dogs, taking their kids to school. I didn't want to give anyone a chance to notice me sleeping in my car in front of their house. Plus, the longer I waited to get up, the hotter the car got and the more I had to pee.

So, when the sun began to lighten the sky and my alarm went off, I didn't press snooze. Instead, I emerged reluctantly from under the warmth of my quilt, hunched over on the side of the bedframe to get dressed, and Googled the closest coffee shop as I rubbed the crusties out of my eyes.

A few miles down the road, the coffee shop filled up my to-go cup with its house blend and gave me a chocolate croissant, and I was on the road toward Gardiner, Montana, a town just outside Yellowstone National Park. Long stretches of dry plains fading between various shades of brown and gold whizzed by in a blur. Wire fences separated the fields from the road, and at one point, I saw a tumbleweed blow across the road and a plot of land with neatly rolled bales of hay. A tumbleweed! Hay bales! These were things I saw in movies and cartoons about the desert, not in person—until now.

At this point, I'd been on the road for almost fifty days, and I felt as aimless as the tumbleweed. I didn't know how long I'd be on this trip. I didn't know where I'd end up. I didn't know what I might encounter in between. I went where the wind blew me—like the seed from the "flawr" of my very first book.

By the time I got to Gardiner, Montana, the sun had started to lower over the sky-high trees. My plan was to stay in a free campsite a few miles outside of Yellowstone National Park—and I would, just as soon as I could find it. I drove back and forth on the same remote gravel road for forty minutes looking for any sign of the campsite. I was tired, in the middle of nowhere on some random dirt road, and it was getting dark. Why couldn't I find this campsite?

Finally, I spotted a tiny, overgrown wooden sign with faded paint. Just beyond the sign was the slightest semblance of an unmarked, unpaved road, which I followed to a small dirt lot by a lake.

No campsites were marked—just a handful of interspersed RVs and trucks. There couldn't have been more than eight people there. The few folks outside their cars and RVs kept to themselves. No one made fires or sat around tables. No one set up tents. There was no soft hum of conversations or crackling fires. When the sky got dark, the few remaining people disappeared into their vehicles, leaving the campsite feeling eerily quiet. The whole scene gave me the heebie-jeebies. Campsites generally felt remote, but not so remote that I felt alone. And here, I felt completely alone.

It's only scary because it's so dark, I told myself. *You can still enjoy yourself.*

As I strapped on my head lamp, a troubling thought crossed my mind. *Maybe there's a reason no one is cooking or relaxing outside. Are there bears, moose, or something else around here that I might attract if I cook*

Remote Montana campsite.

outside? I'd never been to this part of the country before, and I was not about to start experimenting with the northwestern wildlife. On top of that, I was increasingly aware that I was a young woman camping alone in a place with no cell phone service. *I'll just have some snacks for dinner*, I thought. From under the comforter. Inside my warm, locked, wildlife-free van.

In case you've never experienced it for yourself, let me tell you—eating turkey jerky and Cheez-Its in a remote, dark place isn't the most riveting evening. It was, however, my reality. I checked my phone, thinking it had to be at least 10 p.m.

It was 7:53 p.m.

The sooner you fall asleep, the sooner this will be over.

Eventually, I drifted to sleep, only to wake up from a nightmare so fast that I sat up and hit my head on the roof. My whole body was sweaty. I checked my phone again and sighed to learn it wasn't even midnight yet. This was very out of character for me. I usually slept through the night without waking up once, at home or on the road. The fact that I couldn't settle into a good night's sleep left me disoriented and flustered. I pulled the covers up over my head and tried to forget where I was and that I felt scared.

When I woke up again, pink and lavender shaded the cloudless sky. Everything seemed friendlier in the morning light. The lake was shimmering and silky, while the trees seemed more like protectors than unknown threats. I emerged from my van to heat up some water on my camp stove, pouring it over a small towel and pressing it over my eyes, nose, and mouth, onto the tips of my ears, and the bottom of my jaw. My heart rate lowered, and my mind wound down.

Moving slowly, I changed into a pair of black leggings and the comfiest hoodie I had before slipping a brown beanie on top of my unbrushed hair. Driving toward Yellowstone, I couldn't shake the residual anxiety from the night before. This occasionally happened when I was alone. I either felt free and self-assured, comforted by my own company and trusting in the world around me—or like this, full of skepticism, reluctance, and fear. *Will I get lost? Will I run out of gas in the park? Will my van break down? If it does break down, will I have service to call for help? Will someone try to hurt me? Will I see them coming? Where is my mace in case I need it? Do I know the shortcut to make an emergency call on my cell phone?*

I certainly wasn't the only independent woman traveler to feel this way. A study by the Solo Female Travelers Club[8] revealed that the biggest concern for women traveling alone, across age groups and geography, was safety. As the Club writes, "Females traveling alone have to face a variety of risks, such as unwanted attention, sexual harassment, and social disapproval when traveling in the gendered tourism space that privileges men's movement." A basic Google search of "women traveling alone" pulled up articles with headlines like "Why Traveling Alone Is Dangerous for Women" and "The Ten Things Women Need to Know to Protect Themselves While Traveling."

---

8   "Solo Female Traveler Trends & Statistics," Solo Female Travelers, accessed July 9, 2023, https://www.solofemaletravelers.club/solo-female-travel-stats.

The narrative was entirely shaped by fear. Women were afraid for their safety, while media perpetuated those fears with all the reasons it was dangerous and what women needed to do to stay safe. It was like another version of "boys will be boys," telling women we better learn how to protect ourselves because the outdoors isn't a place we're meant to be.

Before I left, plenty of people had told me about the risks as a young woman traveling alone and the precautions I should take to protect myself. I wish I had a dollar for everyone who told me to buy mace and keep it on my keychain (which I did) or to keep a knife in my purse (which I also did).

In 2016, Jen Rose Smith wrote an article for *Outside* titled "Sleeping Alone in the Woods While Female" in which she writes, "When people say a woman choosing to venture alone in the wilderness is reckless, it's very possibly due to a lack of understanding about the realities of sexual assault. Women are most likely to be assaulted in their own homes or in a private space, according to Jennifer Wesely, who studies violence against women at the University of North Florida. Fear of strangers seems like a misconception too, considering that more than three-quarters of women who are sexually assaulted know their attackers . . . Like a person who fears airplanes and sharks over highways and heart disease, my nervous nights in the woods just don't reflect the world's real dangers. Knowing that makes me determined to take on the things that scare me."[9] At the end, she wrote, "I do my best to enjoy the view, and the peace, and the quiet. It's why I'm there in the first place, after all. And it's why I won't stop sleeping in the woods by myself, even when my nights are sleepless."

That article had stuck with me since I read it. It was the first time I had heard a woman admit to being afraid about being outside and refusing to let that stop her—while also putting it in context of other, more common threats like sexual assault. There was power in how she acknowledged that women face significant, gender-based threats exploring

---

9   Jen Rose Smith, "Sleeping Alone in the Woods While Female." *Outside, December 2016*, https://www.outsideonline.com/outdoor-adventure/hiking-and-backpacking/sleeping-alone-woods-while-female/.

nature alone, but not more than we do in the world every day. Knowing that women—particularly transgender and BIPOC women—have to do so much emotional and mental work to simply exist in open spaces was disheartening.

Cue the growing knot in my stomach.

Breathe. You're safe, I reminded myself as I accepted my Yellowstone map at the entrance of the park. Big, beautiful trees lined the paved road, a sparkling stream to my right. The sunlight glistened on the water, and families with fishing gear waded in with poles and knee-high boots.

I am safe. I am safe. I am safe.

Around the bend presented bumper-to-bumper traffic, which seemed just wrong inside a national park. As I sat with the windows down, listening to my favorite all-female rock band HAIM, a pack of wild bison as big as my car trotted by a few feet away. I marveled at their dark, coarse fur, muscular bodies, and strong horns.

I am safe. I am safe. I am safe, I reminded myself as the traffic began to move, and the bison carried on. Time passed as I took myself on solo tours of various other park attractions and visitor centers. As I learned about geysers, hot springs, and other thermal natural wonders, I came across a feature on forest fires and, in particular, one specific type of pinecone that closes in around the seed and seals itself shut with sap. The only way to melt the sap is with at least 130° F heat—meaning, a fire—at which point the seed is released and new life can begin.

Eventually I stumbled across an old theater running a film about the park's history. As I settled into a seat in the dark room, a man's voice boomed from the theater speakers.

"Everything you see will one day be gone," he said with slow certainty. "It will all change."

As he bellowed about the beauty in nature's ability to adapt and evolve, I found myself feeling the truth in his words. Everything would change. It was the way of the world. Understanding that opened a lot of possibilities—gratitude for the preciousness of the moment, fear of change, and also hope about change. Right then, I fell somewhere in the middle of all three. If change was truly inevitable—not good or bad, but inevitable—then all I could do was accept it, make the best of it, and trust it. Right?

When the short film ended, I had tears in my eyes. I called Erin to tell her about it, and as I verbally processed, she asked if she could ask me a question.

"Of course," I said.

"How do you think nature parallels the abundance of life?"

The question gave me pause. She wasn't asking me how nature parallels life generally; she asked how nature parallels the abundance of life.

"You don't have to answer right now," she said, perhaps sensing my hesitation. "Just think about it over the next week or so until we talk again. Does that feel okay?"

"Yeah," I said, still pondering what to make of it. "It'll be my homework for the week."

"It's your play plan!" she said, which was the term she used for homework that was more fun. "Just get curious about it."

29

*"You were a complete surprise.
A welcome, wonderful, complete surprise."*

SEPTEMBER 18–JACKSON, WYOMING

49 DAYS ON THE ROAD, 3,476 MILES

One of the things no one told me about Yellowstone National Park was that it's connected to Grand Teton National Park. Discovering it for myself was like stumbling into the National Park Service's best-kept secret—discovering the ugly duckling overshadowed by its more outgoing, popular sibling.

Except Grand Teton National Park was anything but an ugly duckling. It was more magnificent than anything I had ever seen. The sun lit the entire park up as if she were putting on a show, showing me her brightest and best sides. Diamonds dazzled on beds of water. None of the trees were the same color. Greens faded to bright yellows, yellows faded to fierce oranges, and reds took my breath away. There were zero traffic jams. In fact, there were hardly any people there at all.

I spent the day immersed in fall beauty, including a particularly long time at the shore of Jenny Lake, watching the reflection of the mountains shimmer in the rippling, ice-cold water. Nothing was crowded.

Everything was perfect.

Erin's question popped into my mind: "How do you think nature parallels the abundance of life?"

I didn't know. But I did know that the water and trees and mountains felt like everything right about the world—even if it would all change someday. My fears and doubts were far away as I watched the wind rustle colorful leaves and dance shadows at my feet.

At one point, I came across a long, paved path surrounded by tall grass that painted the hills around me gold. No one in sight, I pulled off into a small parking lot, took out my old Santa Cruz skateboard, and slipped off my shoes and socks to feel the grip on my bare feet. Even though it had been a while, my muscle memory kicked in after a few seconds of wobbles and shakes. Moving from the balls of my feet to my heels told my body how to subtly shift its weight, and the board quietly obeyed. Just me and my skateboard as I pushed and glided along a winding road on a peaceful afternoon. I didn't feel scared. I felt free.

Another set of four wheels in Grand Teton National Park.

There was only one person I wanted there with me. Since leaving Portland, Devin and I had talked on the phone every day. Sometimes it was a multi-hour conversation. Other times, it was a quick FaceTime call to show her where I was. She always expressed so much excitement about what I was doing or where I was going, cheering me on every step of the way. Heading out of the park into Jackson, Wyoming, I decided to give her a call. As I told her about my day, she mentioned making plans to visit me.

"I have a few days off next week before I go back to school," she said. "I was thinking that would be a good time to come and visit . . . if you're okay with that, of course. I know it's last minute." Her voice sounded more nervous than usual.

"I would love that," I said, finding her nervousness endearing. "I think I'll be in Utah at that point. Would you want to come there?"

"I'll go wherever you are," she said simply.

"Well, Utah it is," I said, blushing at how much of a romantic she was.

As I searched the streets of Jackson for a good urban campsite, she asked me if I'd been looking for a relationship before I met her.

"I never wanted a relationship just to have one," I confessed as the streetlights around me flickered on. "I did want a relationship that felt right, with a person who felt right. If I didn't have that, then I'd rather be alone. And when I met you, I wasn't necessarily looking for a relationship—not because I was against it, but because I was focused on other things, like my own healing. Like returning to myself."

"Same," Devin added. "When we met, I was casually dating but mostly working on myself and learning how to have a relationship within the new boundaries I was building." She paused for a moment before adding, "You were a complete surprise. A welcome, wonderful, complete surprise."

I smiled. "If anyone had told me one month ago, while I was crying on my sister's front steps with a broken-down van, that I would be in a trusting, communicative, kind relationship a few weeks later, I would have laughed in their face." I chuckled at the recent memory. "And somehow, here we are."

"Here we are," Devin echoed.

We sat in silence for a second, before she said, "I was just curious if you were looking for something like this, or if it more so happened to you."

"I think it more so happened to me—and I'm really glad it did."

Suddenly, I started to get a little nervous. Why is she asking this? Is she having regrets?

"What about you?" I asked. "Were you looking for it, or did it happen to you?"

"Oh, you definitely happened to me," she said with a small laugh. "I knew you were different as soon as I met you. Five minutes in, I knew you were someone I wanted to spend a lot more time with, however you would let me."

My whole body was warm. I didn't realize she felt that way.

I am safe. I am safe. I am safe.

"I found it!" I said abruptly, eyeing open street parking along the perimeter of a small neighborhood park. A dense row of homes and cars lining both sides of the street signaled to me that my van wouldn't stand out here, and it would be a fine place to sleep.

We continued talking as I went through the nightly routine. This would be the first night it was expected to get down to freezing temperatures, so I blasted the heat for a few minutes to warm up the inside of the van before turning the engine off and climbing under the covers.

Surrounded by the stillness of the mountain town and Devin's voice coming through the phone on my pillow, I gave myself over to sleep.

"I guess when you meet your people, you just know."

SEPTEMBER 20–OGDEN, UTAH
51 DAYS ON THE ROAD, 3,721 MILES

On a cold September morning, Jackson, Wyoming, was perfect. The mountain town's main street looked like a cross between winter cabins and old western buildings. Everything seemed to be made out of wood and brick with simple signage swinging in the wind. Some of the wooden beams had white Christmas lights wrapped around them a few months early, giving it an extra cozy feeling.

I stepped into a local café to wash my face and use the bathroom, sneaking in a small bag of toiletries and a change of clothes as I often did in the morning so I could wash my face in the sink and get dressed standing up. Afterward, I took a seat at a booth and pulled Devin's manuscript out of my bag, reading it over coffee and breakfast. Her lovable characters quickly drew me in with their humor and humanness.

As I read, people shuffled in and out of the café. There was something remarkably ordinary about watching locals at their local coffee shop. It was a small glimpse into someone's everyday routine, observing an ordinary moment in another life. I especially liked watching the people who knew the staff, like the burly man who belted, "Gooood morning, Brooke!" from the doorway. A barista—I guess Brooke—turned to him and said, "Hi, Mr. Henry! The usual?" He nodded, and the wooden floors creaked as he approached the counter, asking her how her dog was and telling her to say hi to her dad.

Coffee shops have long been hubs for community character. Maybe that's why they'd been a prominent part of my journey in almost every city I'd been to. The mugs, the tables, the staff, the almost inevitable collection of community flyers near the bathroom, the merchandise on display, the art on the walls—not to mention the customers—all say so much about a place. Beyond that, it had been my experience that coffee, or tea, brings people together. Few things were as fulfilling as sitting across from another person and having a rich, meaningful conversation over a hot cup of coffee. In all the homes I stayed in so far—with Mercy, Grace, Erin, and Devin—coffee had been a morning staple and a conversation catalyst.

With a refill in my to-go cup and my toiletries bag tucked into my jacket, I made my way out of Jackson, heading through the Bridger-Teton National Forest. The fall colors were just as vibrant as the day before. I marveled at them as I drove, and a spectacular waterfall caught my eye from the road. Taking the first exit, I made a U-turn and followed the side road to a small parking lot along the edge of the river. Stepping out of my van, I heard it before I saw it—a gushing waterfall spilling turquoise water over a cliff. A smooth boulder invited me to sit, watch, and listen to the river. Much like I had with Coeur d'Alene Lake, I enjoyed the moment without agenda until my heart felt full.

As I left Wyoming and worked my way toward Utah, dense forests became long, uphill mountain climbs. Heading into the city of Ogden, I planned to reunite with my high school friend Andrew and meet his wife, Claire. Andrew and I met through mutual friends in my hometown. For years, we saw each other sporadically—someone's St. Patrick's Day party, a Fourth of July barbecue, the New Year's Eve when everyone came home from college. We didn't see each other often, but when we

Stopped on the side of the road to take in the view.

did, we talked and laughed like we'd been friends our whole lives. When we both left Maryland, we stayed in touch.

As someone who often felt hypersexualized by men, I appreciated and trusted Andrew because he was different. He was opinionated but always listened and made room for others. He spoke with conviction and passion, without talking over anyone or making them feel small. He made people laugh. Everyone loved him—including me—but my love for Andrew felt more like deep gratitude for the person he was.

As I remembered how much I cared for Andrew, I started to overanalyze how long it had been (almost ten years) and wonder if he actually wanted to see me. *Does he feel like hanging out with me is a forced encounter with an old friend he feels obligated to accept? Would my presence be an awkward intrusion into his everyday life?*

I parked around the corner from the pizza spot he had suggested and centered myself. I had no idea what to expect. *All I can do is be myself*, I thought. *If it's awkward, I can always excuse myself and say it was nice to see him.*

The pizza spot had indoor and outdoor seating and a bar inside with at least twenty craft beer taps. I walked slowly toward the outdoor area, and my peripheral vision noticed someone standing up outside, walking toward me with his arms out.

"Andrew!"

In the middle of the restaurant, he wrapped me in the biggest hug, resting his chin on my head. His wife Claire, with wavy blonde hair and big, beautiful blue eyes that immediately seemed kind, leaned in for a hug as well.

"Wow," Andrew said as the three of us sat at the table underneath a black umbrella. "I can't believe you're here! It's so good to see you, Mia."

"I know, I can't believe we're sitting here having dinner together," I said. "Thank you so much for meeting me—and Claire, it's so good to finally meet you."

"Same. I've heard so much about you," Claire said sweetly.

"Oh, gosh," I said. "Good things, I hope."

"Only good things," Andrew said.

Relief flooded me as I realized my fears weren't warranted. Andrew was just as kind and charismatic as I remembered, and Claire was equally warm. We spent the next two hours learning about each other's lives over pizza and beer, asking inquisitive questions that made the conversation feel rich and deep. As I began to tell them about the past month and a half, I realized that for most of the time I'd been friends with Andrew, he'd known me to date men. He wasn't on social media, so even though I'd posted about KC in the past, the chances he'd seen it were slim to none. Did he know?

Suddenly, I was coming out of the closet all over again.

For many queer people, coming out is not a one-time thing—even though it's often framed that way. This first time is undoubtedly a milestone for all of us. But because coming out is the process of sharing our gender or sexual identity and speaking truth to how we feel, this extremely personal experience is often ongoing.[10]

To me, coming out started with admitting who I was to myself first. Then I began to learn how to express that within the context of every relationship in my life. After I began dating KC, I tried to mentally track whom I had told about my sexuality and whom I had yet to tell. Who had liked that one Instagram post? Did that mean they knew I was out? Who else did I need to say this to? As you can imagine, this was not a sustainable or healthy approach. I eventually accepted that if they wanted to know, they could ask. If I wanted them to know, I could tell them. It wasn't my job to keep tabs on anyone else's understanding of me.

Still, talking to people I hadn't seen since I realized I was queer made my heart beat just a little faster.

I am safe. I am safe. I am safe.

"I met a girl on this trip, and we started dating recently," I told them over a bite of pizza. "She's actually coming to visit me in a few days. I think I'm going to take her camping."

"That's so exciting!" Claire said. "Let us know if you need an extra room. You can stay at our place if you want to."

"I want to meet her!" Andrew said. "She must be amazing if she's coming all this way to visit you, Mia."

Their reactions washed my apprehension away. Deciding not to filter parts of myself that had the potential to make others uncomfortable felt like an act of self-love every time.

Full of beer and pizza, I followed Claire and Andrew back to their house a few miles away in the hills of Ogden. It was dark when I got out of the car, and when I looked up, the sky greeted us with a beautiful flurry of stars.

How does nature mirror the abundance of life?

Andrew walked around to the trunk of my van, which I'd opened to grab a few things I'd need for a night inside an actual house.

---

10 Julia Carpenter, "Coming out as LGBTQ: It's Not One Moment, but Several," The Washington Post, June 2016, www.washingtonpost.com/news/soloish/wp/2016/06/30/coming-out-as-lgbtq-its-not-one-moment-but-several/.

"This is it, huh?" he said, pressing his hand into the foam mattress pad. "This is so sick! Is this thing comfy?"

"Very," I said with a laugh, grabbing a few odds and ends and stuffing them into a backpack. "And as much as I'm learning to love Hashtag Van Life, I'm very grateful to be staying in your guest room tonight."

"That's why we have it. I'm glad someone is here to actually use it for once," he said.

The inside of their home was cozy—an open-concept, one-story layout with hardwood floors and lots of books and plants. Their black-and-white dog, Pablo, barked at my feet. The guest bedroom had a queen-sized bed with a blanket draped over the edge, a small bedside table, and a chair in the corner. We hugged each other, and Claire pointed out where certain things were before we said goodnight.

Pulling the thick blanket up to my chin and shimmying under the covers, I noticed my gratitude for their presence in my life, and my amazement at how love can keep people connected despite so much time and distance. I guess when you meet your people, you just know.

31

"Resilience exists all around us."

SEPTEMBER 21–SALT LAKE CITY, UTAH
52 DAYS ON THE ROAD, 3,764 MILES

In the morning, I woke up to the sound of conversation and the smell of something delicious. Claire and Andrew were in the kitchen making omelettes and getting ready for the day ahead. Much like watching people in coffee shops, it was endearing to be part of someone's morning routine.

After sharing breakfast, they went to work like responsible adults. Knowing I likely wouldn't be there when they got home, Andrew gave me a final hug. "Make yourself at home until you go," he said. "Pablo will be happy to have someone around during the day."

Having a house to myself was heavenly. I'd been alone a lot in my van, and I'd been inside people's homes a lot, but I hadn't been inside people's homes alone. What did I want to do with myself?

Turning on American singer-songwriter Maggie Rogers, I made more coffee and danced around and sang into my cup like it was a microphone. Pablo's weary gaze followed me, and sunlight painted shadows of the plant vines onto the floor. I brought my mug over to the brown leather couch and sat cross-legged, cupping my coffee between my hands and feeling its warmth pressed against my palms. Everything was still—even Pablo. Something compelled me to close my eyes and be still too.

As I did, I noticed the corners of my mouth curl up into a small smile, and my mind became a blank scroll. All that existed in my world was the muffled sound of the birds outside and my own breathing. Any worries momentarily lifted as I allowed myself to sink into a moment of levity. I didn't feel any compulsion to be anywhere or do anything.

My meditative moment came to an end when Pablo's fur brushed my leg and his body weight sank on my foot. I opened my eyes and reached down to pet him as he rolled over affectionately.

Very serious snuggles with Pablo.

"Is someone happy to have a little company?" I asked him out loud, scratching behind his ears. "I'm going to have a little company soon too. Yes, I am. Yes, I am."

Company. Company! That reminded me—Devin's book! I was almost finished with it, and I wanted to read the whole thing before she got here. I took a seat at the table and poured through the remaining pages of her manuscript. By the end, the main character, Maggie, had learned how to set boundaries, how to survive a less-than-ideal family vacation, and how to love herself. On multiple occasions, I wanted to pick her up and squeeze her tight, reminding her that she was enough, and her feelings were valid.

Turning the last page, my awe for Devin was at an all-time high. She had turned her most traumatic moments in life into an introspective comedy full of vulnerability and humor.

I stacked the battered pages of Devin's book and slid them back into the manila envelope before texting her.

> Done.

> What? Oh wait—I get it!

> WHAT DID YOU THINK?

> It was amazing. It broke my heart and warmed it all at the same time. You're so talented!

> Yeah, dark comedies will do that. You're the first one to read the whole thing! I can't believe you finished it.

> I told you—I'm your #1 fan. The character development was soooo good. I just want to give Maggie the biggest hug and hold her and tell her everything is okay.

> Well, you can do that tomorrow.

It was surreal to feel so connected to someone I didn't know at all three weeks ago. It was even more surreal to know she was flying to Utah tomorrow.

Taking a shower was another luxury of the morning. I relished every second of the piping hot streams of water against my skin before stepping out into a towel and, reluctantly, into clothes. I could have probably stayed in their home all day, but the pull had returned, telling me it was time to leave. On my way out, I left my generous friends a thank-you note on the counter and hid the key, just like Claire had shown me.

It didn't take long to find a quiet park in Salt Lake City for my weekly call with Erin.

"Amazing Miaaaa," Erin said when she answered the phone.

"Sweet Eriiiin!" I responded.

"I've been thinking about you," she said. "How's it going in Utah?"

I told her about Andrew and Claire—our wonderful dinner and my apprehensive coming out to them. "I've also been thinking a lot about your question from last time," I told her. "You asked me how nature parallels the world's abundance."

"Yes! What have you noticed?" she asked.

I reflected on my interview with Emma and how she'd told me about the seasonal versatility of her job—fighting fires in the summer and prescribing burns in the winter. She'd explained that prescribing a burn clears out the built-up brush that's old and dead, making room for new plants to grow. "It's like giving nature a reset—a fresh start," she'd explained. Emma's words reminded me of the pinecone I had learned about in one of the many Yellowstone visitor centers—the one that only released its seed for a new tree when a fire loosened the sap that had sealed it shut. Fire—something that initially seemed destructive—turned out to be not only good but necessary for survival and new life.

The metaphor was as apparent as walking into a brick wall.

My fire was leaving a company I had helped build for five years. My fire was a toxic relationship. My fire was walking away from the comfortable and familiar into the unknown, alone. And while I was in the fire, I didn't have this pinecone-and-seed metaphor. I didn't see space for growth or newly planted seeds. I only saw what was visible above the ground—which, after a fire, was nothing besides charred branches and a bleak horizon. It looked like death and felt like emptiness. I feared I would always be this way.

But if a small, empty theater in Yellowstone National Park had taught me anything, it was that things would always change. If Emma had taught me anything, it was that new beginnings often appear as endings at first. If Eli had taught me anything, it's that the strongest flowers can grow through the toughest of conditions. And if the people I was interviewing had taught me anything, it was that resilience exists everywhere.

32

"Well . . . I love you."

SEPTEMBER 23–SALT LAKE CITY, UTAH
55 DAYS ON THE ROAD, 3,912 MILES

It was all so easy with Devin. So easy, in fact, that I was extremely nervous for her arrival in Utah.

Just wait until the other shoe drops, my skepticism whispered, creating a pit in my stomach and causing my body to react as if something bad had already happened. But it hadn't. It was just the thought that something bad might happen.

This, my friends, is called anxiety.

As a young woman alone in new places every day, I saw a little fear as a healthy thing. It kept me alert, mindful of my surroundings as I did my best to stay safe. "I'm trying to protect us," I could hear it say.

I wasn't trying to eradicate fear. What I wanted was to get a better handle on the fear-based thoughts that chimed in when I felt happy— whether they came from a place of guilt, like I had discussed with Erin, or from a place of worry about when the good would inevitably end, like with my van and KC. I wanted to enjoy the lovely, precious moments without feeling anxious. I wanted to fall in love with Devin without questioning what might happen. I wanted to reach out to new women and gender nonconforming folks without worrying what they'd think of my project and in turn, me. I wanted to explore new places and try new things without a low hum of fear about whether I was safe.

As Tracie said, "What happens if you do break? Maybe it can be fixed, maybe not. But chances are you will be fixed."

And life will go on.

I pulled up to the arrivals gate at Salt Lake City International Airport feeling like I might throw up.

Devin emerged from the airport in a checkered sweater, jeans, a teal beanie and the familiar black Velcro shoes.

She looked freaking adorable.

As I jumped out of the car and into her arms, she lifted me into the air, giving me a kiss that made butterflies swirl and settle down all at once.

"How was your flight?!" I asked, full of adrenaline and nerves.

"Actually, it was terrible. I almost didn't come," she said.

WE KNEEEWWW ITTTTTTT! my inner voice shouted.

"After I got home from work yesterday, I spent the whole night vomiting," Devin said, rubbing her hands over her face. "It didn't stop until three o'clock this morning, and at that point I was so exhausted that I worried I would miss my flight if I went to sleep . . . so I just didn't. I thought about not coming, but I really wanted to see you."

"Oh, no!" I said, shocked. "What happened? How do you feel now? What do you need?"

"I'm pretty sure I got the stomach flu from this freaking ninety-eight-year-old woman at work who clearly didn't realize I had a date today," she said, managing a wink. "The perks of working in an emergency room." She closed her eyes and reclined her seat. "I still don't feel good. I think I just need to close my eyes."

"Just rest," I said as she reclined in the passenger seat. "I'll drive."

Ready to be around fewer people and in more nature, I drove us out of town and up a mountain dirt road toward Wasatch Mountain State Park to camp for the night. Every once in a while, I looked over to find her doing that nodding thing people do when they're falling asleep sitting up. I laughed quietly to myself, just grateful that she was here, in my van, in Utah, with me.

The campsite was beautiful—high enough to see above the tree line. As I started opening doors and unloading cooking and camping equipment, ready for our date to begin, Devin promptly climbed from the front seat into the bed without getting out of the car. By the time I looked up from lighting the stove, she'd curled up into a ball and fallen asleep inside the van.

My anxiety had prepared me for the worst—not for her to have stomach flu and fall asleep at 5 p.m. *What do I do now?*

I laid down next to her for a little while, hoping that after a few minutes I could get her to wake up. That didn't happen. After about an hour of gently nudging her and her gently brushing me off, it was time to face facts: she was out for the night.

I put away the camping gear and crawled into bed next to her, putting in my headphones and trying to fall asleep while it was still light outside.

"Well, that took it out of me," she said in the morning with more color in her face. "What happened last night?"

"You fell asleep at five," I told her with big eyes and a cheeky smile.

"So I slept for thirteen hours?! No wonder I feel better."

As I gently teased her about how early she had passed out yesterday, she laughed and heated up water for instant coffee. It seemed natural, as if we had been doing this morning routine for a long time.

Neither of us knew what to do around Salt Lake City—I don't think either of us had gotten past the initial anticipation of spending time together. But we knew we wanted a big breakfast, so we packed up the campsite and headed down the mountain to a café.

"Does your stomach hurt?" I asked Devin as she drove.

"No, not really anymore," she said, eyes on the road. "Where do I turn next?"

The van and the mountains.

"Make a right up here at the light," I told her. "Do you think there was something weird in our camp coffee?"

Devin glanced over at me with a concerned look on her face before her eyes got big. "Oh, you're so white," she said. "Whiter than normal. Are you going to throw up?"

"No," I told her, now starting to sweat. "I just don't feel good."

She side-eyed me with skepticism. "Okay, because you look like you're about to throw up."

As we talked, my fingers and toes began to tingle. Feeling the sudden gulp in my throat, I realized she was right. I needed to vomit. Now.

"Pull over!" I blurted out, starting to heave.

Devin cut across three lanes of traffic and turned into a Target parking lot. She slammed the brakes and before she even got to a full stop, I opened the door and ran inside with both hands over my mouth. I spotted a big red trash can next to the entrance. Good enough.

Bent over it at a ninety-degree angle, I spewed all over the inside of the trash can. Despite the scene I was making, no one seemed to notice me projectile vomiting into a trash can. When it was over, Devin was standing next to me, rubbing my back.

"We okay?" she asked. "That looked rough."

I looked up at her, removing both of my hands from the trash can and wiping my mouth with the back of my forearm in the least cute way.

"Should we get you some Gatorade and soup while we're here?"

"Yes, please," I murmured.

She put her arm around me, and I leaned into her as she kissed the side of my head. Nothing like going shopping with your new girlfriend after you've vomited in front of her—and a bunch of other people, for that matter.

Devin seemed cool as a cucumber while I walked through the aisles of Target like a zombie. Was this what it was like dating someone who worked in an emergency room? Watching her ask me, "What's your favorite kind of Gatorade?" and pile light blue bottles of Glacier Freeze into her arms was comforting, like being held by a person I could count on. We checked out with four Gatorades and four cups of Top Ramen.

"I don't want to sleep in the van tonight," I told her when we got back into the car. "I really don't want to. Can we get a hotel?"

She squeezed my hand. "Of course."

As we walked into the lobby of the nearest hotel, my head pounded against my temples and my stomach rumbled again. I wanted to get upstairs to the room as fast as possible. Whatever was about to happen needed to happen in private—not in a public trash can.

A man in a navy blazer with short black hair stood behind the front desk as we walked in, eyeing us without saying a word. We both picked up on his weird vibes immediately.

"Hi there," Devin said, approaching him. "Question for ya—do you happen to have any rooms available tonight?"

"I'll see," he said, drawing his words out very slowly. I sat across the lobby, watching him avoid eye contact with Devin. "We have a room with two twin beds," he said, still looking at his computer screen.

"Do you have anything with just one bed?" she asked kindly.

He looked up with just his eyes, glaring at her as if to say, "Two girls don't need one bed."

As he returned his attention to the computer, Devin glanced over her shoulder at me with widened eyes. I shook my head.

"You'll be in room 220," he said reluctantly, putting the key card on the counter. Devin asked him simple questions like where the ice machines were or if there was a microwave in the room. He acted like he didn't hear her, choosing to be unhelpful and pretending to be important.

I walked up to Devin and squeezed her hand. When she turned to look at me, her face was red, and her eyes looked angry. She slapped her hand down on the key card and slid it off the counter as she put her arm around me and we walked toward the elevator. "Fuck that guy," she said, not quietly.

"People like that aren't worth it," I told her.

Even though we knew there were people in the world who chose to remain ignorant and closed-minded about queerness, it never made it easier to encounter.

In Room 220, the first thing I did was run a hot bath. As the water collected in the tub, I turned on the fan so Devin wouldn't hear me vomiting. I lurched over the toilet on my knees, realizing what had happened—I had gotten Devin's stomach flu.

It took all the energy I had to move my body into the bathtub and pick up the brush to try to run it through my hair. My arms were so heavy that even the smallest movements felt impossible. I let out a cry of frustration and exhaustion before Devin tapped on the door and peeked her head in.

"Everything okay?" she asked.

I'm sure it was quite a sight—me sitting in the tub, sobbing, with the hairbrush stuck in a patch of knots in my wet hair. Without saying a word, she sat next to the tub, carefully removed the brush from my hair, and gently began to tease out the knots until my hair was smooth against my back. Then, she wrapped me in a fluffy, white towel, walked me to the bed, tucked me under the covers, and gave me Top Ramen.

Despite feeling absolutely terrible, I felt very loved.

The following morning, we both felt like we'd been hit by a bus. The Starbucks across the street from the hotel came through with two of the biggest iced coffees we'd ever had, kick-starting a new day for us—hopefully, one without either of us being sick.

Devin's trip to Utah had been nothing like I thought it would be so far. I expected camping, outdoor exploration, and romance. Instead, we both got the stomach flu and spent the night in a homophobic hotel.

In a way, the unpredictability was actually refreshing. Any expectations that either of us may have had about our time together were so quickly obliterated that now, it felt like we had a clean slate. An expectation-less road ahead of us, versus me trying to guarantee that Devin and I had some kind of perfect experience. I was in Salt Lake City with my new girlfriend, driving wherever, doing whatever, both of us enjoying being together and trying not to throw up. *Maybe this is what's possible when you trust the process—and yourself,* I thought.

Feeling alive again, Devin and I spent the sunny day looking for hot springs, taking photos, prancing through ankle-deep water at the edge of the Great Salt Lake, and skinny-dipping in turquoise rivers we discovered off the side of the road. We ate snacks and listened to pop music like Betty Who and MisterWives. We pulled over on empty roads to skateboard down the double yellow lines. We moved at the whim of what we discovered around us.

Over the past few days, I had seen so many sides to her—the sick side, the caretaker side, the adventurous side. As I watched her ride my skateboard, affection bubbled up in my chest. I found myself watching her laugh as she hop-skipped on to the board, lost control, and went to chase it down. She came back with it tucked under one arm, smiling like a little kid.

I think I love this person.

I rolled those words over in my mind. *I think I love her. I think . . . I love . . . her.* Yeah, that felt right in my body. No stomach pains or sweaty palms or anxiety. Just a quiet happiness that felt a lot like contentment with sprinkles of adoration.

She bounced over to me, out of breath. "Ready to keep rolling?" she said.

"Yep," I said, holding out my hand. She grabbed it and pulled me up, giving me a quick peck on the cheek.

The Utah sun was exceptionally hot as we drove along the two-lane highway outside of Salt Lake City. When Devin noticed a big white screen in an open field to our left, she shouted, "DRIVE-IN!" Turning to me, she took my hand.

"Would you like to see a movie with me in the middle of a random field in Utah?"

"Of course I would like to see a movie with you in the middle of a random field in Utah!"

We pulled onto the grassy field, backing the van up to the screen so we could watch from the bed with the trunk open. We pulled out my small camp chair, the cooler, and cooking equipment.

She flew all the way from Portland while she had the stomach flu to chop potatoes with me at a random drive-in. Love.

"What?" she said when she noticed me looking at her.

"Nothing," I murmured. "Just watching you."

She smiled to herself as she continued to chop potatoes. "Well, okay," she said.

As the sun started to set and the mountains turned pink, Devin stood and looked around, noticing a small, white building with a red-and-white-striped awning and picnic tables. A few people were walking away from it with hot dogs, sodas, and popcorn.

"The movie will probably start soon, once it gets dark enough," she said, turning to face me. "I'm not going to kiss you or hold your hand here," she told me in a whisper. "It's not because I don't want to, okay? I just don't trust people."

I nodded, understanding the desire to avoid ruffling more potentially homophobic feathers—especially in a remote area at night. The juggling act between being proud of my queerness and not hiding it to make others comfortable, while also selectively concealing it to avoid danger, seemed backward, confusing, and—not to mention—like a privilege. As a white woman who presents femininely, I know I have the option to conceal my queerness and, in doing so, more likely avoid targeting and harassment often experienced by my community. Camouflaging is possible for me, and I don't know how to feel about that. Devin's short haircut and androgynous style made me keep an eye on her as she walked toward the snack bar.

People hate what they don't understand, I thought. Eli's coworker sprang to mind—the tremendously qualified mechanic who got consistently rejected because of how she expressed herself and showed up in the world. All the people who rejected her were the tragedy—like the front-desk man at the hotel, living in a small world of heteronormativity and hate.

When Devin returned with a container of buttered popcorn, a small wave of relief washed over me. Everything was fine and the movie was about to start. (Which movie, we still didn't know.)

We climbed into the back of the van with our plates of roasted potatoes and popcorn, lying next to each other with the trunk open. The electricity flickered on, and the screen lit up as *Slender Man*, the latest horror movie, began to play.

"I can't believe it," Devin said, laughing and pressing her face into the bed. "I hate horror movies. This could have been anything else!"

"Oh, no," I said, laughing. "I keep forgetting it's almost Halloween! I don't even know what month it is anymore."

"Dammit," she said, picking her head up to reveal a red face and a smile.

"I don't think it would be so bad if we weren't out in this field in the middle of nowhere," I said, not helping the situation.

The movie couldn't have mattered less to me. I loved her. I loved her!

I loved a lot of people in my life, and I wasn't shy about telling them. I said, "Love you" to my friends and family all the time. Growing up, I would shout it to my parents when I left the room. When I dated people, I had to actively refrain from saying, "Love ya" out of habit in the early stages. A few times I almost said it getting off of work calls with colleagues.

With Devin, it would be more than a casual phrase I called out from room to room, and saying it now would mean we were more than a casual relationship. I had been feeling it build since she got here, and now it felt like it might burst out of me. Now on the tip of my tongue, I could hardly think about anything else. I couldn't imagine waiting until tomorrow to tell her. But to tell her during *Slender Man*? Then again, we had wholly abandoned the idea of some perfect trip since the second she'd gotten to Utah. There were no perfect moments to wait for. There were just moments, right now.

I rolled over to my side to face her. "I have to tell you something."

Seemingly grateful for the distraction, she peeled her eyes off the screen and looked at me, rolling on to her side to mirror me. "What's up?" she said.

Even in the dark, I could feel her green eyes looking at me tenderly. A horrible scene I tried to not pay attention to played in the background.

"Well—"

"What?"

"Well . . . I love you."

I held my breath after I said it, partially in shock and partially scared she wouldn't say it back. I thought about burying my face in the pillows the way she had when she asked me to be her girlfriend. She grabbed my hand.

"Well . . . I love you too," she said slowly, every word placed carefully.

In four words, everything opened up—possibility, safety, excitement, the unknown. Her love felt like the right kind of love—the kind that I'd been looking for. Not the scary kind but the trusting kind. The kind that didn't leave me empty but filled me up. The kind that didn't take away from who I was but made me more of myself. The kind that didn't feel gray but full of the most vibrant color.

Two months ago, I would have never thought I'd find myself saying

"I love you" to someone in Utah while watching a B-grade horror movie in a field after sharing the stomach flu. I could have never planned it. It was absolutely, imperfectly perfect.

Swept up in each other, we completely forgot to plan where we would sleep. When the movie ended, we laughed and shrugged, deciding to drive around and find a place to camp. We were filled with hope—hope we would find a campsite, hope for each other, hope that everything would work out just fine.

The sky was completely dark, and the rural roads had zero streetlights, which meant we could see a sky full of bright stars. I stuck my head out the window as Devin drove, looking straight up to the sky, feeling tiny and alive.

Upon discovering a small string of campsites in the Uinta-Wasatch-Cache National Forest, we drove through only to find that every spot was full. Tired and ready to curl up next to each other, Devin parked the van at the entrance of the campsite.

"Think we can get away with this?" she asked, turning the car off and unbuckling her seat belt.

"I honestly don't know," I said, looking around. It was late and dark, and the dirt roads were empty. The only way people would see us parked here was if they were coming in or out of the camping area. I figured if we left around sunrise, like I normally did, we should be fine. "I guess the worst that could happen is someone wakes us up and tells us we can't be here, right?"

"Exactly," Devin said, already getting into the bed. I followed her lead, locking the car from the inside out and climbing under the covers.

Snuggled into the comfort of the van bed, we held each other tightly. I put my head on her chest, listening to her breathe and feeling her pulse on my ear.

"I love you, Mia Bolton," she said as she closed her eyes.

Everything felt warm.

"I love you, Devin Hiller," I whispered back.

33

"It won't always be this way."

SEPTEMBER 25–OGDEN, UTAH
57 DAYS ON THE ROAD, 3,952 MILES

For Devin's last night in Utah, I decided to surprise her with an Airbnb. Before she woke up, I quietly booked a one-room stone cabin for us in Ogden. Scrolling through the price tag, worries about my dwindling finances began to surface. *That's an after-Devin-leaves-Utah problem*, I thought, effectively buying a little peace of mind.

Devin started to stir as the sun came up, streaking through the car windows and giving her messy curls and shoulders an orange hue. Eyes still closed, she said good morning and threw her arm over me.

"It's time to get up," I told her. "I have a surprise for you."

She opened one eye, then the other, then reached for her glasses. Squinting at the screen, I watched her make sense of what I was showing her.

"We're going to stay here tonight!" I said, like a kid on Christmas morning.

"Oh, my god," she said. "It looks dreamy! Are you sure it's not too expensive? I can help pay for it."

"Nope," I said, wanting to treat her to something. "This one's on me."

The cabin was everything I had hoped for. The outside had a chiminea and a few plastic chairs overlooking a stunning valley with a beautiful, icy-blue river cutting through trees that looked like they'd been dipped in cans of cherry red and blood orange paint. The front door was round, giving it a hobbit-like feel. We wiped our feet on the doormat and stepped into one room with a bed, a small furnace, a ladder that led to a tiny loft above us, and a bathroom with a clawfoot tub. Tonight, we would enjoy the luxuries of running water, electricity, and walls. *Yesss.*

Devin and the coolest Airbnb there ever was.

As I unloaded our stuff from the van, Devin sprang into action to make dinner. She loved to cook, and I loved that she loved to cook. She was in her element, chopping kale and garlic, mixing them in the cast iron pan, squeezing a lemon on top. I changed into a favorite nighttime outfit on the road—sweatpants, sweatshirt, socks, red Birkenstocks, and a beanie—and pulled up a green plastic chair.

"Do you want any help?" I asked her, already knowing the answer.

"Not at all," she said. "You just relax and enjoy, little lady."

"Okay. Love you."

"Love you."

Kicking my feet up onto the other chair, I pulled out my journal and began to write. Journaling had always been my way of making sense of the thoughts circling in my mind. I had gotten away from it a little bit on this trip because I had been so busy driving, planning, interviewing, even hosting. As I cracked my journal open for the first time in nearly two months, I had no idea where to begin.

My mind replayed the day before like a movie, and I kept pressing rewind to watch my favorite part: lying next to her in the van at a horrible drive-in movie, telling her I loved her, and hearing her say it back.

Something had shifted between us in a beautiful way—a deepening in our understanding of each other while also deepening our commitment to each other. She wasn't just a random girl I'd met on a road trip. She wasn't just a chapter in my story. Without knowing the ending, I knew she was already so much more.

A few minutes later, Devin presented us with plated chicken sandwiches, complete with garlic-lemon kale and sautéed mushrooms. I ate it so fast that I don't think I said one word to her—and to this day, I think it's the best sandwich I've ever had.

The next morning, Devin woke up before me to start a fire in the chiminea and make coffee. I wandered out of the cabin and poured a hot cup from the French press and sat beside her, holding her hand in my lap. We didn't say a whole lot, just looked out over the valley and warmed our toes in the heat from the chiminea.

How come everything seemed so easy? Early stages of past relationships had definitely included more playing it cool, more awkward silences, more cryptic messages and mixed signals. We didn't have that. There was no room for any of that in the van, on this trip or in this stage of both our lives.

Before long, the time came to take Devin to the airport for her flight back to Portland. She'd only been here for four days, but for the first time, the idea of continuing on this trip alone felt lonely. I started to cry as I loaded the French press and our pajamas into the car. She walked over to stand in front of me and let me rest my forehead on her chest.

"It'll be okay," she said softly, stroking my hair. "You have so much left to explore and so many people to meet. And when you're done, you can come right back to Portland. To me."

Nodding, I could taste the salt water on my lips.

"Okay."

The energy was low on the drive, both of us eager to talk about anything other than our rapidly approaching goodbye. She took the lead, telling me about how she was nervous to start classes tomorrow.

"Being here has been so refreshing, just to have a break from juggling full-time work and full-time school at the same time."

"How do you manage to do that?" I asked.

"With incredibly strict boundaries and really good friends," she told me. "All I have to do is get a few more As and then I'll have the minimum GPA to apply to PA school."

"I know you can do it," I told her, trying to be supportive, even though my heart hurt.

"I know I'll get back into the swing of that life after a few days, but it's going to be a rough transition—especially from this."

She took my hand and kissed my knuckles as we followed the signs for departures.

"It won't always be this way," she told me as I slowed down at the curb and airport employees shouted at us to keep it moving.

"I know. It's only temporary," I said without fully understanding what I meant. *Am I saying it's only temporary that we're apart? Knowing that she lives in Portland and I live in San Diego, what does that mean?*

She moved slowly, opening the door and slinging her duffel bag over her shoulder. I got out to give her a big kiss, both of us soaking in one last moment until whenever we would see each other again.

"Call me when you land, okay?" I said.

"Okay," she said, wiping her eyes. "Love you."

"Love you too," I responded, the words as effortless as morning coffee. After a few looks back, I watched her disappear through the airport doors.

Driving away from the airport, my mind was hazy and absent. I wondered what it would have been like to have done this trip with another person, someone to share the highs and lows with, to revel in the beauty of new places with, and to reminisce with when it was all over. For just a minute, I thought about asking Devin to meet me again and stay with me longer, but I knew that wasn't the answer. She was dedicated to her goal just like I was dedicated to mine. We were proud of each other for that, and neither of us would have asked the other to give any part of it up. But damn, did I feel lonely now that she was gone. Compared to the past few days of companionship and love, today was unbearably flat and dull. *I was on the road for two months alone just fine up until now*, I thought.

Well, except for the calls with Devin.

And the calls with Erin.

And all the people I got to know.

And all the friends I spent time with.

And all the family who let me stay with them.

Maybe I haven't been alone as much as I thought, I realized. I'd been traveling alone, but thinking back on it, I suppose I'd actually had people with me in some form or another the whole way.

I needed something to rejuvenate me for this post-Devin-visiting phase of my trip. I searched "hair salons," and my GPS led me to a small salon in the city that was able to fit me in for a last-minute appointment.

A woman with bright red hair sat me down and whipped a black cape over me. I took my scrunchie out and let my thin, dirty-blonde hair fall to the middle of my arms. She tousled and fluffed it, tilting her head to the side. "So, what are we doing today?" she asked me.

"Cutting it," I told her, pulling up a few pictures of chin-length bobs I'd found on Pinterest. She nodded as I swiped through, still touching my hair occasionally. "I was also hoping to get some pink," I added spontaneously, eyeing her red hair.

She smiled, meeting my eyes in the mirror. "Red is a pain in the ass," she said. "Pink is a good choice."

Two hours later, I walked out of the salon with significantly less hair and pink streaks in what was left. My short bob bounced as I walked out to my van, catching my reflection in the window.

"Well, hello there," I said, mimicking the tousling and fluffing I had seen the hairdresser do.

Cutting my hair felt symbolic, like a physical manifestation of everything changing inside. I was shedding the version of me that began this trip—stuck in heartbreak, slipping away from everything around me and myself. Two months later, I was more in touch with and more secure in myself than I could remember being before. Somewhere along the way, my general enthusiasm for life had started to return, and with it a subtle sense of potential and possibility. I'd started to see in color again. I wanted that to show on the outside too.

A well-lit, residential Salt Lake City street became my urban campsite for the night. As I went through my routine and laid my head down on the pillow, I had a perfect view of the full moon.

I wouldn't forget my time here. And this would be my last night in Utah.

34

"I am a fiercely independent person, and I am no one's pawn."

SEPTEMBER 27–FORT COLLINS, COLORADO
59 DAYS ON THE ROAD, 4,407 MILES

In the morning, I woke up with the sun and got an early start out of Utah, headed toward Fort Collins, Colorado—a place that had been on my bucket list since I won the bike from New Belgium Brewing.

There were a few ways to get from Salt Lake City to Fort Collins. I chose the shortest route—seven hours on the I-80, through northern Utah, dipping into southern Wyoming, and then finally, into Colorado. Memories of my time in Grand Teton National Park and Jackson resurfaced as I passed snowcapped mountains that reached into the sky, surrounded by long stretches of golden fields. I continued to marvel at Wyoming's beauty.

Some days, the long drives were my companions. Today, my mind was anxious, and the drive felt more laborious. After the happy distraction of Devin's visit, some fears about money and the second half of my adventure had surfaced, and I spent a good part of the drive overthinking them.

At Bindle Coffee & Roastery in Fort Collins, yellow flowers sprouted from clay vases and from coffee beans in Mason jars. I plopped on a wooden stool, exhausted. Perhaps it was the long stretch of driving I had just finished, or the comedown from my time with Devin, or maybe living out of my minivan for nearly two months had started to take its toll. The novelty of my trip had begun to wear off.

I wrapped my hands around a mug of coffee, struggling with how to uproot these seeds of stress I was carrying. Usually, writing was my best bet at finding clarity with my own thoughts, so I pulled out my notebook and began listing my fears and potential solutions.

Fear #1: I'm going to run out of money.

Potential solution #1: I will make minimum payments on my credit card and save the money I have left. I will get a job when I get home. I can take out loans or borrow money if I have to.

Fear #2: I'm going to have expensive car problems in a remote place.

Potential solution #2: The worst car problems are behind me. I have insurance. I am doing the best I can to take preventive care of my van. If anything happens, I trust that I will figure it out in the moment.

Fear #3: I'm going to get to the other side of the country and be too sick of driving to make it back.

Potential solution #3: This is the adventure, and I'm going to find a way through no matter how exhausted I feel. When it's over, I'll go back to riding my bike as much as possible.

Fear #4: I have no idea what happens when this trip is over, and that's scary.

Potential solution #4: I don't have to know what comes next right now. I trust that I will know when the time comes for me to make those decisions.

Transferring my thoughts to paper felt like water turning into ice—something that had been flowing without shape became crystalized and contained. As I stared at the pages, I realized how some of what I wrote were actual solutions, but mostly they were just intentional perspective shifts and trusting the process. I was clearly having anxiety about the future, and the advice I gave myself was to not try to know all the answers now and to surrender to the journey.

I am safe. I am safe. I am safe.

As I put my journal away and got ready to leave, I overheard a girl at the table behind me talking about Dr. Christine Blasey Ford's testimony that would take place in front of the Senate Judiciary Committee against Brett Kavanaugh that day. I knew of Dr. Ford's case and didn't want to miss this historic moment for women's rights. Change of plans. I ordered another coffee, got the Wi-Fi password, put in my headphones, and immersed myself in NPR's livestream of the hearing.

"I have been accused of acting out of partisan political motives," Dr. Ford said as I tuned in. "Those who say that do not know me. I am a fiercely independent person, and I am no one's pawn."[11]

My entire being was captivated by Dr. Ford's unwavering testimony. She proceeded to give a detailed account of the night Brett Kavanaugh assaulted her, speaking about the subsequent impact on her life with impossible grace. Watching her stand up to a man who would potentially be given a lifetime appointment to one of the most powerful positions in our country, accountable for delivering justice of the highest caliber, captivated my entire being.

Listening to her speak, I learned that she grew up just outside Washington, DC, and spent many summers swimming, just like me. A feeling of redemption surged within me—redemption for all the women who had been taken advantage of, including a younger version of myself. I remembered the men who had disregarded my youth, boundaries, and new understanding of my sexuality.

A National Sexual Violence Research Center study[12] related to the #MeToo movement shows that more than 81 percent of women in America have reported experiencing some form of sexual assault or

---

11   Politico Staff, Full transcript: Christine Blasey Ford's Opening Statement to the Senate Judiciary Committee, September 2018, https://www.politico.com/story/2018/09/26/christine-blasey-ford-opening-statement-senate-845080.

12   Holly Kearl, "The Facts Behind The #MeToo Movement: A National Study on Sexual Harassment And Assault," Reston: Stop Street Harassment, 2018, https://www.nsvrc.org/sites/default/files/2021-04/full-report-2018-national-study-on-sexual-harassment-and-assault.pdf.

harassment, while the 2015 US Transgender Survey Report found that nearly half (47 percent) of respondents had been sexually assaulted at some point in their life.[13] Multiracial and Indigenous women, in particular, were significantly more likely to experience sexual violence and rape in their lifetime.[14] And that's only the people who have reported it. I didn't report it. Young Dr. Ford didn't report it. How reprehensible would that number be if it reflected us all?

As Dr. Ford pointed out, recovering from sexual assault takes decades, if it happens at all. Research from the Rape, Abuse & Incest National Network reports that survivors of sexual assault are likely to experience post-traumatic stress disorder, suicide contemplation, drug use, increased problems at work and school, and more.[15]

By the time she concluded, I was sobbing publicly, my feelings ranging from grief and anger—why did she have to get up here and recite all of this to a panel of old, white men, anyway?—to tremendous redemption. How could anyone dismiss that?

In the bathroom, I dabbed my face with a cold paper towel, pressing it into my skin and feeling my heart rate slow down. Dropping my hands to the sink, I looked at myself in the mirror. Puffy hazel eyes. Red cheeks. Dirty hair. Strong arms. Sensitive. Independent. No one's pawn.

One more cold paper towel to the face and I left the coffee shop, stepping into the afternoon light. At my van, I moved seamlessly, listening to my body as she told me what to do.

---

13   S. E. James, J.L. Herman, S. Rankin, M. Keisling, L. Mottet, M. Anafi, "The Report of the 2015 U.S. Transgender Survey," National Center for Transgender Equality, Washington, DC, 2016, https://transequality.org/sites/default/files/docs/usts/USTS%20Full%20Report%20-%20FINAL%201.6.17.pdf.

14   K.C. Basile, S.G. Smith, M. Kresnow, S. Khatiwada, and R.W. Leemis, "The National Intimate Partner and Sexual Violence Survey: 2016/2017 Report on Sexual Violence," Atlanta, GA: National Center for Injury Prevention and Control, Centers for Disease Control and Prevention, 2022, https://www.cdc.gov/nisvs/documentation/nisvsReportonSexualViolence.pdf.

15   "Victims of Sexual Violence: Statistics," Rape, Abuse & Incest National Network (RAINN), https://www.rainn.org/statistics/victims-sexual-violence.

Put on your tennis shoes. Lace them up nice and tight. Pull your hair into a ponytail. Lock your van and tuck your keys into your shoe. Head for the dirt path and start running. One foot. Then the other. Breathe in. Breathe out. One foot. Then the other. Breathe.

I traced a trail behind the coffee shop alongside a river that moved slowly over rocks and branches. I made it about two miles before I got a side stitch, and for the first time since hearing Dr. Ford's testimony, I stopped. I stopped thinking, stopped moving, stopped doing. I stood still, facing an even more still creek and water as smooth as glass.

She did it, my inner voice said. *She did it for all of us.*

After a few long, slow breaths and gratitude for Dr. Ford's bravery and sacrifice, I jogged back to the van and decided it was time to leave this coffee shop behind.

35

"Had I stopped at all to recognize how far I'd come?"

SEPTEMBER 30–ROCKY MOUNTAIN NATIONAL PARK, COLORADO
62 DAYS ON THE ROAD, 4,482 MILES

The patter of rain on the van woke me up the next morning in a tree-lined Fort Collins neighborhood, and the wet ground outside implied that it had rained all night. As I put on clean clothes and tidied up the van, I realized how much I enjoyed urban camping. It had been so expensive to spend the night at actual campgrounds, like in Seattle. If I had kept doing that, I would definitely be out of money by now. Of course, there were some things I couldn't enjoy while urban camping, like setting out my chair and reading by the fire, or cooking dinner outside. But that was okay. So many campgrounds I'd encountered were RV parks packed to the brim with trailers, which made me feel like I was sleeping in a parking lot anyway. If I were going to sleep that close to other cars, I'd rather do it on a random street for free. Now I only wanted to spend money on campsites like the one Devin and I had found in Utah—far away from other people, immersed in nature. I would spend money on that.

After going through my morning routine and finding a coffee shop for breakfast, I was on the I-25 freeway, following a wide two-lane road surrounded by a tunnel of trees toward Boulder, Colorado. A big brown sign for Rocky Mountain National Park caught my eye.

Well, why not?

Turning onto Route 34 toward the park, I found myself on winding, uphill mountain roads that eventually opened up to a dazzling fall spectacle that rivaled Wyoming and Utah. Sprinkles of bright yellow, orange, and red colored the side of the magnificent Rocky Mountains. The air was crisp and refreshing with a chilly bite to it. There were very few people there—tourist season was largely over by now.

It was perfect . . . until I got pulled over.

A park ranger approached my window and sternly asked me why I didn't have license plates.

This again?

I showed him my registration and tried to give him the short version of the story. "I'm on a trip across the country, and I bought this car in LA after my first van broke down several times," I explained. "It was kind of a crisis situation. Anyway, when I finally bought this one, the people at CarMax told me I would get the plates in the mail in one to two months. I haven't been able to check the mail, so my roommate in San Diego plans to send them to me as soon as they come in."

He eyed my registration without saying much.

"And they haven't arrived yet," I added.

"It's not good to be driving around without a license plate," he said, his voice softer but still stern.

"I know," I said. "I wish they would show up already. You're the second person to pull me over."

"Well," he said as he looked around. "I suggest you have your roommate mail them to you as soon as possible, however you can make that happen."

With that, he headed back to his car and drove away.

I sat in my van for a moment, frustrated. I had never bought a new car before, and this whole license-plate process had felt unnecessarily complicated. If I had known it would be such an inconvenience, I would have insisted CarMax provide more clarity about exactly when and how I would get the plates.

How am I going to get the plates once Kaley gets them, anyway? I thought. I'll probably ask her to mail them to my parents' house in Florida. My mind fixated on the logistics of the license plates as I continued driving, surrounded by monstrous gray mountains and empty roads.

The cold wind floated through the window, and as the road climbed higher and higher, a wave of unexpected emotion started to wash over me. From San Diego to Rocky Mountain National Park, so much had changed. I had a new car, a new partner, new relationships with new friends, and a new relationship with myself.

Had I stopped at all to recognize how far I'd come?

Suddenly, and for the first time on this trip, I allowed myself to feel proud. It wasn't a loud, ego-driven show, but a quiet hum of acknowledgment from me to myself for all the minutes, hours, days, places, faces, situations, and conversations I had experienced—and would experience—and how I could feel them changing me.

36

"I'm the best version of all the women that I have been."

OCTOBER 2–DENVER, COLORADO
64 DAYS ON THE ROAD, 4,550 MILES

After the beautiful, emotional whirlwind that was my drive through Rocky Mountain National Park, I made it safely through the remaining seventy miles to Denver, Colorado. Sitting in a local coffee shop and researching Denver women and gender nonconforming people who might be interested in speaking with me, I discovered Confidence.

Articles featured her as an internationally ranked slam poet—someone who writes and performs poetry on a stage in front of live audiences, often with intensity and liveliness. When I watched a few videos on YouTube, her powerful words and delivery brought tears to my eyes. She was outstanding.

To my surprise, she responded to my email fairly quickly. Her sign-off, "The ink in my veins never dries," gave me full-body chills. We agreed to meet at a coffee shop she loved near her home.

As soon as Confidence walked in, I recognized her. She had short, turquoise hair, a beautifully patterned poncho, and long, violet nails.

We both ordered tea, which came in small, colorful teapots, and found a seat outside.

"I'm happy to share my story with you," she said directly as we began talking. "I believe in the power of story to change lives. I have built my life on it. But I'm weary of my story being used in a way that I'm not intending it to be. I don't want to be a soundbite in someone else's story or a conveniently used quote in an already preconceived narrative. So, tell me a little more about how you found me and the work you're doing here."

I was grateful for her candor and could understand her skepticism. White people had a long and terrible track record of exploiting and taking credit for the work, creativity, and culture of Black people. I wanted Confidence to feel comfortable knowing that wouldn't happen here.

I reciprocated her transparency by thanking her for sharing her apprehensions with me and by telling her more about who I was and why I wanted to meet her.

"The narrative women and gender nonconforming people often see rarely depicts all that is possible. That's how all of this started for me—wanting to find inspiration for my life at a time when I felt lost and stuck. I'm hoping to uplift the stories of real people living brave, big, bold lives so others who identify similarly can feel not alone, and more than that, inspired to do the same," I said. "What matters most to me is that you feel comfortable sharing your story, and you feel good about the way it's represented. I will only share what you choose to share, and I will ensure you have the chance to review anything before it's published."

She listened intently as she poured tea from the orange kettle into her cup. "I appreciate that," she said.

"I realize I know very little about you," I said. "There's only so much you can know about anyone without meeting them. But I have watched your poetry slams and read interviews with you, and I feel compelled to start by saying thank you for your bravery. The way you use poetry to respond to trauma is an act of courage, and it's incredibly moving."

My eyes started to well up. *Shit. Don't be that white girl who cries.*

"I'm not going to cry," I said, more to myself than to Confidence, looking away and blinking.

"I'm going to go get napkins," she said as she leaned forward. "Because the thing is, you might cry, and I will."

Returning to the table with a handful of napkins, Confidence began to tell me about herself and her life. As she spoke, her grace and wisdom commanded my attention. Her voice danced rhythmically over her words, each of which she chose with precision.

"This life, in one way or another, has reduced my body and soul to rubble and ash again and again and again," she said. "By all accounts, I should not be here, let alone in my right mind, let alone a leader, let alone a mother. There are so many things that I should not be capable of that I am. I think a lot of us have been trained into thinking that being wounded makes you somehow less than. That isn't even a little bit true."

Confidence described the many times she'd faced trauma and thought, *I can't deal with this because if I do, I will come unglued, and nobody will ever be able to put my pieces back together.* Then she would face the issue head-on, come entirely unglued, and, as she described it, "Watch the spirit and the ancestors put a new version of me back together."

"It's not that I have faith in myself to not break open," she explained. "It's that I have confidence that I will break open, regrow, heal, and rise again and again and again. This is the way I want to help people move into their transformations, knowing that it's not about how strong you are but about trusting that there's a power greater than you that will pick you up and help you put the pieces back together. Every time, I'm newer, stronger, and more beautiful inside and out than I was in the last iteration."

As Confidence spoke, I drew parallels to what Tracie had shared with me in Ventura. Both weren't moving through life with a fear of breaking or being broken, instead regarding it as unavoidable – and something that makes you more.

"I like thinking about who we are like that," I added, "as iterations."

Tea and happy tears with Confidence.

"I feel like I'm the best version of all the women I've been because I had to kill a couple versions of myself along the way. I have had to lay an axe to the root of versions of myself that helped me survive certain periods of my life that no longer serve me. We all do. Yet the "hoodest" version of me is ever present," she said with a joyful laugh. "She fought the battles that made it possible for me to speak my truth.

"So many women, and mothers particularly, exist in survival mode. They don't have the privilege of being able to sit back and examine their trauma because they're trying to get everybody up on time, pay for daycare, and keep food on the table. I understand survival mode because I was in it for years. But survival mode won't end until you fix you and let things die. And most people are just not willing to die or let anything die. They want to champion growth. But growth demands certain deaths—deaths that you have to endure in order to survive and move forward in life. There are relationships that you will have to end.

There are friends you will have to say goodbye to forever. There are things in your life that you will have to say no to if you want to fully manifest."

This idea of certain deaths reminded me of my conversation with Erin in Utah about the controlled burns that clear everything out so new life can grow. Of course we don't want to let things die. Facing the unknown with a blank slate, especially when you feel cracked open, is terrifying. I felt it at the very beginning of my trip, and I still felt it some days now. Yet Confidence was helping me further understand the necessity, unavoidability, and beauty in the raging fires.

"Your poetry references these certain deaths often," I observed. "What makes you feel drawn to slam poetry?"

"I have to say that a portion of my zeal in poetry slam was looking for someone to tell me that my writing, my life, my voice, had value. It used to be that I was at every open mic, I was in every competition, and I was slamming all the time," Confidence explained. "Then I found my worth, and after that, I didn't need the validation of winning. Yes, I could win, and I usually did win, but I stopped needing it."

As we talked, I found myself soaking up every ounce of Confidence's hard-earned wisdom. Her reflections on her own life and poetry segued into expressing her many other identities: playwright, executive coach, and mother to her five beautiful children, whom she called the light of her life.

"I am often having experiences with my children that I never had with my parents," she told me, with a smile that lit up her whole face. "I sent myself off to college alone at seventeen years old. There were no parents celebrating or putting money in my hand. It's crazy to have these experiences where I give [my children] the world, and then sit still and recognize it's because no one did it for me."

She paused and looked off into the distance. When she returned her gaze to me, she kept the smile but had tears in her eyes—as did I. At this point, I was so far forward on my chair, I thought I might fall off. I put my hands out across the table, palms up, and Confidence placed her hands in mine.

"When my son left for college in Missouri three months ago, he sent me a message asking me what advice I wish someone had given me when I went off to college. I told him, 'Trust your gut,'" she said, one tear rolling down her cheek. "Know your worth and know you can choose your way out of any situation you chose yourself into. You just have to be willing to choose again. If you choose the wrong thing, it may utterly devastate you—and you still get to choose again. That has gotten me through the most challenging places in my life. That is how I have survived."

Trust yourself. Know your worth. Choose. Examine your choices. Choose again. Repeat.

"I don't know if you know who Lucille Clifton is, but she has this amazing quote that I consider to be the anthem for my life," Confidence said, pulling her hands away to retrieve a notebook from her purse and flipping to a page that she began reading from: "'Look at this life that I have fashioned from dust and starshine. Who did I have to be but myself with no blueprint?'"

After reading it, she closed her eyes and let the words wash over us both in silence. As she went to put the journal back in her bag, I spotted the tattered binding of a book that looked familiar.

"Are you reading *Women Who Run with the Wolves?*" I asked.

"I'm rereading it," she said, flashing a smile.

"Someone I love gave me that book recently," I told her. "I've been carrying it around with me, but I haven't started it yet."

Confidence encouraged me to dive into it without hesitation, and I took it as a sign from the universe that I was exactly where I was meant to be. To trust.

After several hours and empty tea pots, we hugged and parted ways. I got in my van and didn't even try to stop the tears. Sitting in the driver's seat, I closed my eyes and just let them fall off my cheeks. I already knew Confidence's words would stay with me for a long time. I felt them burrow into the fabric of the new version of myself I was stitching together as the old version of myself faced its own necessary death. With Confidence's perspective, I understood the iterative process of self-growth was only a series of choices, which leads to endings and new beginnings before we choose again. The choice to leave a familiar place. The choice to let an old relationship go. The choice to try a new one. The choice to keep going. The choice to let things die. The choice to begin again.

Eventually, I dried my face and turned the car on before pulling up directions to the address of my next stop. Erin had introduced me to her long-term friend Marisa as a potential place to stay in town, and Marisa was kind enough to let me spend the night in her guest room.

It was dark out when I pulled onto the quiet street in the suburbs of Denver. My body and mind were exhausted, and I felt guilty wondering how quickly I could get into bed without appearing rude to Erin's friend.

When I knocked on the door, a woman in pajamas answered and introduced herself as Marisa. She gave me a hug and welcomed me into her home.

"Thank you for letting me stay with you tonight," I said. "I appreciate it."

"Thank you for coming!" Marisa replied. "My husband and son are downstairs watching a movie right now, but they'll be up soon. Can I get you something to eat, or are you thirsty?"

I thanked her for her generosity and politely declined. I could feel my social muscle fading fast. Before excusing myself, I mentioned Erin.

"Erin told me you're one of her oldest and best friends," I said. "She's such a wonderful person—you've got a good one."

"Don't I know it," Marisa said, leaning against the kitchen counter to face me. "We've been friends since high school. She's one of those people you can tell anything to, and regardless of how much time has passed, it always feels like you just talked yesterday."

That's exactly how I felt about Erin too—about all my closest friends.

After a few more minutes of light conversation, I asked Marisa if she'd mind if I headed to bed.

"Of course," she said. "Just head down the stairs, pass my husband

and son, and make a left into the guest room."

I thanked her again and awkwardly descended the stairs, feeling like an intruder into family movie night. Father and son turned around and gave me a wave before I disappeared into the guest room. Shutting the door behind me, I felt guilty for not spending more time with Marisa and her family on the heels of their generosity—but not guilty enough to interrupt family movie night.

After a luxuriously hot shower, I climbed into bed and checked my email to find a message from *ROVA* magazine—a magazine about traveling the roads of North America. The editor had given me the green light to write a piece about my trip for the next issue—and the deadline was in a month.

I buzzed with momentary excitement and then almost immediately became overwhelmed. When I pitched the story back in August, I hadn't even left on the adventure yet. Now, two months into it, I had no idea how to write about what had happened. Where would I even start? How could I possibly begin to capture it all? The responsibility of describing this experience and explaining it seemed daunting—especially while I was still in the middle of it. I didn't feel ready to write it, and I didn't know when I would feel ready to write it either.

Not a problem for tonight, I told myself as I sunk into the soft pillows and chose to figure it out later. Then, I was out like a light.

37

"It's important to teach girls how to advocate for themselves."

OCTOBER 3–DENVER, COLORADO
65 DAYS ON THE ROAD, 4,559 MILES

There were a few places that I typically defaulted to when exploring a new city—coffee shops and breweries, to start. In San Diego, also known as "the craft beer capital of America," almost everything had a connection to craft beer. Mixte even had some craft beer clients at one point. My time in that city taught me to appreciate the art of craft brewing and the artists behind it.

When I discovered Lady Justice Brewing—a community-focused brewery that supports and empowers women and girls—I had to learn more. What did it mean to use craft beer as a catalyst for change?

After a short email exchange, Jen, one of the cofounders, agreed to meet me in their Denver tap room. When I arrived, she was serving large cans of beer to-go to a steady flow of people at the side door. Jen greeted each person with friendliness, asking, "Hey, how's it going? What can I get for ya?"

When I asked Jen what they were doing, she explained that people were picking up their Community Supported Brewery (CSB) "crowlers," short for canned growlers.

"It's the same as a Community Supported Agriculture program, but with beer," she told me as she wiped down the counter. "You buy a membership for three months, and each month, you come pick up a crowler."

"What does the crowler money go to?" I asked her.

"All the money from this program funds grants that support community programs for women and girls," Jen replied. "Wherever we go, we want to make sure the community that has supported us since the beginning continues feeling the love. If people still feel like supporting us in that grassroots way, we want to make sure they have a way of doing it."

This model of locally made beer that went right back into the community made my craft-beer-loving heart happy. Sipping my strawberry cream ale, I asked Jen about the beginning of Lady Justice Brewing.

"The other cofounders and I all moved back to Colorado in 2016 after service in AmeriCorps and got the idea to start a community-focused brewery. We all thought, 'Should we actually do this?' We started brewing together in our kitchens at first. I had only brewed a couple of times, and it always ended in exploding bottles in the basement," she said with a reminiscent smile. "We were scrappy."

Jen continued to explain the importance of the words GOOD BEER, BETTER WORLD—the phrase on all their cans and merchandise.

"We want to make sure that the way we're structured commits to social justice, which has bled through everything we do," Jen said, sipping on her own beer with a small towel draped over her shoulder. "From the beginning, we've committed to giving grants and donating beer. Whatever we have left after that goes back into the company. We haven't had any significant profit so far, and we're okay with that. Periodically, we find ourselves saying, 'Okay, we need to sell some beer before we can give away more beer.'" She laughed and set her beer down on the counter as another customer walked in. "But it's a beautiful problem to have!"

Jen and a pint of Lady Justice Brewing.

After a short conversation with a young couple who came to collect their crowlers, Jen picked up right where she left off.

"If you're a young woman between the ages of twelve and eighteen, you can apply for a grant," she explained. "This is an opportunity for them to write out why someone should invest in them, and that process teaches them self-worth they can carry with them the rest of their lives. It's important to teach girls how to advocate for themselves."

"You must get to know your community well through the CSB program," I said, watching more people show up for their crowlers.

"Oh, definitely," Jen confirmed. "I remember right after the 2016 election, we had one woman who was pretty visibly distraught pick up beer from us. She had a sense of determination about her purchase—like, 'I'm buying this beer, and that's something small that I'm doing right now to make an impact.' It was remarkable to realize that she saw her beer purchase as a step in the right direction of what she believed our community should be."

As we continued talking, it got dark outside, and the steady pace of people coming to pick up their crowlers slowed. I was curious about how others in the craft beer industry responded to Lady Justice Brewing.

"People question our beer, who we are, what we're doing, and our business model every day," Jen said. "We haven't had any full-on sexism thrown our way—it's more microaggressions, undercutting comments, and lack of cultural and gender awareness. Or just general awareness, really. Institutionalized assumptions have gotten so deep into our culture, expectations, and norms that people don't even realize they're acting on them."

I thought about the cultural standards impressed upon women from such a young age by everything around us—family, friends, community, culture, school, religion, society, mainstream media—the patriarchal pond we're all swimming in. And in this pool, we're all affected. We're told there's a right and a wrong, a good and a bad, a worthy and a less-than-worthy. We accept things as truth about the world and each other. How harmful this is. How much damage it does us all.

As Jen began turning off the taps, I thanked her for taking the time to talk with me, and she gave me a Lady Justice Brewing sticker, and a hug goodbye.

Jen's so right, I thought, finding an urban camp spot for the night. Outdated expectations about how we should look and act, how our businesses should run, and what we should do with our lives drive the world around us. It was designed this way.

At least there were people like Jen, redefining what breweries could do; and Eli, redefining what auto repair shops could do; and Ava, redefining what art could do; and Beth, redefining what filmmaking could do; and so many more redefining so much more. Their stories could remind us that the world isn't binary—right or wrong, good or bad, black or white, male or female—and no one is more or less worthy. Their stories could remind us how much possibility exists and how connected we are. When we realize how connected we are, we realize our power. And when we realize our power, we can finally begin to reimagine what was designed to keep us separate and small.

38

"You've untethered yourself from so many things that hold people in one place."

OCTOBER 4–AMARILLO, TEXAS
67 DAYS ON THE ROAD, 4,993 MILES

Leaving Colorado and entering the unexpected beauty of northwest Texas reminded me of the soft spot I'd always had for country music. When I was young, my babysitter used to play exclusively country, and I learned to love the catchy tunes of artists like JoDee Messina, Kenny Chesney, Keith Urban, and the Chicks.

Rolling the windows down, I put my arm all the way out to feel the eighty-five degrees on my skin. It was humid and hot when the car was stopped but just cool enough when the car was moving. The roads were long and flat, and the land was the same. There was less color here than in Utah and Colorado; everything seemed to be shades of brown, gold, yellow, rust, and gray, with the exception of small bushes and patches of green that popped up throughout.

My country music moment ended with the sound of my phone ringing. Jamie!

I picked up right away, and we launched into conversation like we always did—easily, effortlessly—as we caught up on how things were going on the road for me and what life had been like for her back in San Diego. The scenery became a golden blur as I smiled and drove, excited to talk to someone I knew and who knew me so well.

"Hey, what are you going to do when this trip is over?" she asked after a while.

"I don't know," I answered. "Probably come back to San Diego and try to figure out what I want to do with my life."

"So you think you'll come back?"

I paused. I hadn't thought about not going back to San Diego, but then again, I hadn't thought about what would happen after this trip at all. I'd given myself permission not to plan that far ahead. San Diego seemed like the default decision; it was where my community was. And while San Diego was familiar, it was also the place I couldn't wait to leave not that long ago. I'd assumed that this adventure would wipe away the sadness from San Diego and that I would feel refreshed and reinspired enough to go back and rebuild.

But would San Diego feel different? If so, for how long? Would I truly be able to live into this next iteration of myself I had been building in a place that held so many pieces of the old me?

I fumbled through this thought process out loud with Jamie, and she listened patiently. Then she asked, "Have you thought about moving to Portland?"

The question startled me, not only because I hadn't thought of it but also because Jamie lived in San Diego. As my friend, didn't she want me to return? In my heart, I knew she did. But she also wanted what was best for me, and she could see before I could that it wasn't in San Diego.

After growing up in Maryland for the first twenty years of my life, moving to San Diego had taught me how to live alone, helped me develop my career, and showed me what I loved in myself and my community. Almost a decade later, I had managed to cultivate a home and family in a place that had once been so new to me. Perhaps it was time to do that again.

"I'm just thinking," Jamie said, "You've untethered yourself from so many things that hold people in one place. You're going to put roots down wherever you go after this. Why not do it with Devin, somewhere new?"

When Jamie and I hung up, I entertained the idea of Portland. It was like trying something new for the first time, trying to decide if I liked it. *There's no rush to decide right now*, I reminded myself. *But what an interesting idea.*

39

*"This is a beautiful place—but only when
we choose to see it that way."*

OCTOBER 5–AUSTIN, TEXAS
68 DAYS ON THE ROAD, 5,420 MILES

It was a smoldering hot morning in Austin—close to 100° Fahrenheit—and I had two interviews scheduled. The first was with Deb, a director, screenwriter, and producer specializing in telling stories of queer women of color. She was also an entrepreneur, having recently founded Myth of Monsters—a mission-driven film and television production company dedicated to upending deep-seated myths about women, BIPOC, and LGBTQIA+ individuals.

When we met at a coffee shop near her office, she asked me not to call her Deborah. It was too formal.

"Deb it is," I said with a smile as we settled into our seats at an outside table. I asked her, just like I asked everyone I interviewed, if she was comfortable with me recording the interview and taking a few photos.

"Yes, and I clearly forgot that you were taking photos. I would have worn a different shirt," she said, looking down at her gray T-shirt. "Oh, well. Just caption them 'Mom of two toddlers doesn't sleep very much.'"

"How about, 'Mom of two toddlers is a badass'?" I asked.

"That's fine too," she said, smiling.

Deb began telling me about her parents, who emigrated from Cuba. "To them, there's a particular way to be in the world," she said with pain in her voice. "Shockingly, my father was the one who was fine with me dating women. Now my mom is okay with it too but only because she's a grandma. My sister has never met my children, and that's not the easiest thing."

She paused for a moment, as if she were finding words for something indescribable.

"As I've become a parent, I've also realized that my parents are doing the best they can," she shared. "They're human beings with their own struggles and emotions. This realization has brought me closer to them. Imagine others who haven't been able to transcend this barrier within their families—those who get outcasted or come out of the closet only to realize that being who they are is not as easy as they'd hoped. It took an extremely long time for me and my family to get here," Deb said. "And along the way, I learned a valuable lesson: family truly is about the family that you make. It doesn't have to be the family that you inherit."

Deb explained that so many of these insights came while working on her film, *Southwest of Salem*, which helped exonerate four incarcerated women known as the San Antonio Four.

"It's about a family that we found and made in each other, which is something queer people often do," Deb said. "Sometimes you're shunned from the family you've been given and have to make your own."

I thought about the reactions from my friends and family when I came out—positive, kind, celebratory. I didn't have to choose between my freedom and my family—which wasn't the reality for so much of the LGBTQIA+ community.

A study from the University of Miami found that more than 70 percent of lesbian, gay, and bisexual folks experience rejection from their parents resulting from their gender identity or sexual orientation.[16] The Journal of Nursing Scholarship published a recent study that documented the connection between parental rejection and increased depression and suicidality among transgender and nonbinary youth, noting that high rejection from both parents was correlated with suicide attempts from the past year.[17] And, in its 2023 National Survey on the Mental Health of Young People,[18] The Trevor Project, an organization dedicated to preventing suicide in LGBTQIA+ youth, found that 41 percent of LGBTQIA+ young people had seriously considered attempted suicide in the past year. The Trevor Project also noted that queer youth who experience family acceptance are "half as likely to report suicidal thoughts in the last six months and nearly half as likely to report suicide attempts."[19]

Deb held out her left forearm to show me a small tattoo in navy ink that read INNOCENT followed by the numbers 11-23-16.

"Two of the girls from *Southwest of Salem*, Anna and Cassie, got this tattoo with me," she said, gazing down at it. "For me, it's a reminder that life has no limits."

Deb explained that for the rest of her life, she would remember the four women of that film and her role in chronicling their journey toward freedom. With every odd against them, justice had prevailed in the end. Perhaps this was what Deb meant by "Life has no limits." It

---

16   B. E. Richter, K. M. Lindahl, and N. M. Malik, "Examining Ethnic Differences in Parental Rejection of LGB Youth Sexual Identity," Journal of Family Psychology 31, no. 2 (March 2017): 244–49, https://doi.org/10.1037/fam0000235.

17   Jordon D. Bosse, Kristen D. Clark, Kimberly A. Dion, and Lisa M. Chiodo, "Transgender and Nonbinary Young Adults' Depression and Suicidality Is Associated with Sibling and Parental Acceptance-Rejection," Journal of Nursing Scholarship: An Official Publication of Sigma Theta Tau International Honor Society of Nursing 56, no. 1 (2024): 87–102, https://doi.org/10.1111/jnu.12917.

18   The Trevor Project, "2023 US National Survey on the Mental Health of LGBTQ Young People," https://www.thetrevorproject.org/survey-2023/.

19   The Trevor Project, "Behaviors of Supportive Parents and Caregivers for LGBTQ Youth," https://www.thetrevorproject.org/research-briefs/behaviors-of-supportive-parents-and-caregivers-for-lgbtq-youth-may-2022/.

felt like a profound message of hope.

Deb described filmmaking in intricate detail, explaining that while the medium can be compelling, it can also be exploitative and horrific—especially in the documentary world. She reminded me of Beth and the way she described uplifting the voices often left out in filmmaking, and handling every person's story with intention and care. It was also the way I tried to approach sharing stories on this trip—decentering myself and ensuring those I interviewed had the space to express their stories and that I was doing their stories justice when I shared them.

"Recently, I was on a panel called Decolonize Docs, which was all about how documentaries historically come from the notion that a privileged individual goes to a country and takes photos and videos of the Indigenous population," Deb explained. "That snowballed into predominantly white filmmakers making films about people of color. They extracted those stories and exploited them for their own gain while victimizing people along the way. Now, there's a movement from the inside. Now, people who are of those communities are saying, 'You can't tell our stories anymore. And if you do, you better do it with the utmost respect and integrity.'"

Deb elaborated on how her experiences in the film industry and the obvious gaps in representation had led her to start her own production company, Myth of Monsters.

"Where did the name Myth of Monsters come from?" I asked her.

"There are a couple of meanings," she said, "one of which is how BIPOC and queer people have been perceived as monstrous or deviant. Secondly, there is the way we choose to see the world. Einstein once said something like, 'The most important decision you make is choosing whether the universe is kind and benevolent or dark and ugly.' I believe that. I live that every day. When I choose to see the world as benevolent, it's reflected that way back to me. If I choose to see it as ugly, that's what I get."

She leaned forward, elbows on the table. "I want to defy the perception that the world we live in is monstrous—which it's not—and

Einstein's wisdom reminds me that I have the power to decide." She looked around, gesturing to our surroundings with open arms. "This is a beautiful place—but only when we choose to see it that way."

A happy Deb.

I looked around. A few people at the table behind us got up and walked away, holding hands. More people arrived, talking and laughing. People walked by with their dogs and on cell phones. Cars came and went. Birds chirped. Clouds rolled along above us. Deb smiled. *This is a beautiful place*, I thought.

"I'm past this idea of asking too much of people, with my films and in general," Deb said. Her eyes were big, and she moved her hands as she spoke. "I love the idea of creating something because we want to do it for ourselves, and not asking anyone to do anything anymore. I don't need everybody to love my work or for everybody to go to one of my screenings. I don't have any interest in changing anybody, and I don't need anything to be fancy. It's enough if people who see my work feel moved in a small, private way. I'm lucky that I get to do what I love and that it feels good when I do it. I know that when I feel good, that affects how my kids feel when they come home from school, because if they feel loved, then that affects how they treat others, and so on. I can't control much, but I want to do work that makes me feel happy to be in the world. Otherwise, why be here on the planet, you know?"

I do know.

Glancing down at her phone, Deb realized she had to head to her office, which was on the same block. She thanked me for finding her and flashed me a smile before briskly walking around the corner and into her office building, a cup of coffee in hand.

I stayed at the coffee shop for another two hours, ordering breakfast and thinking about what Deb had shared. Her clarity around what mattered in life—chosen family, representation for the underrepresented, happiness at work—brought the blurry picture of what I wanted for the next chapter of my own life a little more into focus.

Approaching the afternoon, I texted my younger brother, Nathan, and his girlfriend, Daniela, who lived in Austin, and made plans to see them for dinner.

Daniela's parents' house, where she and Nathan were temporarily living, was a big, beautiful brick home on a street of other big, beautiful brick homes. Nathan answered the door with the outstretched arms I knew so well and missed so much. He wrapped me in an all-encompassing bear hug and kissed the top of my head. Even though he's my little brother, he towers over me at six-foot-two. I hugged Daniela, too, thanking her for letting me stay while I was in town.

"My parents are so excited to have two Boltons here," she said with a laugh. "We're having a big dinner, and some of the neighbors are over too. Are you okay with Mexican food?"

"More than okay with it," I told her, knowing that her parents were from Jalisco, Mexico.

Inside, Daniela's parents were welcoming and kind, as were the neighbors. They made space for me around a table in the kitchen as we indulged in margaritas and chicken tacos with onions, cilantro, avocado, salsa, and radishes. At the table, I noticed the sweet and supportive glances between Daniela and Nathan as Daniela's parents happily assumed the role of hosts, ensuring everyone had everything they needed every few minutes. I smiled as the conversation bounced fluently between English and Spanish, reminding me of Camila.

This ordinary moment soothed a piece of me and also made me feel homesick for these everyday moments with people I loved—like sitting around the dinner table and laughing. It's what I'd cherished about being on Orcas Island with Andy, Sandy, Chris, and David. For the first time since leaving San Diego, I noticed a shift from my desire for newness and adventure to a desire for the comforts of home and people I knew.

After dinner, I excused myself to the guest bedroom Daniela had generously made up for me, wrestling this longing for "home"—the feeling more than a place. I missed being around family. I missed sitting on the couch in pj's, watching movies. I missed my mom's laugh, and cooking with my dad. I missed feeling safe and still.

Florida, where my parents lived, was only a few days' drive away, but I had a stop planned in Louisiana first. I found myself considering if I still wanted to stop, or just drive through instead. Funny how strong nostalgia and family—whether given or chosen—can be.

40

"Know who you are, and don't let anybody try to tell you otherwise."

OCTOBER 6–AUSTIN, TEXAS
69 DAYS ON THE ROAD, 5,439 MILES

Nathan and Daniela were enjoying a cup of coffee in the kitchen when I came down the stairs with a bag over my shoulder. Everyone had known I was only staying one night, but still, it seemed too short. They walked me to my van, all of us sad to leave each other so soon.

"Wait!" I said, digging through the containers under my bed. I pulled out the print I'd bought from Camila that said BAE LINGUAL. "Daniela, I got this from a wonderful Latine printmaker in Portland. Do you want it?"

Daniela gently took the poster in her hands and read the words out loud with a laugh. "I love it," she said, glancing at my brother, who was also smiling his relaxed, handsome smile.

"All right, you two," I said. "Bring it in."

We shared a hug, and I dried my wet eyes on my brother's shirt discreetly. I didn't see him enough. Driving away, I blew them kisses, shouting, "I love you!" out the window.

Fueled by the happiness of seeing Daniela and Nathan, I arrived at Settle Ceramics in Austin feeling optimistic and open. I'd messaged the owner Sammi a few days before to coordinate the interview. Now, she answered the door in an apron stained with clay.

Inside the studio, sunlight poured through the windows. Kilns lined the back wall. Mugs, bowls, plates, and pots rested in stacks on shelves. Sammi casually sat on a stool to face me and began telling me about how she discovered ceramics.

"I found clay when I was five years old," she told me. "I was one of the silly, nonsocial children working in a journal full of clippings and collages. I didn't know I could make that into a career. After school, I ended up working in a local clay studio as an assistant, and at the same time, being a terrible waitress. I'm clumsy, and I get upset under pressure, which made my life as a waitress just . . . bad." She closed her eyes and laughed, embarrassed at the memory. "I was lost for a while," she confessed. "Settle was a twinkle in a very faraway eyeball of mine for many years before I ever started my business."

"I love the part on your website where you explain what makes your business different," I said, reciting, "'We live in a disposable world, and the idea of objects being precious has lost a bit of its luster to most people. I want to change that.'"

"You have to understand, I am a nester through and through," she said, stretching out her hands to her knees. "When I move into a new place, I have the ability to unpack in two days in a way that makes it look like I've been living there for fifteen years." She chuckled and gave a small shrug. "I associate home with comfort, food, and communal gathering." Sammi's words resurfaced in my chest the warmth of yesterday evening with Daniela's family.

"I think it's because of my grandmother. She was a home cook, always had so much food. I have a vivid memory of her stockpot—it was dark blue with white speckles, and the majority of Americans probably owned one like it—and the deliciousness that always came from it. With Settle, I wanted to replicate that feeling, the feeling of an object that's nostalgic. It goes back to the idea of creating heirloom items, like that dark blue dish with white speckles. They're one of a kind," she said. "I would rather make a handful of things that can be passed down for generations than push for more, more, more."

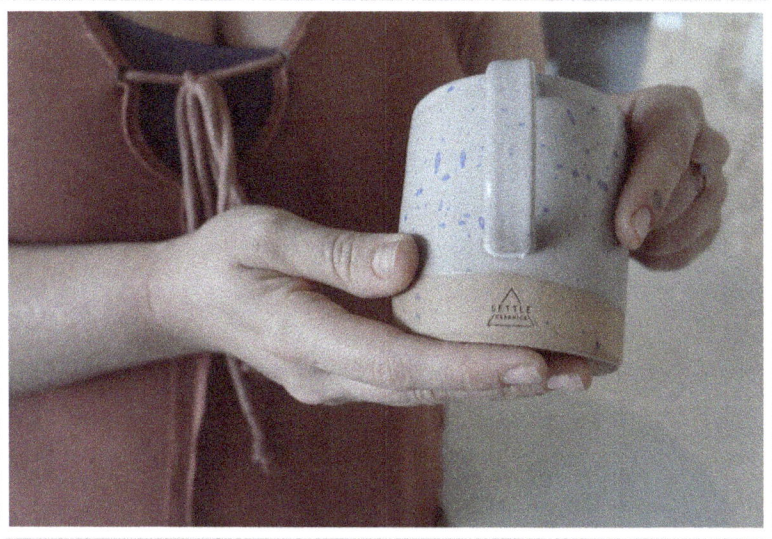

The hands that shaped Settle Ceramics.

As a one-woman show, Sammi described how much she loved being able to say that she made every single thing that came out of her studio.

"When people buy something from me, they're buying directly from the person who's making it," she said. "My advice for people ordering from handmade businesses is simple: remember that you're ordering something handmade. Realize that it's inherently going to be flawed in some way because that's what "one of a kind" means. Respect that there's a human being behind this piece, and it's not perfect because people aren't perfect—and it's the imperfections that make it irreplaceable."

The imperfections make it irreplaceable.

Many times on my trip so far, I had abandoned the idea of perfection, but I hadn't yet thought about the imperfections as making something one of a kind. I had been focused on letting go and detaching from perfect, but that's not the same as acknowledging how special imperfect actually is. One was the act of releasing; the other was the act of appreciation. I remembered what Kim had said about everyone being imperfect together—which, in turn, makes us all perfect. Our imperfections differentiate us. They give us our identity. They make us one of a kind.

"Do you have any advice for other small business owners or creative people who are looking for a place to start?" I asked Sammi.

"That's easy," she said confidently, leaning forward and looking me right in the eyes. "Know who you are, and don't let anybody try to tell you otherwise. Make the choices that align with the vision you have for your company. Choose the clients that like your work the way you make it, and don't work with anyone who wants you to make things that you don't make. You don't have to be everything to everyone."

I imagined the other entrepreneurs I'd met so far would agree.

Before I left, I bought a gray hanging planter with blue swirls for Kaley and two mugs, one solid blue for me and one gray with blue speckles for Devin. Sammi wrapped them up in thick brown paper to keep them safe on the road while I thanked her and we said goodbye.

Back at the van, I stored my delicate presents carefully in one of the Tupperware containers to keep them safe. When I closed the trunk, the yellow CARMAX license plate cover stared back at me.

Knowing it was only a matter of time until I got pulled over again, I called CarMax in Burbank, California, and hit a series of numbers to direct my call. A kind young man answered after a few rings.

"CarMax Burbank, how may I help you?"

"Hi, my name's Mia. I bought a car there a few months ago," I started out, using my best stern voice. "Your team told me to expect my license plates in the mail. But I haven't gotten them yet, and I keep getting pulled over because I don't have actual tags on my car. Do you know when I can expect them?"

"Oh, I'm sorry about that," he responded. "But I don't think your CarMax tags are in the mail."

"What?! How have they not been sent yet? It's been two months!"

"No, what I mean is—we don't mail license plates."

Now I was frustrated and confused. *They don't mail license plates? I don't understand why they would tell me to check for my plates in the mail if they don't mail them.*

"Help me understand," I said. "If you don't mail them, then how do I get my license plates?"

"Umm . . ." His voice trailed off. Just as I was silently cursing the entire "CarMax—the better way to buy a car" slogan, he cautiously said, "Did you . . . did you check under the CarMax tag?"

"What do you mean, did I check under it?"

"I mean, did you take off the piece of yellow paper that says CarMax? There should be a plate underneath."

My stomach dropped. Was he telling me that my license plates had already been on my car the entire time?

"I haven't checked that yet," I said, as calm and collected as possible.

"Do you want to take a look and let me know?" he responded, trying to remain helpful.

"One second," I said, walking around to the back of my van and glaring at the little piece of yellow paper that had taunted me for miles. I lifted it. Sure enough, there were shiny new California license plates underneath.

I took a deep breath, thinking about how to recover with this poor employee. "They're there," I told him evenly. "Thank you for your help."

I hung up quickly and ripped the yellow pieces of paper off both the front and rear plates. Beneath those flimsy, yellow rectangles, the white, navy, and red California plates glittered in the sun.

For fuck's sake. They've been here the whole time. I've literally been driving around with them. As I shook my head in disbelief, I started to see the humor in it. I guess it was a little funny. At the very least, it was a ridiculous story once I got over the embarrassment of telling it. *Kaley is going to make so much fun of me,* I thought.

As I pulled out my phone to take a picture and send it to her, a news alert on my home screen stopped me dead in my tracks. It was from *The Washington Post*, and the headline read: SENATE VOTES TO CONFIRM KAVANAUGH TO THE SUPREME COURT.

I completely forgot my license plates as I sat on the ground in front of my car in the middle of the parking lot. How? How could anyone, after hearing such heartbreaking testimony from Dr. Ford, think that this man deserved a lifetime appointment with so much power? Someone so astonishingly inept didn't deserve to practice law, much less rule on cases that would impact every person in America, if not the world. I had been so filled with hope—for Dr. Ford, for women, for future generations—since that day in Fort Collins. For everyone with hope, this news was a punch in the gut.

I ignored the heat of the black asphalt on my legs. Anger boiled inside of me. The water welling in my eyes made my vision blurry. Putting my head between my knees, I wept and watched my hot tears make tiny pools on the ground.

41

"I hoped for better for us. I hoped we would have changed."

OCTOBER 7–BATON ROUGE, LOUISIANA
71 DAYS ON THE ROAD, 5,880 MILES

The café cashier smiled at me as she asked how I was doing tonight. I snapped out of my fixed gaze on the counter and returned her eye contact.

"Oh, okay," I lied.

If I were feeling more honest, or perhaps more vulnerable, I might have said, "Knowing that Brett Kavanaugh has just been made a Supreme Court justice feels like taking a baseball bat to the ribs. I've been in a nauseating daze since yesterday, and my heart is broken for the message this sends to women and every person silenced by this decision."

She smiled back. "That's good. What can I get you?"

I felt like I might cry. Or scream. But everyone around me in the café appeared calm. The music was low, and the lights were the same. People sat with their headphones in and kept to themselves. Maybe they're just as upset as me on the inside. Perhaps we were all on the verge of a mega meltdown, just barely keeping it together in this café in Baton Rouge, Louisiana. After all, I had pretended I was fine when talking to the cashier. Maybe everyone else was pretending too.

Almost thirty years ago, in 1991, Anita Hill fought this battle as a Black woman, asserting that Clarence Thomas had sexually assaulted her. Then, and today, the verdict favored men in power. I knew true change and justice was a long (I mean, intergenerationally long) game, but it was still hard not to feel defeated in these moments. When I finished my tea, it was raining and dark outside, which seemed fitting. Before I left, my friends in San Diego had joked that I could always sleep in a Walmart parking lot if I ever needed to. Tonight, I had zero emotional capacity to explore the streets of Baton Rouge for a good place to urban camp, so I plugged Walmart into Google Maps and let the familiar British voice guide me there. I didn't want to be too close to the store or the customers, nor did I want to be in the back of the parking lot with all the other car campers. The middle of the lot felt just right.

I went through my routine methodically before I started to cry. I cried for Dr. Ford and the other women who spoke up about Brett Kavanaugh. I cried for Anita Hill. I cried for my sisters and my mom. I cried for the people I'd interviewed. I cried for all the people who were unheard. I cried for all the people who stay silent and all the reasons our country gives them to. I cried for the generation of young folks growing up and watching a patriarchal system work exactly the way it was designed to.

I buried my face in the pillows and let it all out in the middle of a Walmart parking lot in Baton Rouge, Louisiana.

42

"We're just doing our own thing because we love to do it."

**OCTOBER 8—NEW ORLEANS, LOUISIANA
73 DAYS ON THE ROAD, 5,964 MILES**

The woman in her car next to mine was listening to the news so loudly I could make out every word of the journalist describing Brett Kavanaugh's appointment before I even opened my eyes. I groaned, rolling over to look out the window. A few pickup trucks and a brightly colored school bus looked like they'd gotten the overnight Walmart memo too. The overcast sky released rain droplets that dotted my windows.

I covered my head and ears with the blankets. I'm not ready for today. My emotional hangover from the day before had left me feeling like I hadn't slept in days. This Supreme Court news was like the spillover point for all the challenges I had managed to keep at bay—my decision fatigue, my physical exhaustion, my dwindling finances. I felt like a mess.

Inside the van was uncharacteristically scattered, but I found some pants and shoes on the floor and my toiletries bag under the quilt. I tossed it in my backpack with a change of clothes before wandering across the Walmart parking lot to a coffee shop. Inside, I ducked into the bathroom to wash my face, brush my teeth, and change my clothes.

It didn't make me feel holistically better, but at least I felt clean.

Back in the car with hot coffee, I called Devin to confess that I was tempted to drive straight through Louisiana to Florida, to Maryland for Steph's wedding, and then back to Portland again to be with her.

"I could be at my parents' house today if I left now," I told her.

"But don't you have an interview in New Orleans?" she asked.

"I do, with the Caramel Curves. I really wanted to talk to them too," I said, as if I had already skipped it.

"Why don't you do that one interview and then go see your parents?"

"I don't know if I can be social right now," I said. "I feel the opposite of social. I feel depleted—and it's not just the Kavanaugh news. Being on the road is taking a toll on me. Every day, there's a thousand small choices to make: where to go to the bathroom, where to get food, where to get gas, where the wildfires are, which route to take, who to talk to, where to meet, what's safe, what's not safe, where to sleep, where not to sleep . . . it's exhausting. I miss having a bathroom. I miss having a shower. I miss having a room I can stand up in to change my clothes. I want to be inside a house. I miss you, I miss my family, I miss my friends. And I feel so far away from everything."

I stopped myself and took a deep breath. Devin seemed to do the same.

"I know you're exhausted," she said. "But you've been looking forward to this interview with the Caramel Curves. I think you'll regret it if you don't go."

This wasn't the answer I wanted. I wanted her to say, "There's nothing you have to do. Go to Florida and be with your family. Or better yet, come back to me."

At the same time, I knew she was right. She knew this trip and these stories were important; she knew how excited I was to have connected with the Caramel Curves after I read about them in *The New York Times*.

"Just go, be present, power through, and know that as soon as you're done, your parents' house is only a few hours away," she said. "You only need to hang on a few more hours. Do you think you can do that?"

"Yes," I admitted. "I can do that. Thank you. Love you."

"Love you too," she said. "Call me when you're on your way to Florida."

I hung up and got directions toward New Orleans to meet with Nakosha Smith, cofounder of Caramel Curves Motorcycle Club. After exchanging messages over Instagram, she had invited me to meet her and the Curves at a neighborhood park for their annual winter coat drive. Before hitting the road, I went into Walmart to buy a few pairs of gloves and beanies.

After a short drive, a handful of glamorous pink-and-black motorbikes clustered along the side of the street told me I was in the right place. Parking the car and opening the trunk to get my things together, I heard two voices getting louder.

"Did you get that shot?" the woman said to the man.

"The lighting was perfect," he responded. "I just need to switch my lens. What's up next?"

"Let's get one of them lined up by the motorbikes," she said.

My curiosity had been piqued. I peered around the van to see people standing by the car parked in front of me, decked out in camera gear. The man was shorter and older, wearing a fedora and fumbling through the trunk. The woman was taller and leaner, resting against the car and focused on a clipboard in her hands. She wore black combat boots and a loose gray T-shirt tucked into black jeans.

"Excuse me," I said. "Are you here taking pictures of the Caramel Curves?"

"Yes," the woman said, her eyes snapping up. "We're from *O, The Oprah Magazine*. They're going to be in the January issue."

"Oh, my god!" I exclaimed. "That's incredible. They must be so excited."

"What about you?" she asked, scanning me and noticing my camera. "Who are you with?"

"I'm actually just meeting up with CoCo to learn more about the Curves for a book I'm writing," I said, still getting used to saying that.

In my fantasy world, this very hip photographer in combat boots would ask questions, find herself intrigued, and bring it back to Oprah, who then would get it published and choose it for her book club. We would sit across from each other on the couches on her stage, talking and laughing about how hilarious and synchronistic it was that I ran into her magazine photographers one day in October.

"Oh," the woman said, uninterested. "Well, good luck." She turned back to her clipboard and the fedora man.

Inside the park were a few tables with piles of hats, gloves, scarves, and snow pants, and some coat racks with jackets hanging from them in all sizes and colors. I swung my backpack around and pulled out the beanies and gloves, placing them on top of one of the piles.

"Thank you so much!" a woman in a stunning navy spandex jumpsuit said to me. She had dark skin and short, black hair, long nails, and an eye-catching silver necklace. "This all makes a difference for the families around here."

"Of course," I said. "Thank you for hosting this!"

"It's just what the Curves do," she said with a big smile. "We're like family in this neighborhood."

Family. My family. My family was in Florida. My family was in Florida, and I would get to see them so soon. I tried to keep myself focused on the present moment.

"Are you CoCo, by any chance?" I asked her.

"No, girl. CoCo is over there." She pointed to a woman with long, blonde hair sitting at a table by the park entrance.

CoCo sat with her back to me, talking to two other women, all of them wearing the same navy spandex jumpsuit. They laughed big, bodacious laughs, the contagious kind that I loved. I always admired people who allowed themselves to laugh big and joyously.

I took a deep breath and walked up to the women. "Hi, ladies—hi, CoCo," I said. "I'm Mia. We've been messaging over Instagram for the past few days. Is now still an okay time to chat?"

"Hiiii! Yes!" she said with enthusiasm before introducing me to the other women as "the girl writing the book about women who do badass things."

I loved it.

As we started talking, CoCo told me she was one of the founding members of the all-women motorbike group. The group formed in 2005, right before Hurricane Katrina.

"After the storm came, we had to rebuild our community," she said. "Who would have thought? We're all just a bunch of chicks who ride bikes."

She pointed around the park to all the women in jumpsuits, naming each member of the club and telling me a little bit about them—where they worked, what their families were like, how they got into riding motorbikes. Sometimes she would call out to them, and they'd wave or strike a pose.

Coco with the winter clothes donations.

"We wanted to do something different," CoCo told me. "We wanted to pull up looking cute and stand out. We came up with the name Caramel Curves because we're caramel complexioned, we've got curves, and we take curves better on the motorbikes than the guys do."

A member of the Caramel Curves rocking her magenta hair.

At this, she laughed again, and even though my heart still felt heavy, I let myself do the same. It felt healing to be surrounded by the joy of the Curves.

"The jumpsuits are incredible," I told her. "Do you always dress like this together?"

"Well, we're doing a photo shoot today for *O Magazine*, so we tried to get cute," CoCo told me. "But honestly, figuring out what outfit to wear and finding something everybody agrees on is such a challenge as a group. It is not easy to get thirteen women to agree on an outfit. Some people just don't see the vision at first. But majority rules, so if seven out of thirteen of us like it, then it's a go, and we all wear it. Period."

"What do you like to wear?" I asked her.

"For me, I like whatever you're not expecting me to have on. I like the kind of clothes that get your attention. That's what I want to wear," she said.

"Hey, CoCo!" a man shouted from across the park.

"Hey, baby!" she said, getting up to give him a hug as he approached. They chatted for a second before he walked away to help another Curve bring industrial-sized speakers into the park. When CoCo returned to her chair, she tossed her long, blonde hair over her shoulder and adjusted her jumpsuit.

"That's Chad," she said, still smiling and watching him set the speakers up. "He's an honorary Curve. But back to what I was saying," she said. "We're just doing our own thing because we love to do it. None of this was ever done for the fame. The recognition just happened to come. Now, Caramel Curves has gone way past what I thought it would be."

"What did you think it would be?" I asked, intrigued.

"I always thought it would stay a local New Orleans thing," CoCo said. "It's not outside New Orleans yet, but it's going to be. We have a lot of women who want to start Caramel Curves chapters in other cities. So far, we haven't gone out looking for any women to do this, but they've been coming to us asking to do it." She looked around and waved to someone else in the park. "It won't be long before we have Caramel Curves all over the world," she said, eyes following what was happening around us.

Some more people shouted, "CoCo! Get over here!" and I didn't want to keep her from her own party any longer. I was grateful for CoCo's time, especially during the community event she was hosting. "Thanks so much for taking the time to talk to me, CoCo," I said.

"Happy to have you," she said. "Stick around and enjoy—there should be some food and music soon!"

With that, she headed toward a group of fellow Curves and posed for a photo in their shimmering jumpsuits. Kids played and ran around the park. Chad continued setting up the speakers. The pile of winter gear on the tables got higher and higher. People hugged and laughed everywhere. *Chosen family*, I thought, thinking of Deb's words. Community was truly the best balm for tragedy—from Hurricane Katrina to Supreme Court Justice Brett Kavanaugh.

Suddenly, hip-hop filled the air as Chad, the honorary Curve, started dancing. I walked over to him on my way out, and we talked for a few minutes about how amazing the Caramel Curves were.

"Their meaning is just so positive," he said, putting his hands on his chest. "Their hearts are so full." Then, out of pure excitement, he started clapping and yelled, "Let's go, Curves!" like he was at a sports game cheering on his favorite team. "I love to help, but this is their thing, you know?" he said. "It's a sisterhood. I love it."

They were powerful together. In a moment where I felt despair for women everywhere, the joy of this group reignited my sense of hope. There was good. There was community. This had been a setback, not the end.

A quote from one of my favorite authors, Alex Elle, came to mind:

"Women forget how much we can inspire each other.

No one understands us like us."

43

"I was looking forward to just being home for a little while."

OCTOBER 9–DESTIN, FLORIDA
73 DAYS ON THE ROAD, 6,219 MILES

It didn't take long for me to get from New Orleans to Destin, Florida. The landscape rushed by in a brown-and-green blur until the Gulf of Mexico darkened and blended into the navy sky. When I pulled onto my parents' street, the light-wrapped palm trees lit up their front yard, swaying in the wind.

As I got out of the van, humid air whipped through my clothes, and relief filled my body. Finally, a place to rest.

I am safe. I am safe. I am safe.

Walking through the front doors, I plopped my bags down in the bedroom right off the hallway and headed up the stairs to give my parents a hug.

"Mia!" my dad said when he saw me appear, throwing both hands up in the air. "I heard the door open. I hoped it was you!"

"If it wasn't me, you might be in trouble, Dad," I said, letting him swing his arms around me. It reminded me of when Nathan hugged me in Austin, strong and loving. "Where's Mom?" I asked, scanning the living room. Empty white couches sat facing the TV, and all the chairs in the dining room were neatly tucked under the table. Fan blades that looked like palm leaves whirred silently overhead, just like I remembered it.

"She's in the bedroom," my dad said. "I'm so glad you're here!"

"I'm so happy to be here, Dad," I said, everything in my body exhaling. "I'm going to go say hi to Mom."

Dad on film.

The bedroom was dark with the exception of the TV. My mom sat wrapped in a cozy brown sweater. When my dad and I walked in, she looked over at me and said, "Hi, Mia, honey."

"Hi, Mom," I said, sitting on the armrest of her chair and hugging her. "I would like to kindly inform both of you that I love you very much—and I will be asleep for the next twenty-four hours."

Downstairs in my bedroom, the last thing I remember before falling asleep was how much I loved the color of the walls, which were painted robin's egg blue.

❋

When I opened my eyes, light filled the room. Blinking and squinting, I checked my phone. It was noon. I had slept for fifteen hours. Upstairs, I found my dad standing in front of the TV with the remote in his hand, watching news about the incoming Hurricane Michael. "The governor says we need to evacuate today," he said, eyes fixed on the screen.

"John, I really don't want to do that," my mom said from the kitchen. "Remember last time? We evacuated, and nothing ever happened. Why don't we just close all the shutters and wait it out?"

"It's expected to hit in two days, and it's a category four hurricane, Norah," he responded logically. "We can't stay. We have to assume the worst. I'll book us a hotel room further north for a few nights, just to be safe."

A few nights?! No, no, no. I just got here. All I want to do is stop moving.

Mom muttered something about the hurricane shutters as I looked at the window. Trees swayed even more than they had the night before, and the ordinarily calm Gulf of Mexico roared with messy waves. My surf-deprived brain started to think the choppy hurricane waves looked kind of fun.

Being here brought back all the good memories of this place. The porch where we drank coffee in the morning together. The table that my dad joked was our shared office. The kitchen where we did dishes—I washed; he dried. The living room where we watched the *Lord of the Rings* trilogy on New Year's Eve. This was where I let go of all the pressures of life outside of this house, where I always felt safe.

After a long night's sleep in an actual bed, I started to notice the toll that more than two months of driving had started to take on my body. Aside from the bike ride on Orcas Island and the run I went on in Fort Collins, I hadn't exercised or moved much at all. Between driving and meeting people for interviews, almost my entire day was spent sitting. To save money, I'd stopped eating out as much and started trying to buy more food to keep in the van, which was largely snacks because they wouldn't go bad as quickly, and they didn't require a fridge. My diet had become mostly dried fruit, granola bars, Cheez-Its, and beef jerky, and I was certain I wasn't drinking enough water.

My mom seemed to pick up on this, the way mothers do. Convinced I had a protein deficiency, she had already started giving me vitamins and leftovers with meat. I didn't resist.

"Dad, do we have to go?" I asked him. "I wanted to just be home for a little while."

"We have to go," he said.

44

"Step one."

OCTOBER 10–CRESTVIEW, FLORIDA
74 DAYS ON THE ROAD, 6,259 MILES

When the mandatory evacuation order finally came, Dad showed Mom and me how to close the hurricane shutters on all the windows. We went around the house, quietly tending to every window as we fastened the blue shutters down. My parents packed bags for a few days, and I simply zipped my bag up and put it by the door. Who knew how long we'd be gone, hoping the house would be there when we got back. I looked around at the normally lively street. Sidewalks typically filled with people jogging or riding bikes were eerily lifeless. Every home had its windows covered, and there were almost zero cars on the road. Rain pelted the ground around us, and the Gulf of Mexico churned like a washing machine. "You better be here when we get back," I said, looking at our boarded-up house.

My hands clutched the wheel tightly as I followed my parents an hour north in my van, both my arms stiffened as I drove through the pouring rain, windshield wipers on the highest setting. My biceps began to twitch, reminding me of the drive from Ventura to Grace's house.

Trying to avoid another bilateral bicep strain, I loosened my grip on the wheel. *Try to relax*, I urged myself. *We're going to be okay.*

At the hotel, every TV in the lobby had the same station on. The TRACKING MICHAEL headline flashed as a live reporter covered the Category 5 hurricane that had made landfall a few minutes ago. When we got to our room, a palm tree slapped against the hotel window, making such a loud thud that my mom jumped and clutched her chest. My dad sat quietly on the bed with his legs outstretched, eating a butter croissant he'd brought from home and heated up in the hotel room microwave.

Trying to find space from the barrage of newscasters to FaceTime Devin, I curled up in a chair in the hallway. I'd been thinking a lot about the potential move to Portland that Jamie had suggested—but I hadn't mentioned it to Devin. I wasn't sure how she would react. I imagined she'd want me to make that decision for myself, not for her, which made the question: *Is moving to Portland something I want for myself?*

Feeling brave, I FaceTimed her. "Hey, I need to tell you something," I started.

"Oh, okay," she said, surprised.

"I've been thinking about . . . moving to Portland," I said. "There's lots to figure out and talk through, but I wanted you to know it's on my mind as an option when my trip is over."

I held my breath for her reaction, studying her facial expressions closely through the screen. She lifted her eyebrows. "Okay," she said. "Let's have this conversation."

"I feel detached from San Diego," I said. "My job, relationship, and community there are all at a turning point where making a change would be easy. Wherever I go, I'll need to rebuild . . . so why not do it in Portland? It's been one of my favorite places on this adventure so far—for obvious reasons."

She smiled. "You're biased."

"True. But you aside, I liked the culture of the city, loved all the small businesses, and I feel like the people share my values. Besides, I can do so many things that I already love to do there, like bike and surf and be in nature. Of course, you're a factor," I admitted, "but there are also so many other things that make me think it would be a good place for me."

When I finished, she was smiling.

"What?" I said. She was never this quiet. Why was she being so quiet?

She leaned back on her bed, putting one arm behind her head. "I want you to make the choice that's best for you," she finally said. (Called it.) "And if that's Portland, that would make me very happy."

"Really?"

"Of course," she responded. "I wanted you to move here after our time in Utah, but I didn't want to pressure you into anything. You have to make this decision on your own."

Now, we were both smiling. "I wish I could hug you," I said, pulling the phone into my chest. "We have a lot to figure out still," I said, holding it out again so I could see her cute face. "But this feels like step one."

"Step one," she repeated back.

When we hung up, I sat in my chair, filled with gratitude. I silently said thank you for a communicative, vulnerable partner who prioritized my happiness and understood the importance of allowing me to make my own choices about what that meant.

The next day, the storm had faded just enough for us to venture outside. There wasn't much around except a few chain restaurants, including Panera Bread. We enjoyed turkey and wild rice soup as everything outside remained gray and wet.

My dad pulled a set of cards out of his pocket, and for the next few hours we played at least a dozen games of rummy while my mom responded to texts from people who were checking in on us. Every once in a while, my dad pulled her into the game, asking for her help with a certain move. I knew he didn't actually need help. He just never wanted anyone to feel left out.

Sitting at Panera Bread, I realized that this was what I had longed for since Austin—ordinary moments with people I loved. I had filled my cup with adventure, exploration, new faces and places—and still, what I longed for was the company of people my heart knew. My dad, in his gray sweatshirt and khaki shorts and sandals, analyzing his cards and refilling his iced tea. My mom, in her black exercise jacket, black leggings, and black Crocs, texting and occasionally suggesting rummy moves.

Home.

"This can at least bring them some small amount of joy."

OCTOBER 12–DESTIN, FLORIDA
75 DAYS ON THE ROAD, 6,301 MILES

The following morning, the newscasters told us that Hurricane Michael had moved past northern Florida. Destin was reported as safe and largely untouched, but forty-five minutes south, the Panama City area was decimated. Pictures of buildings that had either collapsed entirely or were stripped down to their bare bones flashed across the screen. Cameras panned around what had previously been a marina, revealing stumps that once held up a pier and boats turned upside down and on their sides in piles of wreckage. Popular roads had been torn up, the pavement raised in sharp, jagged pieces and crumbling off to the sides. An aerial view showed piles of wood and rubble where homes, businesses, and schools used to be. The once-popular beach destination had been devastated. A TV reporter called the damage "unprecedented" as we left the hotel, grateful to be alive.

Driving back to the house, we saw some of the destruction firsthand. Trees littered the roads as people drove cautiously around them. Some buildings looked beat-up but salvageable. Every few miles, we passed a roadside donation stand collecting supplies, with signs that read: HURRICANE MICHAEL RELIEF—PLEASE HELP.

We stopped at a store and silently split up to collect towels, clothes, socks, and canned food. My mom grabbed toys, and when she saw my curious expression, explained, "There are going to be kids that lost their homes. They're just kids. This can at least bring them some small amount of joy."

These were the moments when I remembered how big my mom's heart was.

We drove back to one of the donation stands we'd passed where a man and his young daughter were stacking supplies behind a pop-up table. "It's not a lot, but hopefully it helps," my mom said, handing over the bags.

"Anything helps," the man said. "Thank you. God bless you."

When we got back to our house, it looked exactly the same as when we left it—blue shutters sealed tightly and all. It seemed surreal. How radically different would our lives be right now if we lived just forty-five minutes east? I considered my parents. How would they have handled it?

My dad has always been calm and level-headed—a fact-checker and steadfast planner at heart. Nothing seems to rattle him, but it isn't because he doesn't care. He just deals with life as it comes, makes logical decisions in the moment, and doesn't stress out much about things he can't control. He is analytical and able to remove emotion from decision-making without being callous, and has a brilliant mind that has studied incredibly complex topics ranging from medicine and computer science to outer space and history. Amidst all of this, he has a goofy sense of humor and is almost always smiling. I know without a doubt that I got my unbridled optimism from him.

I'll never forget the time we ate together at a restaurant in San Diego. There was a fish tank next to our booth. "Did you know fish hearts only have three ventricles?" he said excitedly, staring at the fish. "How cool is that?"

My mom smiled and mouthed, "I don't care" to me, making me laugh.

"That's very cool, Dad," I said, and he went on to explain it further, comparing it to the human heart and enthusiastically drawing an anatomical diagram on a napkin.

My dad is the person who spends two months doing market research on all the options before buying a new cell phone. He taught me how to drive and how to stay safe on the road, and gave me an emergency kit to keep in my trunk at all times. He showed me how to invest money and write a good resume. A father of four daughters, he made sure that I knew from a young age that girls can do anything.

My mom, on the other hand, falls more into the right-side-of-the-brain categories of spiritual, artistic, musical, and empathetic. She has a big laugh, just like the women of Caramel Curves do, but I don't hear it as often as I want because she has struggled with anxiety and depression. But whenever something really makes her laugh, the rest of the family stops and soaks in the moment. Her laugh lights us all up.

My mom has always creatively expressed herself in one way or another. We had a piano in our house growing up, which she would occasionally play. Less frequently, she would strum on the guitar. One time, I heard her singing "Amie" by Pure Prairie League, and telling me after, "I used to sit on the mall at the University of Maryland and play this song on the guitar with my friends." When I miss her, I listen to that song.

More than music, she loves to paint and sketch. Over the years, I'd saved paper bags and scraps of paper that she doodled on, even though she always told me to throw them away. "They're not worth keeping," she'd say. I kept them anyway.

No one has a more selfless heart than my mother. She taught me about compassion and generosity, about caring for others and helping people who need it without judgment. One time we were in a store, and a woman complimented my mom's shoes. My mother gave that woman her shoes on the spot and walked out barefoot.

"I don't need them," she said when I asked her about it. "They're only shoes. What's the big deal?"

She has often paid for the groceries of the people behind us in line, and she never walks by a person experiencing homelessness without asking if they are hungry. She always treats people with dignity and believes we are all connected.

In addition to all of these wonderful things, my mom is also notorious for being very intense. She almost always wears all black, paired with her long, black hair, and she doesn't care about managing her feelings to make anyone else comfortable. She says what she thinks and stands by that righteously, which I admire.

Only in the last few years before this trip had my relationship with her transformed. I began to see her as a whole person, complete with her own life and experiences that shaped who she was outside of her identity as my mother—just like Deb had described with her own parents. While I once disregarded her advice, now I actively sought it. If something happened that I needed to talk through, she was one of the first people I called.

My mom liked to say that we used to fight because we're so similar.

"You may look like your father, but you're like me on the inside," she'd say.

Now, I just nodded and said, "I think you might be onto something, Mom."

They weren't perfect, but I wasn't looking for perfect anymore, anyway. Looking up at our house, still intact, I hugged them tight.

46

"The secret of life is love, and it is as simple as that."

OCTOBER 14–DESTIN, FLORIDA
76 DAYS ON THE ROAD, 6,301 MILES

Instead of setting up interviews with women and gender nonconforming folks in Florida, I gave myself permission to enjoy quality time at home with my parents. In doing so, I got the crazy idea to interview them. After going around the country learning about other people, how much did I actually know about my own parents? I dedicated the rest of the day to learning about who they were—and, in turn, who I was as a result of them.

My dad was sitting at the dining room table with two chocolate chip cookies stacked on a napkin and a glass of milk. I sat across from him and asked if he had time to talk.

"Sure, what's up?" he said, mid-bite.

"I just realized I don't know a lot about Gran and Pop, or your life growing up as one of ten kids," I said. "Will you tell me about them—and about you?"

"Well, there's not much to tell about me," he said with predictable humility, "but I'll do my best."

I started by asking about his parents, whom I'd always known as Gran and Pop. As he began talking, I pressed start on my phone's voice recorder and slid it between us. I didn't want to miss a word.

"They were the greatest generation," he began. "They never asked for or felt like they were owed anything. They risked and often gave everything they had for their families. They were selfless."

After the Vietnam War, where Pop was a bomber pilot, my dad recalled him spending every day out in his greenhouse.

"He took orchids that everyone else thought were dead and made them bloom. There was this one that only bloomed once a year. I remember him telling me to come see it one night, but I slept through it. When I went into the greenhouse the next day, it was closed shut. 'You'll see it in 364 days,' he told me." Switching to his mother, he continued. "Gran was fluent in French. She became a French professor, teaching at the University of Maryland for many years."

Me and Gran in Baltimore, Maryland

Hearing my dad describe Gran and Pop made me wish I had known them better while they were alive. As he continued, he got so animated recounting his childhood, recalling how he used to get stuck in drawers, hitchhike, and spend all day in the woods or on the roof. According to his stories, my grandparents rarely intervened.

I could also tell when my dad didn't want to talk about something because he would skim over the details and default to telling a funny story instead. This time, when I asked about his Catholic upbringing, he told me about the games he used to play with his friends at church.

"My friends and I were altar boys," he said. "We used to have this scoring system where we could earn points, depending on how many things we did to slow down the sermon. We would do silly things like put the Bible bookmarks in the wrong place or intentionally let our robes get stuck in the fan." He laughed at the memory. "Oh, we were just kids," he said.

"Why didn't you stay religious?" I asked him. "I mean, you and Mom didn't raise us to be religious, so I'm assuming you didn't."

"You know, I went to Catholic school for twelve years, and none of it made sense to me, even when I was a kid," he said. "There was so much guilt and fear about everything that didn't match up with what I experienced at home. At home, we were happy, and we loved each other. We had fun. To me, that was a better model for a healthy life. Mom and I wanted you to have that."

Even though my mom would say I'm like her on the inside, that's not entirely true. I think I got my optimism from my dad. Despite being a big feeler, I tended to always find the silver lining and choose to focus on that—like my dad.

Hours passed, and more cookies made an appearance as he answered all my questions. I learned that he loved Baltimore, which was where he went to school and worked for decades. He told me about moving to the Bay Area, marrying his first wife, having my three older sisters, and how much he loved being a dad.

"I just felt like the luckiest dad in the world," he said. Even when he and his wife got divorced, having children was the highlight of his life. At the time, he lived in Palo Alto, California, and worked at Stanford Children's Hospital as a premed student before getting rejected from Stanford's school of medicine.

"Wait, I didn't know that," I said. "Why?"

"Since I already worked there, they knew me," he began. "One day, one of my coworkers took me aside and told me I wasn't going to get in—not because I didn't have the grades, but because I was a single dad. 'They know you won't have enough time to be a dad of three young kids and a full-time medical student,' they told me."

In my millennial righteousness, I wanted to demand justice for my dad and tell him how not okay that was—but he didn't see it that way.

"Look," he said calmly. "I was never going to not be a dad. So if they wouldn't take me because of that, then that was just the end of it."

When I'd exhausted him with questions and the cookies had run out, I hugged him tightly. My dad had lived a full life and had made choices based on love, family, and what he felt to be genuinely right.

The interview with my mom went differently. When I found her, she was wading in the pool, wearing an old swimsuit from my competitive swimming days. It was black with the word TERPS—the University of Maryland mascot—written across the chest in red letters.

I sat on the side of the pool, watching her move her arms back and forth in the water as she told me about our Ashkenazi Jewish lineage—how our ancestors were part of the Jewish diaspora and ended up planting roots throughout Central and Eastern Europe, which eventually led to my mom being born in New Jersey.

"So, what was it like growing up in New Jersey with an identical twin sister and a little brother?" I asked, getting curious the same way I had with Dad.

"I wouldn't say I had a happy childhood, Mia, and I don't want to get into it," she said. "The secret of life is love, and it is as simple as that. I've had to learn that. No one taught it to me the way I teach it to you.

No one gave me any of the things I've given you. You and your siblings are what I'm most proud of in my life. I know that my purpose was to break the cycle of abuse with all of you, and that's what I did."

Her answer took me aback. I imagined my mom as a young girl, her black hair pulled back into a ponytail with a ribbon; she and her twin sister, my aunt Laney, in matching dresses, smiling for the photos but feeling alone and scared on the inside. The vision broke my heart.

She stayed focused on the ripples her arms were making in the water, answering every question I asked with the same cryptic honesty. My dad had described his childhood in such colorful detail, full of stories and personalities like he was reading from a book. With my mom, there was no funny storytelling or elaboration. No joyful memories of pranks of playfulness—at least that she shared with me.

At first, I started crying softly. Then it became a full sob. *My mother only wanted love her whole life*, I thought. Like many of the resilient people I had interviewed, she'd had to blaze that trail for herself. How lonely that must have felt. I wish I could've been there for her the way she had been there for me.

She broke her gaze on the pool water and looked up at me sitting at the edge of the pool, my knees curled into my chest and my arms wrapped around them.

"Are you crying? Oh, don't cry," she said in her mom voice. "Baby, I don't want you to cry."

She got out of the pool and wrapped herself in a fluffy, white towel hanging over the chair. Sitting next to me, she put her arms around me, coaxing me to lean into her. I curled up in her arms and cried for a person I loved deeply, who'd experienced so much of life without love from others or from herself. I wiped my eyes, startling myself by asking a question I didn't expect.

"What am I going to do when you're gone?" I asked, wiping the hair out of my face.

"You don't have to worry about that for a long time," she said. "And besides, I'm always with you."

"Even when I live across the country?" I said, attempting levity. It worked. She smiled, just a little bit.

"Yes," she said. "Even when you live across the country."

47

"There's no right way to move through life."

OCTOBER 17–WASHINGTON, DC
79 DAYS ON THE ROAD, 7,273 MILES

Scrolling on Instagram one night before bed, I discovered Senna. Her striking photography caught my eye—in particular, a beautiful portrait of dozens of women of color dressed in bright yellow. The picture felt bold and unapologetic. I reached out to Senna to tell her how beautiful it was, and after a few messages, asked if I could meet with her when I got to DC.

After a multiday, traffic-filled drive from Florida, Senna and I met for an afternoon coffee. She wore a black dress with a gorgeous red-and-fuchsia scarf and big silver jewelry. As we sat in the café, she asked me about the project and how I intended to use her story. I shared with her what I'd shared with Confidence.

"I'm here to listen and share your experience only as you want it shared," I told her. "This is about you and your journey."

"Thank you for saying that," she said. "It's a really important thing to address upfront, especially for women of color. I feel like I can talk to you vulnerably now that we've gotten that out of the way."

"Oh, good," I said. "Let me know if anything else comes up as we start talking too."

Senna nodded and began describing how she went to a four-year university in Virginia to study English and become an English teacher. When she started school, she realized she wasn't prepared for the university environment, which led to a lot of mental health challenges.

"Going through that, I felt disappointed—like I had failed myself," she recalled. "Looking back on it now, taking a break was the healthiest thing I could have done. Still, I have moments every now and then where I wish I had stayed in school and pushed through it. I look at my peers and see where they are, and I compare myself to them. But then I have to remember, there's no right way to move through life. That's something that I'm learning."

Senna's inner dialogue felt familiar. I'd been learning that too.

"It's a hard thing to remember," I told her. "Somehow, we get this idea that we're doing it wrong, especially when we compare ourselves to others. But shouldn't we be the ones deciding what's right and what's wrong for ourselves?"

"Exactly," she said.

"The idea that there's no right way to move through life is in large part what sent me on this journey in the first place," I shared. "I knew there had to be more ways for people challenging gender norms to live full, happy lives. I believe there are lots of ways to live a happy life."

Senna nodded, leaning forward and smiling. "I couldn't agree more," she said. "And it takes a long time to understand that because that is not the culture we live in."

Senna did end up going back to school—part-time at first—for graphic design. She put her hands on the table as she emphasized the importance of starting slowly.

"My father always tells me that the first time I swam in a swimming pool, I jumped into the deep end without any idea of how to swim," she said, a glimmer in her eye. "He says I do this in life too. It's been important for me to recognize that you don't learn how to swim in an eleven-foot-deep pool overnight. It took practice and a lot of time to figure all of this out," she said. "I went through anxiety and depression for a while. When I started to heal from that, I began to learn about myself and my voice. I remember thinking, 'The most important thing for you to do right now is to be aware of yourself and what you feel is right and wrong. Have that vision for yourself.'"

"How do you do that, especially with social media?" I asked.

"When it comes to Instagram, there's a few things to remember," she said knowingly. "First of all, no one's paying much attention to you. People are going through your Instagram story while they're sitting on the toilet."

"That's so true!" I shouted as we laughed together. "You're right—no one cares that much."

Senna and her contagious laugh.

"Right?" Senna said. "Okay, second of all, it only takes one authentic person to encourage other people to be authentic as well. I want to not feel so much pressure on social media so others can do the same. For example, I'm practicing drawing and writing in Urdu right now. I speak it pretty fluently and I can read it a little bit, but I can't write it, and I'm terrible at drawing. I'm just learning something that excites me, and sharing it on Instagram is my public way of practicing. It's helped me in so many ways."

Senna sharing her art was not only a way to draw out authenticity on social media—it was an act of taking up space. She described the male-dominated photography and design industry despite the abundance of women doing incredible work. So Senna posted her frustrations on Instagram. She posted about situations she'd been in as a creative woman of color and how alone she had felt. She posted about how she wanted to see more people who looked like her in positions where they felt like they could thrive while supporting one another instead of competing with each other. She posted about not wanting to be "one of the boys" or harden herself the way toxic masculinity teaches us we need to do to succeed but instead to say: I'm struggling, this person's struggling, and we're going to get through this together.

"I got a variety of responses to that post," she said. "Some men responded wondering how they could do better. A few people were negative, but mostly they were positive. A lot of creatives said they shared my feelings and that they wanted to address the challenges and choose projects that would change things."

One such project was known as Unity in Color, started by Jasmine Solano in California before it spread to chapters across the country. In 2018, Senna and her friends played a part in the DC chapter, bringing women of color together at the Capitol Building, all wearing the color yellow.

"I loved that photograph," I told her. "It's what inspired me to reach out to you."

"Thank you!" Senna said. "Bringing us all together was a great way to show that we're not afraid, and that being an ally comes in all different shapes and sizes. It felt empowering to be in a space filled with positivity. And these weren't random women. These were women who we felt had dedicated their lives to justice via policy, creative work, advocacy, etc. This helped me feel like I was 100 percent part of something and connected to other people."

"The opposite of how you felt a few years earlier on social media," I noted.

"Yes," Senna said. "The world we live in now doesn't cherish connection as much. This very capitalistic way of living where everyone is competition is toxic. A lot of us have this desire to be on top or win, a habit of competing that was instilled by the patriarchy. For me, it's essential to unlearn these things."

"What takes their place?" I asked. "When we unlearn them, what fills that space?"

"Community that uplifts each other and looks at each other with compassion and kindness," she responded. "Let's see what we can do all together and the fantastic things we can create when we come together and support each other."

Around us, the café staff had started to stack chairs and close the doors, a not-so-subtle hint that it was time to go. Even though we were last to leave, we didn't want to say goodbye.

"There's a little market just down the street," Senna said. "Do you want to walk through with me?"

"That sounds wonderful," I told her.

As we stepped into the market, all my senses were bombarded. The air smelled like a field of wildflowers mixed with fresh meats and cheeses. Specialty vendors stood behind counters of beautifully displayed products; everything from locally sourced honey to artisanally crafted soaps.

Senna bought a bouquet of flowers as we strolled, burying her nose in the collection of purple, red, yellow, and green. We took our time, taking slow steps and enjoying every inch of what surrounded us until we had walked the whole market.

"If you're ever in DC again, give me a call," she said.

"Thank you, Senna," I said. "I will."

We parted ways as she walked toward her home, and I walked back to my home on wheels. Yellow leaves rustled on the ground, collecting against curbs and buildings. Looking up, I noticed the trees had started to shed for winter.

48

*"You're going to do this, and it's going to matter.
I just know it."*

OCTOBER 19–BEL AIR, MARYLAND
81 DAYS ON THE ROAD, 7,344 MILES

Almost three months and more than seven thousand miles into my trip, the cold had officially set in, and the novelty of the trip had officially worn off. I found myself almost rushing through my time on the East Coast, feeling torn between wanting to make the most of my time on this side of the country and wanting to get back to a new chapter of my life that was unfolding. With the energy I had left, I chose to spend time with people I loved instead of planning interviews. It felt like what my heart needed at this stage of the journey.

One such person I loved was Steph, my college roommate. Steph was the greatest kind of friend—she was supportive, kind, and made everything fun. I was also close with her parents, siblings, and cousins, who were equally wonderful. Steph was also getting married this weekend to the love of her life, and she kindly offered to let me stay with her at her parents' house in Bel Air, Maryland. Pulling up to their big, cozy home with a huge yard and outdoor patio, my longing for family and home resurfaced.

Inside, I found Steph and her family in the kitchen, leaning against the cabinets and laughing over cups of coffee like I had seen them do many times before. Steph's mom gave me a big hug and pointed me to the full pot of coffee, while Steph continued talking with her twin brothers. Their dad was sitting on the couch recliner in the living room, watching football.

"Is that a Bolton?" he shouted.

I smiled and walked into the living room, bending to give him a big hug. "Sure is, John," I said. "I'm so happy to see you. Thanks for letting me stay for a few days."

We drank coffee and watched football until it was time to drink beer and watch football. The Baxters set up a homemade bar on the outdoor patio and a few tables covered in newspapers to enjoy something my East Coast heart had truly missed—eating Maryland-style crabs. It was one of those evenings where everyone was just plain old happy. People hugged, joked, and gave each other a hard time out of love. They caught up over a game of darts or standing outside by the bonfire and reliving memories that made them laugh so hard, they had to lean against something—or each other.

I moved through the party, saying hi to people I remembered from years ago before finding myself next to Steph's brother, Ty. I'd always felt close to Ty—he was laid-back, genuine, and humble.

"What's uuuuuupp, Mia?" he said, pulling me in for a hug. "What have you been up to?" he asked, resting against his dad's work bench, taking a sip of his beer.

"Oh, you know, just living in my minivan," I told him. "I wouldn't miss your sister's wedding, though."

"Yeah, that's pretty cool that you made it," he said. "I think it means a lot to her."

I glanced over at Steph, who was across the room now, playing darts with her dad. She made a great throw, sending the dart right down the middle as John shrugged and took a sip of his beer. People milled around, laughing and catching up like no time had passed.

Probably done getting smoked in darts by his daughter, John interrupted us to introduce me to a friend of his.

"Mia, this is Tim," John said, walking right in front of Ty with his arm around a man who had a gray goatee and a faded baseball cap.

"Don't mind me, Dad," Ty said, laughing and moving out of the way.

"I've been telling him about your book," John continued. "He thinks it's a damn good idea. Tell her, Tim," he said with a hard pat on Tim's back.

"Well, John told me about what you're up to and the book you're writing, and I just think that's really fucking cool," Tim said, now on the spot. "When can I buy it?"

I laughed, flattered that even though I hadn't spoken a word to this man, he was willing to buy a book that didn't exist yet.

"Well, when it becomes a book!" I said. "Right now, all I have are audio recordings. But I'll put you on the VIP list if you'd like." (I didn't have a VIP list, but it felt like a clever thing to say.)

Tim smiled and dug into his wallet, fishing out a business card. "Here's my email," he said. "Let me know when I can buy one. I'll be your first customer."

I took his card graciously and slipped it into the pocket of my jeans.

"Mia," he said, turning to walk away, "what you're doing is important. You're going to do this, and it's going to matter. I just know it."

Tim's conviction about my project reminded me of the moment Cori had grabbed my surfboard in San Diego, and when Dana told me to write the book—a moment of intention among casual conversation and jokes to ensure I knew that it mattered.

I knew it inside, but hearing someone else say it unprompted felt meaningful in a new way.

49

"The slow, steady feeling of coming home to myself."

OCTOBER 20 – BEL AIR, MARYLAND
82 DAYS ON THE ROAD, 7,351 MILES

The next morning, everyone in Steph's house was just a little bit hungover—nothing some coffee and a hair of the dog couldn't fix. People milled around, recapping the night before as they stretched out on the sofa in their pajamas. If I didn't know differently, I would have thought it was just another slow fall day.

Then Steph put her wedding dress on, and it was far from an ordinary day. She stood in front of an oval wooden mirror as lace in the shape of flowers delicately shimmered against her back. An ornate silver clip at the back of her head held up half of her short, wavy hair, and the rest fell at her shoulders.

Today, one of my best friends was getting married.

The ceremony was short and quaint, outside a small church. There were no more than twenty-five seats, each taken by friends and family. A small, petal-lined walkway funneled toward the end of the aisle, where two beautiful ferns spilled out of ornate cement vases in front of an enormous willow tree and where A. J.'s sister, Megan, waited patiently to marry her brother and Steph. They each recited a short series of vows, holding hands and promising to always love each another. With the exchange of the rings, Megan pronounced them husband and wife, and they kissed as everyone cheered, clapped, hooted, and hollered. Turning to face all of us for the first time, they raised their hands in the air, laughing and smiling from ear to ear.

Only a few months ago, I would have cringed at a beautiful moment like this. Witness two people declare their unconditional love? No, thank you. I was way too bitter for that. I didn't need to be immersed in someone's happiest moment only to feel my own loss. Now, all I could see was someone I loved, happy and enjoying a beautiful moment. My own heartbreak suddenly felt like a fading memory.

Third wheeling Steph's new marriage.

The wedding after-party was at Steph's favorite local sports bar. She might have been the most elegant person to ever drink a Coors Light—sitting in her wedding dress and a gray cardigan, sipping a beer and laughing. I cried happy tears during the father-daughter dance, watching John spin his daughter on the self-made dance floor.

In all my years coming to the Baxter house, so much had remained the same. Life here was reliable and easy, the way so many of us want the place we call home to be. We want to feel safe. We want to feel loved. It's remarkable how much of that comes not from the place we call home, but from the people. It's why I felt at home with David on Orcas Island, with Erin in a house that wasn't hers, with my brother in Daniela's parents house, in Panera Bread with my parents, and in Portland with Devin. And it's what this adventure had given me—the slow, steady feeling of coming home to myself.

Despite my temptation to stay longer, I still had more to do and a lot of journey left in front of me. I soaked up the moment as Steph twirled in a white dress in a sports bar, knowing I'd leave Maryland the next day.

50

"Your feelings are valid—and they're also temporary."

OCTOBER 22–QUEENS, NEW YORK

84 DAYS ON THE ROAD, 7,536 MILES

Growing up on the East Coast, I'd been to New York many times, and every time this city felt different. One of my favorite memories here was taking the subway out to Rockaway Beach, New York, for the Women's Annual Surf Film Festival. Despite going alone, I ran into a handful of friends and got to know the organizer of the festival, Davina. I even won a surfboard that year in their raffle, which I'd brought back to Brooklyn on the subway.

These memories compelled me to reach out to Davina again, asking if she would be open to an interview.

After a few hours, she texted me back.

> I'd love to meet up tomorrow
> Come to my house in Rockaway.

From where I sat in one of the Queens Library parking lots, I could see the boardwalk and the Atlantic Ocean. It felt peaceful, until I realized how hungry I was and how much research I had to do. I reluctantly headed inside the library, where the harsh, fluorescent lights made me feel so far away from the warmth of the Baxter home and all the moments on this trip that felt like comfort. I found a table and tried to will myself to ignore the pit in my stomach.

Why are you even sad? my inner voice asked. *Just be in the moment, remember?*

But I was angry at myself for feeling sad, and my inner voice telling me to enjoy the moment wasn't helpful. I wished my dad were here to help me see the silver lining. I wished my mom were here to comfort me. I wished Devin were here to stroke my hair. It all felt like too much, and I felt alone. I stepped outside for fresh air.

Erin. Call Erin.

Even though Erin always offered to talk outside of our regularly scheduled calls if I needed it, I very rarely took her up on the offer. Tonight, I did.

"Hi, sweet Mia!" she answered. "Is everything okay?"

As soon as I heard her voice, I started to cry. I confessed that I was tired, broke, and ready to go home—except that home was in a bunch of different places. Not here. Not in New York. Not in the freezing cold, living in my van.

"I want to feel adventurous and Hashtag Van Life-y, but I just feel lonely and exhausted," I told her.

"Even endurance athletes need to rest," Erin offered with kindness.

"Are you comparing me to an endurance athlete?" I asked, sniffling and wiping my nose with the back of my jacket. It made me laugh. It felt like the exact opposite of what I was right now.

"I think I am," she responded, laughing lightly. "What can you do for yourself tonight that will feel good?"

I looked around and noticed a small ramen restaurant across the street.

"Get dinner," I said. "There's a ramen place right here that I could go to."

"Great!" she said enthusiastically. "I bet soup will feel good on a cold New York night."

"Yeah, I'm going to go do that now, I think," I told her. "Thank you for picking up."

"Of course. Everything is going to be okay," she offered. "Your feelings are valid—and they're also temporary. You've got this."

"Thank you," I said, already walking across the street. "Love you."

Inside the small ramen restaurant were a smattering of two-person tables, a bar, and zero customers.

"We're closing soon," a young woman shouted, emerging from the back with an armful of dishes. When she noticed my red eyes, she softened a bit. "But you can sit for a few minutes if you want."

"Thanks," I said, taking a seat in the back. I was grateful for the chance to sit in a warm building before going outside to heat up my icebox of a van. I thought about how I would spend the next few days here, how I would eventually make it back to Portland, and how I should probably just go to sleep and start over tomorrow. Sometimes, you just need a new day.

Sitting in the restaurant, I waited for the young woman to reemerge and tell me it was time to leave. Instead, she brought over a menu. The look on her face was surprisingly kind.

"It's no big deal," she said, handing me the menu. "You can hang out while we close up."

51

"As women, I think we sometimes take for granted all the things that we do just to keep everything afloat."

OCTOBER 23–ROCKAWAY, NEW YORK
85 DAYS ON THE ROAD, 7,550 MILES

The bitter cold of New York in October woke me up. "Thirty degrees," I read off my phone's weather app. Yikes.

Keeping as much of my body underneath my comforter as possible, I slipped into a pair of thick leggings and a sweatshirt as I opened the side door of the van to gusts of salty wind. The morning air gave me a chill as I pulled a beanie over my unshowered hair and layered on a puffy jacket, zipping it up to my chin.

Rockaway was quiet this morning, which felt unexpected, yet welcome. At a nearby café, I ordered a coffee and a New York-style everything bagel, enjoying it as I tinkered on my phone, trying to find more local people to interview. A few articles mentioned a catering company called Just Soul Catering that hired previously incarcerated women caught my attention. As soon as I watched the introductory video, I messaged their Facebook page. Tucking my phone into my pocket, I refilled my coffee and headed out for a walk along the ocean.

The Rockaway boardwalk was wide and empty, and the Atlantic Ocean lapped at the shore to my right. The first ocean I ever loved. I had so many good memories in this ocean with my family. Even now, despite feeling so far away from everyone, being near the ocean gave me an indescribable sense of familiarity and comfort.

I closed my eyes and let the wind swirl the smells of sand and saltwater around me. My hands wrapped around my coffee cup, warming my palms. *I'm okay*, I thought.

Davina only lived a few miles away, and it didn't take me long to get there. As I walked through a small, white gate and knocked on the door, I felt a pang of nervousness. I hadn't seen Davina since I was at the Women's Surf Film Festival years ago. *What will it be like to spend time with her one-on-one, years later? Will we have good rapport, or will it fall flat without all the excitement of the festival buzzing around us?*

Davina opened the door with excitement, wearing her pajamas. "It's so good to see you again!" she said in her Australian accent.

"It's so good to see you too—and oh, my gosh, you're pregnant!" I said, noticing her baby bump.

"Yeah, with my second," she said, smiling. "Come inside. It's freezing out here!"

She took off her shoes by the door and walked barefoot into the kitchen, asking if I'd like some coffee. I nodded, placing my shoes neatly next to hers. The hardwood floor felt good on my feet, and the heat in her apartment soothed my chapped skin. Surfboards hung from the ceiling, and colorful fins lined the shelves. Her walls collected posters from surf events and other surf-related art in a variety of forms, frames, and colors. Suddenly, I realized how good it felt to be around another surfer. Just being in the presence of someone who appreciated the art of surfing like I did filled up my cup.

As I gazed around her surf-tastic, sunlit home, she poured hot water from a kettle into a French press.

"Sorry, it's decaf," she said with a laugh, motioning to her belly.

"I already had a few cups, so decaf is perfect," I said, taking a seat

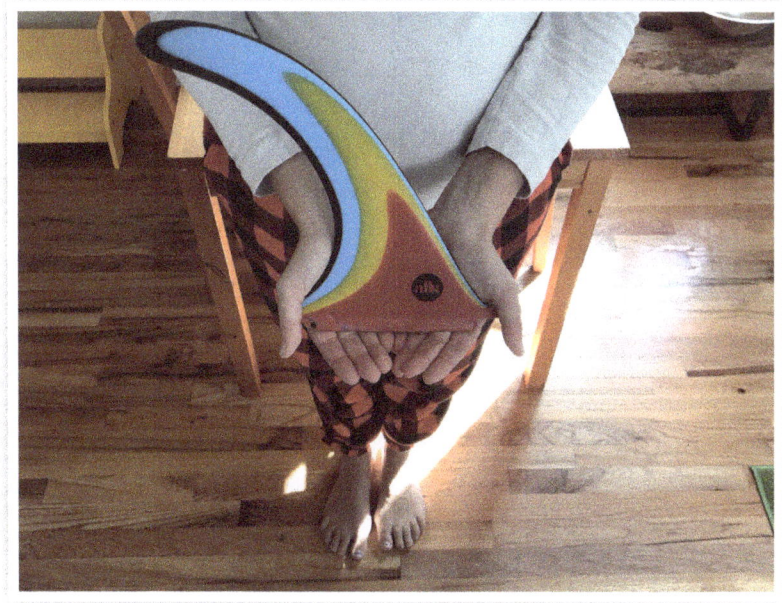

Davina presenting one of her favorite surf fins.

in the corner of a big gray couch. "I have to tell you, I'm in love with your apartment. All of the surf artwork is so beautiful."

"Well, thank you! I feel like I haven't been surfing enough this pregnancy," she said, pouring coffee into two mugs for us. "During my first pregnancy, I would paddle on my side because I couldn't lie on my belly! While that isn't the most fun, you do get all the waves. Just shout, 'It's so much fun surfing while you're pregnant!' And watch—no one will drop in on you."

"Now I know the secret!" I said, laughing as I felt my nerves fade away.

"I know, who would've thought that was all it takes?" she said. "This pregnancy, however, has been kind of a doozy. To be a mother, an entrepreneur, and a surfer is an exciting chapter. As women, I think we sometimes take for granted all the things that we do just to keep everything afloat."

Davina and I started talking about the many roles women play and how little space there has historically been for our many identities, particularly in surf culture.

"It was the norm to have an eating disorder in my high school," she recalled. "Thankfully, all that is changing now. People don't want to see women in tiny bikinis surfing, and the big brands are going to need to reflect that. They're going to need to change the way we're depicted, both in and out of the water."

"There has been some positive change recently," I said. "Did you see the news about pay equity?"

She nodded enthusiastically. "Oh, yes," she said. "It's a big deal. Finally, women have a division in big-wave surf competitions, and the pay is equal for men and women. Those are two enormous milestones for professional surfing." She paused to take a sip of her very strong, very decaf coffee. "Honestly, I was in shock when that happened, and I think the rest of the women's surf community was too, to an extent," she continued. "It was a mixed feeling of shock and 'It's about time.' I hope it sticks."

"Me too," I said.

Much like when Tim had given me unexpected words of encouragement, being able to talk to Davina about surfing was something I didn't know I needed. It felt so good to be in community with another surfer, talking about the latest news and what it meant for surfers around the world and how we felt when it happened. I found my eyes wandering around her apartment, admiring the fins lining the shelves around us.

"So, how did you find your way to surfing?" I asked. "I know you founded the Women's Surf Film Festival, and I saw firsthand how fantastic that was. What came before that?"

Davina smiled and settled back into the couch, getting comfortable as she told me about growing up in Melbourne, Australia.

"I didn't actually pick up surfing until my thirty-second birthday, when I drove all around Puerto Rico for seven days by myself, just for fun," Davina recalled. "I took one surf lesson and was like, 'Oh, this is it.'"

After Puerto Rico, Davina bought a board and a wetsuit and came to Rockaway Beach in New York—in the winter.

"I would get up at 4:30 a.m., get out here by 5:30 a.m., get my suit, get my board, go surf for an hour and a half, then go into the city for work," she said, laughing with disbelief. "By ten a.m., I was barely functional. But it was what I felt needed to do, and now surfing and the surfing community have become a huge part of my life."

"Were there other women out when you were learning?" I asked.

"Oh, yes! Around the time I started surfing here, there was an influx of women doing the same," she said. "My husband actually came up with the idea to do a workshop for women that covered all things surfing. It was a great idea because when we're learning to surf, most of us get two lessons and then rent a board, go out by ourselves, and make a mess of everything. So why not do a workshop just for women to make it a comfortable space?"

When it came to fruition, the workshop covered much more than how to ride waves, including ding repair, surf etiquette, reading the ocean, board shape, and so much more. Perhaps more importantly, they provided an opportunity for women who surfed to get to know each other and build community. After such a great turnout and a positive response, Davina wanted to expand the idea to include films, and the Women's Surf Film Festival was born. Telling me about it, she paused and smiled, as if she were feeling all the positivity from the festival all over again.

"The festival always reminds me just how quickly surfing can become a part of women's lives in such a positive way, and how necessary it is that we have a platform too," she said. "Women surf so differently from men, and they bring such a different energy to the water. When I surf with men, I feel competition and more individual ownership of the waves. When I surf with women, we take turns, laughing, talking, and enjoying. Don't get me wrong—I see people of all genders being aggressive sometimes," she added. "But generally, paddling out with women is such a breath of fresh air. That's what the Women's Surf Film

Festival is all about."

I felt the same way when I paddled out with women—less aware of my performance or proving myself, and more able to enjoy the experience and my connection with the ocean in a meaningful way.

As Davina got up to start putting our dishes in the sink, I stacked the mugs in my arms to help her, thanking her for having me to her home. Most people had met me at a public place or where they work. Kim and Davina were the only two so far to invite me into their homes, which felt like an act of trust.

Before I left, Davina picked up a blue tote bag that said Women's Surf Film Festival on it and held it out to me.

"What? No, I can't take this. They're for the festival," I said.

"Please, I have too many," she said, motioning to a box in the corner full of tote bags. "Take it and spread the word!"

I slung the tote bag over my shoulder and gave Davina a hug goodbye, thanking her again and telling her how much joy it brought me to catch up with her.

Walking back to my van in the Queens library parking lot, I felt myself unwind as my shoulder blades slid down my back and my neck loosened just a little. I called Devin to tell her I was feeling better and that I thought I had just needed to spend time with a friend and get out of my own head.

"Oh, that's great, little love," she said. "Tell me more."

Walking along the boardwalk and talking to Devin, I didn't notice the sting of the cold as much as I had before.

52

*"You have to find the good in the bad.
You have to find light in the darkness."*

OCTOBER 24–LONG ISLAND, NEW YORK
86 DAYS ON THE ROAD, 7,566 MILES

It was quiet in Sharon's suburban Long Island neighborhood when I arrived. Opening the door, she pulled me into a big hug and invited me into her home. Pumpkin, cinnamon, and other fall spices filled the air as she motioned to me to take a seat.

"You want some tea? I make a delicious ginger tea with Carnation milk," she said as if I were a frequent guest in her home.

"I would love some," I said. "Thank you."

In the comfort of her kitchen, Sharon floated around making tea as she asked me open-ended questions about myself, like where I was from and what brought me to New York. I longed to learn more about her as the founder of Just Soul Catering, a company breaking down barriers to employment by hiring formerly incarcerated women, but I knew that would come. For now, it was my turn to open up.

I told her about what brought me on this journey, the amazing women and gender nonconforming people I'd spoken with, and of course, the trials and tribulations of sleeping in my van.

"Oh, honey," she said with a bold laugh that reminded me of CoCo. "You can stay here tonight if you want. Don't need to be sleeping in your car out in the winter!"

"Thank you, Ms. Sharon," I said. "But it's okay. I promise."

Everything about being here with Sharon warmed my heart—the kitchen conversation, the genuine curiosity, and the laughter—but I didn't want to overstay my welcome.

"This right here is the truth," she warned me, handing me a mug of milky tea.

"Ms. Sharon," I said after taking a sip. "It's such an honor to be here with you. I hope you don't mind me asking you a few questions about your journey. I'm here to listen to whatever you want to share."

"Well, I think I'd be all right with that," she said, taking a seat next to me. "But my story probably isn't much different from anyone else's."

"How so?" I asked.

"When you put any bunch of women together, and you talk about struggles, fears, pains, trials, and tribulations, you're going to hear some of the same web. Pain is pain. Suffering is suffering. Death is death. You don't have to go to prison to feel that type of stuff," she explained. "But there is something different about being behind a wall when it happens. It makes you realize there is nothing you can do about what you're feeling. You have to tell your mind and your heart and your being to be still, because if you cross over into where you feel, it could destroy you. We were in prison. We did time. It was a painful journey—yes to all of that. But you have to find the good in the bad. You have to find light in the darkness."

Only five minutes into listening to Sharon talk, my words were stuck in my throat. She was in her mid-fifties, and I felt every ounce of her hard-earned wisdom. Ms. Sharon noticed and put her hand on my hand, patting it as she continued.

The wonderful Ms. Sharon.

"I was in prison for twenty years, and I've been home for eight years now," she said, her voice steady and unwavering. "I remember one of the hardest things for me when I first got out was swiping my MetroCard. I could not get it. And I cried one day because it was this thing everyone else did with ease, and it was so difficult for me. Everything was challenging. And as much as I wanted to be home, home was so hard and scary that I almost wanted to go back in. But that's the part of the psyche that plays tricks with you and says, 'You're not going to be able to do this. You're not going to be able to make it.'"

Thanks to research from The Sentencing Project,[20] data shows that the population of incarcerated women has grown more than six times since 1980. Similarly, the National Resource Center on Justice[21] found

---

20   Niki Monazzam and Kristen M. Budd, Incarcerated Women and Girls, Washington, DC: The Sentencing Project, 2023, https://www.sentencingproject.org/app/uploads/2023/05/Incarcerated-Women-and-Girls-1.pdf.

21   "Fact Sheet on Justice Involved Women in 2016," National Resource Center On Justice Involved Women, 2016, https://cjinvolvedwomen.org/wp-content/uploads/2016/06/Fact-Sheet.pdf.

that poverty is a strong indicator for women in the criminal justice system, with 37 percent of women reporting incomes of less than $600 per month prior to their arrest.

I didn't know a single person that could survive on $600 a month.

The same research outlines that recidivism rates for women go up as time passes. About one-quarter of women are arrested within six months of their release from prison, one-third are arrested within a year, and two-thirds of women are rearrested five years after release.

"My pastor says I got out and started running and haven't stopped since," Sharon said with a laugh. "I said to myself, 'There has to be a way to reach people, do things for people, and be able to get people together who have the same type of story that I do.'"

When a friend asked her if she had ever thought about running a business, she remembered saying, "Heck no! I just got out of prison! I have no money and zero credit!"

Still, she admitted that as time passed, she couldn't shake the idea from her mind. When she discovered Defy Ventures, a nonprofit that helps formerly incarcerated people start their own businesses, it got Just Soul Catering off the ground.

"Our menu is southern comfort food," Sharon said proudly, making one loud clap with her hands. "We make macaroni and cheese, collard greens and vegan collard greens, teriyaki honey-ginger wings, jerk chicken, curry chicken, curry goat, shrimp, and of course, breakfast food. We do everything."

"There's something special about bringing people together over food," I said. "Even now, your tea feels so comforting. What is it about feeding people that just feels right?"

Sharon nodded. "You know . . . when my mom got sick, I was taken to the hospital by correctional staff to say my goodbye. My mother was dying, and I was devastated. When I got back to the facility and my housing unit, my friends were sitting around waiting for me with cooked food. We all cried together, and it just worked." Sharon grew a little teary herself. "Food is a life changer. It makes people feel good, and it brings people together. Feeding people is comforting. And it matters. When we're starving in any capacity, food makes a difference. You don't have to be hungry to be hungry. You could be starving from the pains of the day, or just due to a lack of."

I let what she said wash over me. "You don't have to be hungry to be hungry. You could be starving just due to a lack of." Everyone has their own lack of. Lack of acceptance. Lack of representation. Lack of time. Lack of community. Lack of family. Lack of resources. Lack of freedom. While we can't all be lucky enough to gather around a table with Ms. Sharon, how else can we feed each other?

"Women come home from prison, and like all of us, they need to work, and they need a place to live. But what happens to all the people who don't have the referrals, the connections, the community, the know-how, the credit, the job, the money? Where do they go? What are you going to do with all these people who have done their time and are trying to reenter? Put them on another island when they get out? Maybe don't let them come out of prison at all? It's difficult. That's all I can say."

Sitting back in her chair, a distant look crept into Sharon's eyes. "Sometimes, when we're talking about this level of reentry, I sit back, fold my arms, and let my eyes fill up with tears," she said, doing exactly that. "It's normal in life to fall, get up, brush ourselves off, and keep it moving, but not everybody has the capacity to do that. We've had sisters and brothers return to prison for committing terrible crimes—again. What's the difference between them and those of us who have done time, come home, gotten on that straight-and-narrow path, and kept moving?"

Sharon sighed and leaned forward. "I think it's a mindset," she continued. "Listen, it's hard. Transforming and transformation has to do with a multitude of things: changing the mind, changing the heart, changing the spirit, and changing the soul. You do whatever you have to do to get those things together. If you didn't do it while you were inside, then get it done now while you're out."

"How do you know you're in the process of transformation?" I asked her. "What does that feel like for you?"

"I know I'm on my right path when people tell me, 'You're doing good, Sharon. You inspire me.'"

I remembered the small moments of encouragement throughout my trip—like Erin's package of googly eyes, or Tim asking if he could buy my book—and how much those had meant to me.

"You're doing good, Sharon. You inspire me," I said with watery eyes.

She gave me a warm look and brought me in for a hug. I closed my eyes, feeling her soft sweater on my cheek.

"I should probably get going," I told Sharon, realizing it was dark outside. "I don't want to take up any more of your evening."

"You sure you don't want to stay here?"

"Oh, yes," I said, "I'm sure."

"All right, honey," she said, giving me one more hug as I stepped out into the New York night. She watched me from her doorway as I got into my car.

I took the long way back to Rockaway, winding through suburbs and avoiding the freeway. There was one main road that ran straight through Rockaway, all the way from one end of the beach town to the other. I chose a street with bright lights and parallel parked in front of a row of townhouses to urban camp for the night.

I went through the motions of my routine, except now, I left the car on and blasted the heat for about ten minutes as I got under the covers, trying to warm up. People walked their dogs and chatted with each other just outside my window, and I held extremely still in the van, waiting until they had dispersed to move around and turn the car off.

Back under the covers in my sweatpants and sweatshirt, I texted my friend Lee, the one who had introduced me to Devin. He was supposed to be in New York tomorrow.

> Still coming to Brooklyn tomorrow?

> Yes Mia

> Yay! Can't wait.

The end of my East Coast chapter was in sight. Tomorrow, I would meet Lee for a few hours before heading to my aunt's house in Philadelphia for the night. And then, from there, I would finally start the drive back to Portland.

Now, go to sleep so tomorrow will be here faster, I told myself, pressing my eyes shut.

53

"Love you. Mean it."

OCTOBER 25–AMBLER, PENNSYLVANIA
87 DAYS ON THE ROAD, 7,677 MILES

Waking up on the streets of Rockaway, I knew I'd slept later than intended because people were already walking around, and the sun was high in the sky. *Shit, am I late to meet Lee?*

I tried to change my clothes as discreetly as possible, sitting on the floor of my van and shimmying into a long-sleeved shirt, wool-coated jean jacket, and leggings before climbing into the front seat and turning the car on. The engine whirred and stalled before finally switching on—it had gotten cold overnight.

Brooklyn seemed more crowded and chaotic than Rockaway, and finding Lee was a challenge riddled with construction and sketchy detours. Finally, parking along the side of the road, I saw him walking over to my van.

"I can't believe you're here!" I said with a big hug. "It's so good to see you."

"It's good to see you too or whatever," he said. After years of friendship, I knew that meant he was happy to see me.

"Wanna go get some food and talk about our feelings?" I said jokingly.

"Yeah, I could use that," he said, surprising me. "Girl drama," he added.

Wandering down the street, I felt happy to be in this moment with my friend. Familiar faces like Lee's felt like an antidote to the homesickness I hadn't been able to thoroughly shake since Florida. Sharon's words came to mind—"You can be starving just due to a lack of." Seeing Lee felt like comfort food.

Fall in New York draped us in color as we walked and talked. People moved around us, playing music, skateboarding, and riding their bikes, and I let the liveliness of New York fill me up.

We chose a hole-in-the-wall Venezuelan restaurant and took a seat at a bright purple table as I asked Lee what I'd missed back in San Diego.

"It's all pretty much business as usual," he said. "You're not missing much. Even the waves have been flat."

"Well, that's boring," I said with a smile. "Still, I miss it."

"Are you coming back?" he asked.

"I don't know," I said slowly. "You were right . . . Devin is pretty great, and she lives in Portland."

"I knew I shouldn't have introduced you to her, Mia!" he said with a laugh.

"I know, right?" I smiled and looked down, realizing how bittersweet leaving San Diego for good would be—if that was the choice I made. "Who would've thought," I continued, "that you, the guy with all the girl drama, would be such a good matchmaker?"

"For real, right? Fuck."

"What I'm trying to say is thank you," I said, more genuinely now. "Thank you. Love you. Mean it."

In traditional Lee fashion, he refused to linger in the sentimental moment. "Love you, mean it," he said, grabbing a menu. "Now, can we please order?"

New York hangs with Lee.

After lunch, we wandered under the Brooklyn Bridge and along the river. We took photos and walked slowly through coffee shops and corner stores that you only find in New York, talking about all kinds of things until it came time to take Lee to the airport for his flight back to San Diego.

We rounded out our New York experience with rush hour traffic, complete with last-minute merges, honking, and hectic driving that rivaled the DC traffic I'd sat in last week. At the airport, we felt rushed by the chaos around us, so we said goodbye quickly before he disappeared into a sea of people.

After checking my blind spot fifteen times, I happily left the airport, knowing I was trading high-rise buildings and five-lane highways for tall trees and winding back roads in the neighborhoods of Ambler, Pennsylvania.

When I arrived, my aunt's house was exactly how I remembered—an old stone house with perfectly trimmed flowers and a small circular driveway. Laney emerged from the side door and hugged me so tightly that I could barely breathe. Her short, black hair was topped with a stylish beret, and she wore a gray, knee-length dress with magenta leggings underneath. She was my mom's identical twin, and although you couldn't tell them apart when they were little, they looked very different now. The only two things that weren't different were their laugh and their artistic talent.

"I've been in my studio painting all day," she told me, "but somehow I found time to make the most fantastic buffalo chicken soup. I know you'll love it! Go grab some bowls and wine glasses and set the table, love."

She was always just a little bit bossy in an endearing, East Coast family member way. I chuckled to myself. Being all over the country reminded me just how much I loved East Coasters for their directness and sass.

At dinner, I decided to share with her how incomprehensibly disappointed I'd been in our administration over the last two years. "I wish more women would have voted against him," I said. "He doesn't respect us in any way."

"Yes, and so many women didn't vote at all," Laney added, to my surprise. She sounded exasperated. While we were close, we rarely talked about politics. "You know, it just feels like such a slap in the face when women don't vote. The way I see it, if you don't vote, you do not get the privilege of complaining about the way things are."

I thought back to what I read in the Seattle library about women earning the right to vote. White women earned the right to vote in 1920—Black and Native American women, among others, were denied the right to vote until the passage of the Voting Rights Act in 1965. Then I thought about Ms. Sharon and all the challenges facing her as a formerly incarcerated person, including not having the right to vote. I thought about people who do have the right to vote but experience tremendous difficulty in exercising that right for systemic reasons, such as finding access to childcare, transportation, getting to the polls during working hours, understanding the information on their ballot, speaking the language, and so much more. On top of all of that, I thought about corrupt, power-hungry people who intentionally spread disinformation about voting and allow perpetual voter intimidation.

I agreed with the core of what my aunt was saying, but it wasn't that simple. If we needed more women to vote, we should work together to dismantle the system that keeps them from voting, not turn against each other.

We talked a little more about this, listening and sharing our perspectives. *Camila was right*, I thought—antipatriarchy does begin at home. It begins in conversations over soup and wine to shift from women blaming women to women coming together to blame the systems that position us against each other.

When morning came, I sprang out of bed with excitement. Today, I was heading back to Portland.

I wasted no time jumping into a luxuriously hot shower and packing my bags. Before leaving Laney's house, we shared a cup of coffee outside in her garden. Then she followed me out to the driveway and kissed me goodbye. I hugged her big, then backed out and headed west.

54

"It felt so fulfilling just to arrive."

OCTOBER 30–BOISE, IDAHO
92 DAYS ON THE ROAD, 10,178 MILES

The past three days had been a cycle of driving until I had to pee or eat, driving more, and only stopping for the night when I got too delirious to keep going. The I-80 had taken me along the northern part of the country, through the nonconforming plains and rolling hills of Indiana, Illinois, Iowa, Nebraska, and Wyoming—all magnificent places full of rich history and natural wonders I'd love to experience . . . someday. For now, I had Portland tunnel vision, and nothing was going to slow me down.

I found this final part of the trip to be challenging in a new way as time and miles passed excruciatingly slowly. To distract myself, I listened to multiple audiobooks, like *The Hate U Give*, by Angie Thomas. Talking to friends also helped pass the time—like my conversation with Jamie.

"I've been thinking a lot about what you said, about moving to Portland," I told her. "I talked to Devin about it too. She was really open and receptive."

"That's awesome," she said on the other end of the line. "It's like the next few weeks will be a test run."

"A test run of living in Portland?" I asked.

"Yeah, exactly. This will be the first time you see Devin when you're not actively on your trip, and she's actively in school. You'll get to experience what everyday life is like together for the first time," she explained. "Anyone can get along when they're on vacation. What truly matters is how you do in the day-to-day."

In some ways, Devin and I had experienced very real moments together—like having the stomach flu back-to-back. On the other hand, I could see how it would be good for me to experience life with this person in the midst of work and school and everyday life.

Just outside of Boise, Idaho, I had to stop for gas. As the familiar glug chugged into the tank, I pulled out my phone to check my email. Scanning the little bold names, I stopped when I saw an email from KC. My heart dropped into my stomach. Opening the driver's-side door, I sat on the seat and opened the email with no subject line. It read:

> You are up to good things. Proud of you. To attempt to reconcile all things seems fleeting at this point, but I wanted to express that all of us who know and have known you are in full support of you. Job well done Bolt.

After rereading it a few times, I shut my phone and put it facedown on the passenger seat. I closed my eyes and took a handful of long breaths, suddenly sweating. The gas pump popped, signaling it was done.

Back in the car, I called Devin to tell her about it as I resumed directions to Boise, where I was planning to stay with Laney's friend, Jack.

"How do you feel?" she asked after I described the email.

"I appreciate their kind words, but it's not fair," I said. "It's not okay that they can push me out of their life when they want and pull me back in when they're ready."

"What do you want to do?" she asked, careful to let me be the one to decide.

"I don't know yet," I said, pulling into the gravel driveway of Jack's house. "I have to think about it." I let out an audible sigh. "I just want to be with you in front of the fireplace with a glass of white wine with ice in it."

Devin laughed. "You're the only person I know who likes that."

"It's delicious," I said with a chuckle as we said goodbye. I had never met Jack before. He was an old friend of Laney's who'd heard from my aunt about my trip and invited me to stay with him if I crossed through Boise. I wasn't initially planning on taking him up on it, but after sleeping in only semi-safe parking lots off the I-80 for several nights in a row, I was ready to be inside a house.

Walking inside, I was surprised to find myself in the middle of a party. I said hi to everyone and introduced myself to Jack. I did my best to walk the line between being cordial and polite without inviting too much conversation, feeling my social muscle quickly fade to meet my physical and emotional exhaustion. After fifteen minutes, I asked Jack if he'd mind if I excused myself.

"I think I just need to lie down and go to sleep," I told him honestly.

"No problem," Jack said, setting down his beer. "You can have my room."

"Oh . . . I didn't realize . . . I don't need . . . I can sleep in my van in the driveway—"

"No, no, no," Jack said. "I'm gonna hang out with these guys for a while, so take the bed. I like the couch, anyway." He flashed me a kind smile. "Bathroom is right around the corner. Help yourself to a towel. I'll be out here if you need anything."

Out of sheer exhaustion, I accepted, thanking him again and shutting the door behind me. The irony wasn't lost on me that I'd been feeling lonely, yet the first time I was around a group of perfectly fine people, I retreated to be alone. I just needed to be alone, and my mind was too busy to have any meaningful dialogue.

Jack's room centered around a queen-sized bed with dark purple bedding that I flopped onto immediately. The light was dim, and a big-screen TV was mounted to the wall. Staring at the ceiling, I knew I wouldn't be able to sleep tonight if I didn't respond to KC. I had to close the loop. There had been too many loose ends in our relationship since I left San Diego, and I finally felt ready to wrap at least one up.

I opened their email, reread it, and thought about what I wanted to say. Countless thoughts ran through my mind. I remembered all the times I'd been down this road with KC before: the cycle of being so close followed by the unpredictable distance, always on their terms. I never understood how I could seem to mean so little to someone who had meant so much to me.

If I had gotten this email a few months ago, all my love for them would have rushed back in, and I would've leapt at the tiny opening they'd created for me. From there, I'd fall into old patterns of dissecting our every exchange, scanning for hints of their love, and quietly, anxiously wondering when the other shoe would drop. I remembered the van—how hard the decision was to let it go. To let KC go.

My ten-thousand-mile, three-month-long, cross-country journey had changed everything. I didn't want to change anyone anymore. I didn't have anything to prove. Most importantly, I refused to put myself back into a situation that required me to sacrifice myself again.

Now I knew how to let go.

Now I knew how to trust.

Now I knew how to let certain versions of myself die.

Now I knew what it meant to be part of something bigger than myself.

I didn't know what would happen if I said goodbye to KC, or when I got to Portland, or even when I got back to San Diego. What I did know felt like the most important thing of all: I knew me again. I had rebuilt myself one mile, one conversation, one photograph, one country song, one sibling, one piece of artwork, one van, one game of cards, one wedding at a time. It wasn't just the individuals I was interviewing who were courageous; I supposed I was one of the courageous people too.

I had finally begun to see myself the way others had been seeing me, and this gave me strength.

I took a deep breath and drafted my response:

> Thanks KC, I appreciate your words. I have reconciled things on my own and I hold no grudge toward you. That being said, I do not want to talk anymore—even in supportive, small increments.
>
> I hope only the best for you. Perhaps down the line we can be friends again someday.
>
> Until then,
>
> Mia

I reread it once before sending to ensure I sounded firm while still being kind. Most of all, I wanted to be clear that I was not going back.

I hit send and immediately called Devin, who was having her own reaction to the email I had gotten from KC.

"I have to admit, I'm uncomfortable—not because you did anything wrong, but because I have my own baggage around infidelity," Devin said. "At the end of the day, I want you to do whatever you need to do to feel good about this. You are your own free and independent woman. And while I don't think you're going to do anything shitty, and I hope you don't, I know that if you do, I have no control over that."

Devin and I spent the next hour talking about our fears, boundaries, and how she realized she felt triggered that KC had reentered my life. I listened attentively, offering her the same honesty around what I wanted (her) and how I wanted to be in a relationship (monogamously). By the end of the conversation, we felt even closer to each other.

When we hung up, my mind and heart were toast. I needed to tune out. I picked up the remote and flipped through channels until I found *Julie & Julia*, and Meryl Streep lulled me right to sleep.

❈

In the morning, I had a dead phone and no idea what time it was. Peeking out from the bedroom, the house seemed empty and quiet. A note from Jack was taped to the bathroom door:

Hope you slept well, Mia. Help yourself to anything in the house. I'm at work but I'll be home around 4:30 if you want to grab pizza or something. Jack

One part of me wanted to stay until the end of the day to take Jack up on his offer and make up for being antisocial last night. The other part of me knew that waiting until 4:30 p.m. to hang out meant I was spending another night in Boise, when I could be in Portland tonight if I left now.

My mind was made up. I took a quick shower, wrote him a thank-you note, and headed out the door. I felt a pang of guilt for not being a more present houseguest or more thoroughly enjoying this city. If someone were to ask me what Boise was like, I would tell them I had no idea. Much like with Chicago and Minneapolis, I make a silent promise to come back and explore these cities—later.

The final stretch of drive from Boise to Portland looked familiar. I remembered the golden hills and the dark blue of the Columbia River Gorge that I had seen driving away from Devin a few months ago. Facing the last leg of my journey, I summoned every bit of energy I had to stave off anxious thoughts and get to Portland before I collapsed in exhaustion.

When I parked in front of Devin's pink Portland house at 9:30 p.m., she met me outside wearing blue sweats and a white T-shirt, wrapping me up and lifting me off the ground.

"Finally. You're here," she said. "I've missed you."

The string of ten-hour driving days all felt worth it to see her face, smell her hair, and follow her upstairs to her cozy room, where she handed me a glass of white wine with ice.

"See? I listen," she said with a clever smile.

I took one sip of the wine before we climbed into bed together, and she held me as I hugged her tightly. I felt full.

Waking up in Devin's bed felt like everything I'd been hungry for, and also unusual as I didn't have anywhere to be. I didn't have to get up and figure out where to go to the bathroom or try to change my clothes squatting in the van. I didn't have to get on the road or coordinate interviews. I didn't have to plan where I was going to sleep that night. Relief flooded my body as a new level of relaxation set in. My muscles loosened their grip on my bones all at once.

"I have to get up for school," Devin whispered.

"Can I come with you?" I said. "Not to class, but maybe I could hang out in the library?"

"Sure, if you want to," she said excitedly.

The drive to Portland Community College was beautiful. The turquoise rust of the St. Johns Bridge contrasted starkly against the overcast Portland sky and the sea of dark pine trees in the distance. Devin traversed windy back roads through the woods of North Portland, where the fog hung low, stuck within the thick, mossy trees. "Rainbow," by Kacey Musgraves, played as Devin steered with one hand on the wheel. She stole glances at me with a loving smile as I looked out the window at what could be my future home.

On campus, we parted ways as she walked into class and I headed to the library, finding a seat by the floor-to-ceiling window and watching students walk to and from the buildings. Everything felt slow, and I didn't fight it. It felt so fulfilling just to arrive.

55

"For now, just be happy."

NOVEMBER 6–PORTLAND, OREGON
99 DAYS ON THE ROAD, 10,689 MILES

I'd been staying with Devin for about a week in the pink house. To my delight, we'd indulged in all the things you do in an actual house, like sleeping in an actual bed, cooking in an actual kitchen, and bathing in an actual bathtub.

On the days she had school, Devin and I drove to her campus together and parted ways as I took myself to the library. I cherished these hours of solitude, where I read, journaled, and transcribed the interview recordings from the past few months. Being in the same city for more than a few days also helped my mind slow down enough to write the article for *ROVA* magazine.

Begin anywhere, I told myself as I searched for the right way to begin. I wrote about the elusive quest for balance between saying goodbye to people, places, and things I loved in order to make room for the new and unpredictable experiences around every turn. I had no idea if anyone would understand what I was talking about, much less resonate with it.

Morning light with Devin.

When the story published, I took myself to Powell's and flipped to the pages printed with my photos and words. The subheading of the article read, "A three-month, cross-country road trip prompts a solo female traveler to recognize her newest teacher, and discover the benefit of being the architect of her own life," and I felt my lips form a smile as a wave of peace washed over me. I felt proud. I felt brave. And best of all, I felt like I'd given that to myself.

On the days Devin went to work, I woke up slowly and explored Portland without an agenda, wandering in and out of coffee roasters, food trucks, local shops, parks, and all the places that kept Portland weird. One such adventure landed me in a woman-owned surf shop called Leeward. As I talked to the person behind the counter, I told her I lived in San Diego, but that I was considering moving to Portland.

"Oh, right on. I used to live in San Diego, but I couldn't take it after a while," she said casually. "I like Oregon so much better."

"How come?" I asked curiously. She was the first person I'd met in Oregon who surfed, and I was hungry to understand what this part of my life would look like if I lived here.

"The lineups are far less crowded," she said. "and the people are so much less aggro. There's lots of great spots, and it takes longer to get there, but once you do, it's special."

We talked for a little while longer as the final piece in my should-I-actually-move-here puzzle fell neatly into place. I had finally confirmed that there was a surf community in Portland that I could see myself being part of.

Armed with this new, very important information, I made up my mind: I was moving to Portland. And I wanted to tell someone.

Walking two blocks just to get the jitters out, I sat on a curb to call my mom.

"Mom, guess what I just did?" I said when she picked up.

"Mia! What?"

I told her all about the surf shop and how important it was to me that I felt connected to the surfing community to make sure I wasn't moving just for Devin, but that I would be happy here too.

She listened intently until I finally said, "So . . . I think I'm going to move here. I don't need to stay in San Diego anymore. This feels right."

"Well, okay then," she said lovingly. "You're moving to Portland."

Once again, as soon as I said my decision out loud, any lingering anxiety disappeared.

Back in the van, I called Devin to tell her the news. I told her that I was making the decision because I thought Portland would make me happy. Her being there was a real bonus—okay, a super-big bonus—but this was something I wanted to do for myself. It was my decision, and I had made it.

"I just don't want you to give anything up for me," she said cautiously.

"I'm not giving up anything for you," I replied with confidence.

The other end of the line was silent for a moment. I could feel Devin's smile and the subtle joy of choosing each other while also choosing ourselves.

"In that case, when will you be home?"

56

"A few months ago, this would have felt unimaginable."

NOVEMBER 10–PORTLAND, OREGON
103 DAYS ON THE ROAD, 10,723 MILES

The fire crackled in Devin's living room as I called Erin for our weekly conversation—something I hadn't missed since we were introduced. Her endless wisdom had both helped me to find joy and held me accountable for growth.

"Hiiiii, sweet Erin!"

"Hello, amazing Mia!"

"I'm finally going back to San Diego tomorrow," I told her. "I've been here for about two weeks, and I think I'm ready to start moving into the next phase of life."

"That's a big step!" Erin said cheerfully. "What do you think this journey has taught you that you will carry into the next chapter?"

It was an excellent question—they always were.

I began with what I knew. I knew I wanted to move here. I knew I wanted to be with Devin. I knew the Portland trial run had shown me that this could work. But I hadn't reflected on what the journey as a whole had taught me that I wanted to carry with me wherever I went next.

I thought about the thing that had guided me through every moment of the last few months—my intuition. It had held my hand as I said goodbye to a career, a company, a car, and a relationship. It had helped me choose which neighborhoods to sleep in, when to keep driving and when to stop, whom to reach out to and when, and how to navigate the thousands of small decisions in between. It told me to say yes when Devin asked me to be in an actual relationship with her, to come back to Portland when Canada kicked me out, and to build the next chapter of my life here. As everything fell into place moment by moment, my intuition had become my steadfast guide, and somewhere along the way, I had learned to trust it.

I wasn't sure I listened to my intuition much at all in San Diego. I stayed in relationships that I knew weren't honest, even when all the signs were there. I stayed in a job when I knew, in my heart, that I was burned out and needed a break. How long did I drag myself through the mud as my intuition waited for me to catch up? How much time did I spend trying to logic my way through things that my heart and gut knew had ended? I'd resisted my intuition over and over again. I questioned myself and doubted the piece of me that knew the way.

"I think this entire journey was a lesson in surrendering and remembering how to trust myself," I told Erin. "I think I needed to learn that it was safe to trust myself again." Neither of us spoke, allowing the quiet to just be. In it, I felt Erin's understanding of me not only in this moment, but all along.

"You know, I think it's going to be a little strange, Erin."

"What will?" she asked.

"Going back to San Diego," I said. "I feel so different now, and I'm about to temporarily step back into an old version of life. It's almost like time travel."

I paused for a few seconds before adding, "I don't want to go back to the way things were or the way I was when I get to San Diego. I'm afraid I'll lose all the progress I've made."

"And what would your intuition say about that?" she asked.

The words came out of my mouth before I could overthink them. "Trust."

A few months ago, this sense of peace felt unimaginable. I pictured the version of myself who sat in her bed, crying under the covers, feeling stuck and detached from her intuition. She had to completely fall apart first. A necessary death. She had to learn who she was without the validation of a relationship, a job, a home, and a community. She had to learn she was safe within herself first.

I am safe. I am safe. I am safe.

Erin spoke slowly, breaking the silence.

"Well, then, it sounds like you've already got all you need."

EPILOGUE

It's been more than seven years since this journey, and these extraordinary, everyday women and gender nonconforming people have changed my life. Memories of our time together stay with me, with as much vivid detail as if they happened yesterday, and with as much love as if they've been with me my whole life. I remember exactly how I felt sitting across from them, an open and curious audience of one. Their wisdom and words have permeated everything since.

Shortly after returning to San Diego, I packed up my van to move to Portland, Oregon. My mom and my geriatric cat, Annie, joined me on the five-day road trip. My mom laughed so many times over the course of our drive, and I felt overwhelmed with both her resilience and my love for her. I think setting up a new chapter of life with her by my side brought us closer.

I moved in with a friend of Kaley's, who had ironically been at the brewery in Portland the night I secluded myself inside. She had a room for rent in the same neighborhood that Devin lived in. Despite being in a happy relationship with Devin, the first year in Portland was very hard as I had maxed out all my credit cards, didn't have a job, and didn't understand how much Seasonal Affective Disorder was a real thing, and would impact me.

Mom and Annie on the drive to Portland.

As time passed, I began to figure out how I fit with Portland and how Portland fit with me. I became close friends with Georgia, who was the barista at the coffee shop where Devin and I first met. We surfed the Oregon coast together, went to art shows and film screenings and women-led panels and meetups for women and queer people who loved the ocean. I learned the bike routes I liked, which camp spots were best, and which food trucks had the best falafel. I came to enjoy all the things that made Portland special for the two-and-a-half years we lived there.

Southern Oregon surfing is better with friends. *Photo credit: Devin Hiller*

EPILOGUE

Very excited and very cold. *Photo credit: Milad Sadegi*

Just before the COVID-19 pandemic changed every inch of life worldwide, Devin and I moved into a studio apartment together, said goodbye to my beloved Annie, and shortly after welcomed two kittens, Bennet and Granger, into our little family. The four of us stayed inside as businesses around the world shut their doors, face masks became the norm, wildfires nearly evacuated the city, and snow covered the ground outside. In the spring, we attended Black Lives Matter protests, demanding justice for George Floyd, Breonna Taylor, and too many others. I worked from home at our kitchen table as Devin applied to physician assistant schools up and down the West Coast.

After twelve applications and a few months, she was invited to two interviews—one with a school in the Bay Area, and one with a school on the Big Island of Hawai'i. She spent months preparing for those calls, and on the day she interviewed, Joe Biden was elected president of the United States and Kamala Harris vice president.

Being goofy with Devin.
Photo credit: Kim Kirch

That day, we celebrated bigger than we had celebrated in a long time.

Soon after, Devin told me she liked the program in Hawai'i better and asked if I would move there with her, as she held her breath. Move with my dream girl to Hawai'i? Twist my arm.

Around the same time, two other major things happened.

First, I rejoined Mixte Communications in a new leadership role. My relationship with the company and the fast-paced work felt significantly healthier this time around, and I felt more confident in myself and my ability to figure things out. Trusting myself more and knowing it was okay to not have all the answers from the very beginning helped me find joy again at work and use my skills to support changemakers moving the needle on the issues I cared about.

Secondly, I applied for a scholarship to the same life coaching certification program that Erin had gone through. When the application asked me why I wanted to become a life coach, I wrote about how Erin had changed my life and how I thought coaching should be accessible for everybody. I got accepted into the program, and over the course of nearly two years, I made some very dear friends in my cohort from around the world—and got certified as a Martha Beck Wayfinder Life Coach. Erin and I still talk every week, and now I work with women and LGBTQIA+ folks to help them reclaim their power and find more joy in their lives.

EPILOGUE

The process of moving to Hawai'i was both exciting and exhausting. It involved extensive vet visits for Bennet and Granger, coordinating the shipment of all our belongings, selling the van, and moving into a home in Kona.

While many people saw Hawai'i as a vacation destination, I acknowledged the deep pain of colonization and militarization that the US government had inflicted on native Hawaiians, which gave me heartache over our move. I knew it was my responsibility to deepen my understanding of the unique history of Hawai'i and contribute something meaningful to advance justice and equity there.

I got involved with Hawai'i Peoples Fund, an organization supporting grassroots, Hawaiian-led movements for justice across the islands, as part of its annual Giving Project. As part of the six-month program and small cohort, we came together to deepen our understanding of Hawai'i's unique history, examine our personal privilege, and invest our resources to move money to community partners resisting systems of oppression and building a more just and equitable Hawai'i.

For three years, my time outside of Mixte and coaching was spent engaged with local organizations, as well as in the ocean—surfing, diving or taking photos—and writing this book.

Thankful for warm weather and waves.

Life with Dev.

A typical evening featured Devin and me sitting on our big couch with the cats, screen door open, the sunset silhouetting the palm trees outside, with *Law & Order: SVU* playing in the background as Devin studied human anatomy and I wrote.

When Devin graduated from PA school in the fall of 2023, she tried to find a job on the island to support the local medical community. With limited opportunities to work in the operating room on the Big Island, she applied for a job doing liver transplants at Stanford—and a few months later, she was hired. Much like the move to Portland, I knew it would be a good change for both of us, but that didn't make the transition away from Hawai'i any easier. I worried about giving up the slowness and connection to nature I'd cultivated in Hawai'i for one of the most fast-paced, tech-focused cities in the country.

EPILOGUE

Trust.

Now we live in the San Francisco Bay Area of California with Bennet, Granger, and Madeline, a stray kitten we adopted in Kona. We see family often—both Devin's parents and my sisters, nieces, nephews, and cousins—coming together for the simple things like breakfast or someone's birthday. I still surf even though it's much colder, and we still get into nature to rejuvenate our spirits. We're orienting to life and building our community here, and I have learned to have patience with the process.

Nearly one year into our return to California, Kamala Harris became the Democratic nominee for president of the United States. When she didn't win the presidency, our communities grieved and leaned on each other as we searched for words to express what we felt. Many of us are still searching.

In her concession speech, Kamala Harris spoke with the same sense of hope that fueled her short yet strong campaign. "Don't ever give up. Don't ever stop trying to make the world a better place. You have power. And don't you ever listen when anyone tells you something is impossible because it has never been done before." As we navigate the barrage of attacks on human rights by the new administration, I intend to never forget that power comes from the people.

As I put the final edits on this book, KC reached out to me. They had entered their eighth month of sobriety and asked for the opportunity to make amends. The last time I had spoken to them was over email in Boise, and much like then, I was shocked to hear from them. This time, however, I was open to a conversation.

As their picture appeared on my phone at our scheduled time to talk, my heart began to race, and my hands got clammy.

"Hi," I said, picking up the phone.

"Hi," they responded.

Then, something funny happened.

We both began to laugh.

"I'm sorry. I don't mean to laugh," I said after a few seconds. "I just think it's comical how you can not talk to someone for years, and then reconnecting can be as simple as picking up the phone and saying hi."

"Thank you for laughing," KC said. "I was so nervous, it took me two weeks just to send you a message."

It's hard to describe the phone call that followed. KC explained that the process of making amends is contingent on being very specific about what happened, and they warned me that it may feel triggering and that we can stop whenever I wanted to. They validated my theory that I hadn't been the only one—they had, indeed, been with someone else—describing me as a "fix" that always made them feel better.

"I may not have liked myself, but I fucking liked you," they said.

They brought up our last email exchange, and how a little while after that, they hit rock bottom. This prompted them to do two big things: start going to Alcoholics Anonymous (AA) and accept themself as a transgender man who uses they/him pronouns.

My eyes filled with tears as they described how liberating the process was and what a critical step it was toward the self-love they'd never had. Listening to just how much they had struggled when we were together, in so many ways related to their gender expression and addictions that I had never known, broke me open.

Simultaneously, with the help of AA, they had identified the values they wanted to use as their compass through life—one of which was empathy.

"When I think of empathy, I think of you," they said. "You taught me what empathy means, and it's something I strive for every day."

And then they uttered the words, "You matter . . . so much. I should have told you years ago."

Their vulnerability and honesty cut through every defense I had, reaching right out and touching my heart. Tears spilled out as I realized for the first time that they had loved me just as much as I had loved them—they just hadn't been able to show it. All the broken moments had been felt by both of us all along. The heartache I'd felt hadn't been a result of unrequited love but a mutual love that simply couldn't exist

EPILOGUE

while KC experienced such deeply rooted suffering.

Suddenly, it all felt so clear. All the time I had spent agonizing about us had been the only way to get here, to a place where KC could love and trust themselves, and I could love and trust myself too.

In my bones, I know that every moment that hurt, or felt impossible to understand, or pushed me out of my comfort zone was only a catalyst for learning how to grow into this new chapter of life – the one beyond the grey that I dreamed of when first embarking on this journey. Anna taught me how to let myself grieve. Sharon taught me about freedom. Tracie taught me that joy lies in your perspective. Shalem taught me the art of truly listening, and Dana and Sara taught me the importance of boundaries and saying no. Eli and Deb taught me that friends are the family you choose, and Ava and CoCo taught me about community. Chandra showed me that being an advocate looks different for each of us, while Jen taught me the importance of advocating for yourself. Emma taught me about perseverance and determination, and Beth showed me it's okay to be many things all at once. Senna taught me to not compare myself to anyone, and Kim and Sammi showed me that our flaws make us perfect. Camila taught me about responsibility. Confidence taught me how to let things die. Davina taught me to ride the wave. KC taught me how to love deeply and let go. Devin taught me how to water a new seed and watch it grow.

For a journey I intended to be on alone, I'd discovered I was anything but.

In bloom. *Photo credit: Kaley Aposporos*

The End

(for now)

ACKNOWLEDGMENTS

I cannot say thank you enough to the many people whose time and talents brought this book from an idea and a few audio files into what you now hold in your hands.

Still, I will try.

Thank you to my friends and family for continually asking how the book was coming along, and for listening when I said, "We're in the editing phase" for years at a time. Thank you for the unlimited supply of support and love – especially you, Dev.

Thank you to Larissa for reminding me of the importance of my own story and encouraging me to be the "connective tissue." That piece of feedback was the single most important recommendation in the development of this book as it spurred a more powerful rewrite and my own healing journey as well. I hope you know what a difference you've made and that I will never stop singing your praises. Thank you to my queer and dear friend Karina for your gorgeous art throughout the book and on the cover. You took my story and brought it to life in a way I never could, and I'm deeply thankful that you agreed to lend your talents to this project when I asked for your help that one day on that one beach many years ago.

Thank you to the team at Indigo River Publishing for believing in me and for calling in your brilliant editors, designers, and marketers to bring out the best in this book every step of the way. Your expertise coupled with your thoughtfulness and compassion for a first-time author have set a very high bar, my friends. Specifically, thank you to Deborah for your big heart, vision, and patience.

Lastly, a boundless thank you to every person who was a part of this story – who opened up their heart, mind, past, or space to me in some way – and all the pansies of the world. There are many of you, and you know who you are. May your journeys and your generosity ripple outward and plant seeds of joy and for generations to come.

ABOUT THE AUTHOR

Mia Bolton is a writer, water photographer, and Martha Beck Certified Wayfinder Life Coach. Mia contributes to national and international publications, including a cover story for *HiHeyHello Magazine* and features in *Foam Symmetry*, *Pacific Longboarder Magazine*, *USA Swimming Magazine*, *Surfline*, and others. *As We Bloom* is now a book that celebrates everyday, extraordinary women and gender nonconforming people from all walks of life who have found joy in the untraditional and remind us there is no one right way to live a life.

In her role as Vice President of Communications at Mixte Communications, Mia partners with local, statewide, and national social justice organizations to leverage her writing and communications expertise for long-term change. She's especially proud of the campaign she led with the League of Women Voters of California to mobilize BIPOC youth to vote in the 2020 general election, which earned eight national awards and contributed to the critical work grassroots organizations around the country are doing to get out the vote.

Outside of her many perpetual projects, Mia can be found learning to rest; surfing, diving, and taking photos in the ocean; or spending time with her wife Devin, in the San Francisco Bay Area, trying to teach their three cats to walk on a leash.